D1026919

EYEWITNESS COMPANIONS

Horse Riding

MOIRA C. HARRIS
LIS CLEGG

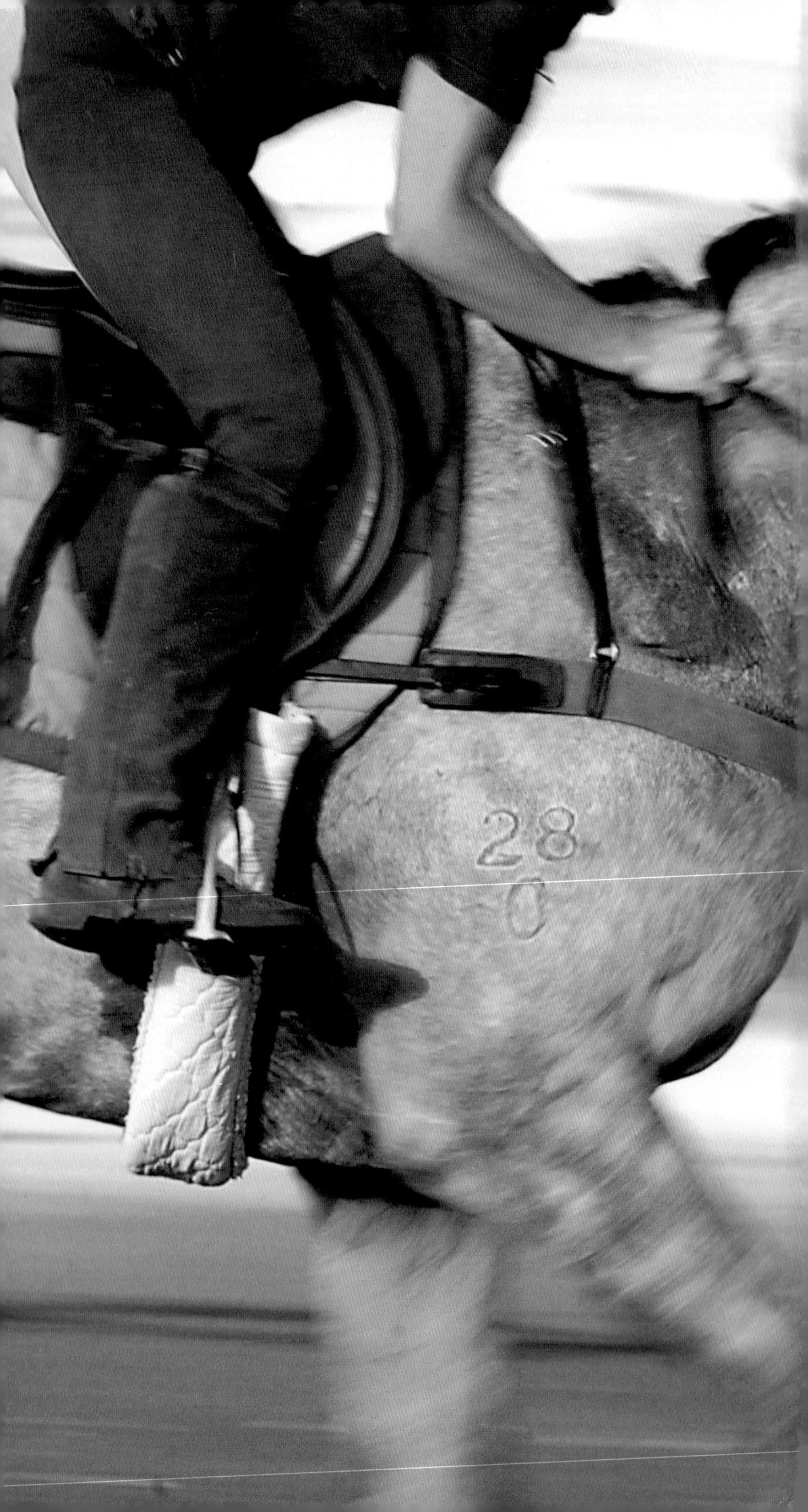
28
0

"THERE IS NO SECRET SO CLOSE AS THAT BETWEEN HORSE AND RIDER."

R. S. Surtees, sporting journalist (1804–1864)

LONDON, NEW YORK,
MUNICH, MELBOURNE, DELHI

Project Editor	Richard Gilbert
Art Editor	Mark Cavanagh
Managing Editor	Stephanie Farrow
Managing Art Editor	Lee Griffiths
Art Director	Bryn Walls
Publishing Director	Jonathan Metcalf
DTP Designer	Vania Cunha
Production Controller	Heather Hughes
Commissioned Photography	Kit Houghton and Bob Langrish

Produced for Dorling Kindersley by
Bookwork Limited

First published in 2006 by
Dorling Kindersley Limited
80 Strand, London WC2R ORL

A Penguin Company

6 8 10 9 7

A CIP catalogue record for this book is available from the British Library

ISBN-13: 978-1-40531-293-6
ISBN-10: 1-4053-1293-9

Colour reproduction by Colourscan, Singapore
Printed and bound by Leo Paper Products Ltd, China

CONTENTS

ANYONE WHO HAS SAT ASTRIDE A HORSE WILL TELL YOU THAT AFTER THEIR FIRST TIME IN THE SADDLE THEY FOUND THEMSELVES INCREDIBLY SORE AND STIFF. BUT ANY DISCOMFORT SOON FADES AWAY, TO BE REPLACED BY THE JOY OF MAKING NEW DISCOVERIES AND EXPERIENCING REVELATIONS THAT ARE FAR MORE LASTING.

When you ride a horse, there are certain muscle groups that get a true workout because this is not like pedalling a bicycle, but rather moving in harmony with a living, breathing creature. During the ride there is a great deal of communication going on between horse and rider, but it is done mostly in complete silence. Riders find that any day-to-day anxieties fall away because the mind is concentrated on what is happening in the moment. With the aching muscles – which will thankfully diminish as skills improve – comes the knowledge that riding is not at all about being a passenger, but being an active participant in a mutually enjoyable activity.

No matter what your level of interest, whether you just want to be able to stay in the saddle during a ranch holiday or intend to tackle a cross-country course at next year's horse trials, you will find this book an excellent resource. It provides great information on riding fundamentals, but it should not be used as your sole method of learning. It is intended as an

TRAIL RIDING IN NEW ZEALAND
The shoreline of the South Pacific is a perfect location for a leisurely walk along the sand or a brisk gallop in the surf.

adjunct to proper riding and horse care lessons, and its aim is to give you an idea of what to expect and aim for and to provide supplementary information to your hands-on lessons. It also explains why so many people are still captivated by horses – even in today's fast-paced, technology-driven world.

There are many reasons why people are drawn to horses. Just look at a horse and you cannot deny its appeal. Its strength, beauty, and intelligence – combined with its willing nature – have given it a unique relationship with humans. No other creature is so impressive in size and speed yet, in most cases, so gentle and keen to do our bidding.

No other creature is so impressive in size and speed, yet so gentle and keen to do our bidding

FILLING MANY ROLES

Historically, the purpose of training horses was to serve humans without complaint. Whether we exploited their strength and obedience to help us plough our fields, to carry our soldiers into battle, or simply as a means of transport, the horses of yesteryear were mostly seen as utilitarian creatures. Today, they are still employed as workhorses by farmers, ranchers, and police forces. Horses also play a role in a number of competitive sports, be it streaking past a winning post, racing across the desert, or tackling the last jump on course at the Olympic Games. For most pleasure riders, however, a horse provides an escape from the workplace, a partner for an exhilarating workout, or even a trusted friend and companion.

While many will argue about the ways in which horses should be ridden, most horsemen and women agree that riding is not easy. There are those rare "natural riders" but most riders are made, not born. Some people spend a lifetime learning to perfect their riding skills, and even world-class reiners and international dressage and eventing competitors work with coaches.

Handling a large, heavy, and muscular animal that has a mind of its own can be a mental challenge as well as a physical one. You will soon learn to appreciate that each horse is unique.

ADVICE AND INFORMATION

ALL-SEASON ACTIVITY
Riding can be an all-year-round activity. This hardy Haflinger horse, with its thick winter coat, is quite comfortable in the snow.

Anyone who loves horses and is thinking of taking up riding, even those merely interested in weekend riding, will benefit from learning more about the horse and how to master basic riding techniques. Selecting the proper attire and equipment is essential for keeping the rider safe and comfortable in the saddle, and finding out about equine behaviour will allow greater understanding when it comes to handling

RIDING WITH FRIENDS
Whether taking a riding holiday or just hacking out with other horse lovers, riding is a joy.

the horse. It is also a good idea for the first-timer to learn how to tackle the tasks of grooming and tacking up the horse. Anyone who takes the time to grasp these basic techniques of riding and horse care will be in a position to enjoy leisure riding in its various forms including trail rides, horse camps, and holidays on a working ranch.

The importance of ensuring safety around horses should be paramount at all times. Good riders never forget that their sport can be a dangerous one. Accidents can happen, but you need to take steps to avoid unnecessary ones and protect the health and happiness of both horse and handler.

SOMETHING FOR EVERYONE

Riders who are interested in pursuing horse riding more seriously will soon discover that they have a great deal to learn about tack and other equipment, and how these can be used to enhance their horse's performance.

There are also a number of different riding disciplines to choose from, including Western riding, dressage, show jumping, and cross-country. Whichever areas of riding are of interest to you, there will be numerous ways in which you can advance your riding, influence your horse, and improve its way of going. Being able to tackle complicated manoeuvres or patterns in the sand-school, jump over obstacles when out hacking, or conquer the trail takes practice, skill, and patience.

Avid equestrians may want to delve even deeper into the different aspects of riding. For those who want to compete, there is a great deal to be learnt about honing skills for the show ring and the psychology behind winning rides. It takes a lot to put equitation (horsemanship or riding skills) to the test and come out a champion.

Horse riding is a thrilling pastime. Many people think of it as an activity mainly enjoyed by children – since owning a horse is a popular childhood wish. Some lucky children do grow up with horses in their lives, but the vast majority of us are not so fortunate. The truth is that riding can be enjoyed at any age, and it is never too late to fulfil that dream of riding into the sunset or galloping through the surf on a beautiful, powerful horse.

THE HISTORY OF RIDING

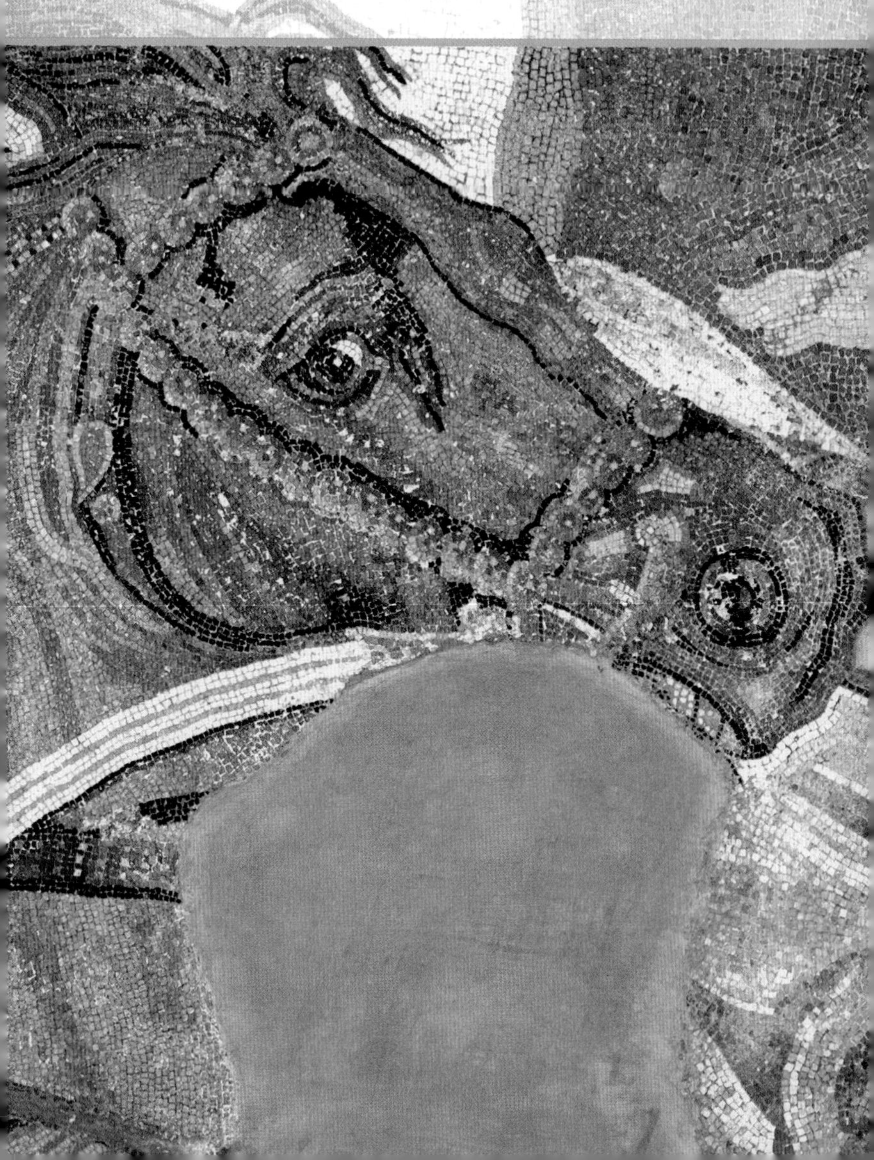

HARNESSING THE HORSE

The first true horse was pony-sized and was hunted for its meat by Cro-Magnon Man. It was fast-moving and agile, however, and was one of the more attractive and gentle-natured creatures of the age. This may be why the horse eventually came to be so much more than simply a source of food.

DOMESTICATION

During the Neolithic era in Eurasia, in about 4,000BCE, early Man moved from life as a hunter-gatherer to farming, raising, and domesticating herds of animals for meat. People at this time are known to have tamed various animals and even kept them as pets. Taming horses probably made them easier to manage as food animals, but their docile nature helped their role with humans to evolve – it was soon discovered that these animals were useful for work.

The horse became an even more valuable resource to early farmers when it was discovered that it was easier to control a herd of horses when sitting astride one. Suddenly, humans had a completely different view of the world.

EXTRA INFORMATION

THE FIRST HORSE

Hyracotherium is better known as Eohippus, which means "dawn horse". This dog-sized animal lived during the Eocene period 55 to 45 million years ago. It was an ancestor of *Equus caballus*, the first "true" horse.

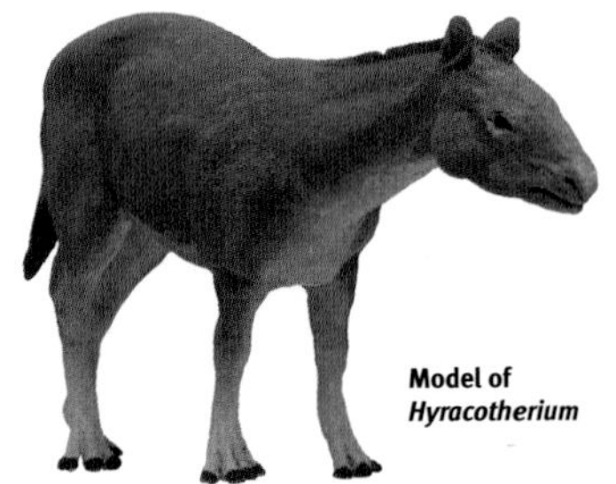

Model of *Hyracotherium*

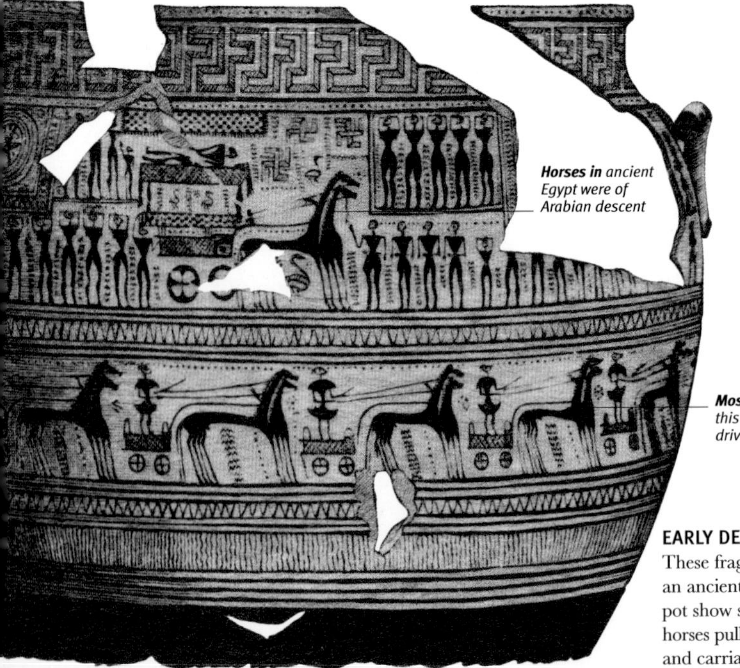

***Horses in** ancient Egypt were of Arabian descent*

***Most horses** of this era were driven not ridden*

EARLY DEPICTION

These fragments of an ancient Egyptian pot show scenes of horses pulling chariots and carriages.

ARAMAEN CAVALRYMAN
The horse became important for early armies in the Near East. This stone relief shows an Aramaen cavalryman from the 9th century BCE.

EARLY TACK

Early riders clung to horses with little say in where they went, but they were determined to establish control. Some of the earliest tack shows that these first equestrians discovered that if they could literally rein in the front part of the horse, the rest would follow. Simple bridles from this time – nothing more than sinew placed round the nose or rawhide looped round the lower jaw – have been found in excavations around the Black Sea.

Once the horse could be controlled, mankind's horizons expanded, with civilization migrating southwards to the "fertile crescent" area of the Near East. By the middle of the second Millennium, horses were pulling chariots throughout Greece, Egypt, Mesopotamia, and even China. In the Near East, humans were sitting astride the horse, too. Horsemanship began to take on a new importance because it was useful in warfare and hunting.

As our relationship with horses developed, so did their tack. The Chinese have been credited with developing the stirrup and the horseshoe. Some of the earliest true bits, developed around 1,500BCE, were discovered in the Near East.

Horses were a commodity enjoyed by the wealthy and the powerful. Chariots, adorned for royalty, were representative of wealth and importance. The horses that pulled them were similarly decorated, with anything from simple head plumes to elaborate bronze harness-work. The horse quickly became a status symbol.

THE HORSE IN EARLY WAR

From as early as 1,500BCE, the power of the horse was being exploited by armies. From the Near East to the Mediterranean, the horse's stamina and strength were used to conquer nations. Horsemanship, spurred on by the needs of warring nations, reached a new level.

The Egyptians and the Hittites were the great empire builders of the time. A cuneiform, written around 1,345BCE, describes how a Hittite horseman named Kikkuli selected, trained, and conditioned horses for war. His writings showed how he selected horses that were free from breathing disorders. He even developed nutrition plans with careful measurements of oats, barley, hay, chaff, and salt. Kikkuli clearly understood the horse's physiology and psychology, and his methods could still be used today.

CHINESE BIT
This bit was probably worn by a cavalry horse during the Han dynasty (207BCE–220CE). Functional equipment of the era was also highly ornamental.

DEVELOPMENT OF BREEDS

Like other domestic animals, horses began to develop into distinct types and breeds as humans started to understand the science of horse-breeding. Climate, soil type and topography, and work purpose all had an impact on how different horse breeds sprung from different corners of the world.

The fourth and fifth centuries saw various Asian tribes invading western Asia on their steppe-bred horses, and these peoples soon met up with the tribes of the deserts on their hot-blooded Arabian horses. These creatures were well suited to travelling long distances in desert conditions. They possessed incredible stamina, speed, and agility coupled with beauty and sensitivity. They were known as hot-bloods, not only as a reflection of their origin, but because of their intelligence and responsiveness.

During the Middle Ages, as European settlements expanded, the need arose for massive, powerful horses that could carry a knight in full chain mail along with their own protective equine armour. Because of their size, the horses had to be bred to be particularly compliant. Originating in the chillier countries of Europe, the heavy, cold-blooded draught horse was created as a gentle giant, from which its knight could do battle.

By the 15th century, mounted soldiers needed to be unencumbered to operate firearms, so their armour was greatly reduced. It was no longer necessary for the soldiers to have such heavy horses to carry them, so horse breeders in Europe began to breed warhorses that were smaller and more agile.

THE TARPAN
We are probably indebted to the tarpan, via the Arab, for the look of our modern horse's head. It evolved in semi-deserts in Europe and Asia.

A colourful *decorated "caparison" covered the horse*

Chain mail *armour covered the rider's body*

MODERN BREEDS

"Heavy" horses, or draughts, were borne out of a cold climate, unforgiving soil, and hard work that required strength combined with a willing nature. "Light horses" (riding, driving, or pleasure mounts) were bred for speed, endurance, agility, and even beauty. Ponies – hardy creatures with great intelligence and resilience – were bred to pull carriages and to ride.

Of course, there are many breeds and types of horses in between. Nearly 400 breeds exist, although a great number are quite rare. Among these unusual breeds are the metallic-coated Akhal Teke of Turkmenistan; the Namib Desert Horse that lives in the most inhospitable conditions of Namibia; Austria's Noriker, a heavy draught splashed with spots; the American Curly Horse, which sports a wavy coat that is said to be hypoallergenic; and the Fallabella from Argentina, which grows no higher than 75 cm (29 in).

EXTRA INFORMATION

RIDING SIDE-SADDLE

Until medieval times, women did not ride horses. It was considered unladylike to sit astride a horse's back, and nearly impossible in the type of clothes they wore. So the idea of riding with both legs to one side developed. The side-saddle rider sat to the side while being led by a courtier. In 1580, Catherine de Medici designed a saddle that had an extra pommel for the rider to lodge her leg under for security. Some 250 years later, Charles Pellier created the "leaping head" pommel, which curved over the rider's thigh allowing the lady to do vigorous riding like hunting.

Woman riding side-saddle

KNIGHTS IN ARMOUR

In medieval times, jousting tournaments were held as military exercises and for entertainment. This is a reconstruction.

***A metal** helm enclosed the entire head and face, and reached down almost to the shoulders*

***A blunt** wooden lance was used to knock a jouster off his horse to begin a ground battle*

***A flowing** surcoat, often displaying a coat of arms, was worn over armour*

BREEDING HORSES FOR SPORT

Since the beginning of recorded time, horse-racing has been a sport of nearly every major civilization. Some records show that nomadic tribesmen of Central Asia may have raced the horses they domesticated as long ago as 4,500BCE. By 638BCE, the ancient Greeks had added chariot-racing and mounted horse-racing to the events in the Olympic Games.

During the 12th century, English knights returned from the Crusades with small, hot-blooded horses from North Africa. By the 17th century, horse-racing was popular with the English nobility, and it was at this time that it gained its soubriquet "the sport of kings". Charles II, aware that the features of these African horses could improve his stock, began to breed them with his English hobby mares. The resulting offspring had speed and stamina. They ran in private match races for the nobility to wager on.

The lineage of all Thoroughbreds goes back to North African stallions brought to England after 1662. Of these, three are found in the pedigrees of all Thoroughbred racehorses: the Darley Arabian, the Byerly Turk, and the Godolphin Barb.

THE BYERLY TURK
This famous painting of the Byerly Turk, by John Wootton, shows that the horse was dark brown with an Arabian appearance.

HORSES IN THE MODERN OLYMPIC GAMES

EQUINE DEBUT

In 1896, the Olympics began once again in Athens, Greece, but the first four Games did not include equine competition. Two equestrian events made their Olympic debut in Paris in 1900, when an equine long jump and *puissance* (high jump) were held for the first and only time. In 1906, equestrian sports were proposed as a permanent addition to the Olympic Games, and they were added in 1912 at the Stockholm Olympics. The Olympic classes include individual dressage, team three-day event, and individual and team jumping classes, with each nation entering a team of six riders. The International Olympic Committee has been considering adding other events – endurance and reining are two possibilities.

EXCLUSION AND INCLUSION

When equestrian events were accepted into Olympic competition, only commissioned officers were allowed to compete in the three-day eventing, and a mere handful of civilians participated in show jumping and dressage. After World War II, the Olympic ban on non-military competitors was lifted, and both women and men were allowed to participate in the same events. Equestrian events are the only Olympic competitions in which men and women compete on an equal basis.

Jessica Kuerten, show jumping, 2004

Blyth Tait, eventing, 2004

Germany team, dressage, 2000

MUGHALS PLAY POLO
Polo was first played on barren fields in China and Persia by nomadic warriors over 2,000 years ago. It proved valuable for army training.

ORGANIZED RACING

During the reign of Queen Anne (1702–1714), horse-racing in England became more of an organized sport, with several horses and riders competing against each other over a course in front of spectators. Racecourses were built all over the country, including Queen Anne's own Ascot course near Windsor Castle, which was opened in 1711. Breeding programmes also became more organized, and a horse that was "thorough bred" for racing developed from England's studs. American Thoroughbred racing is the most popular flat racing in the USA, but races for Quarter Horses, Appaloosas, and Arabians are also held in some states.

NEW SPORTS

Equestrian sport started with racing, but it did not end there. With the invention of the steam engine in 1710 and the new era of the Industrial Revolution, the horse's role in the human world began to change. Our relationship with the horse progressed from one of work to one of pleasure.

Many early sporting events were based on military tests. Military forms of polo go back as far as the reign of the Persian king Darius (500BCE). But it was not until 1869 that polo was played by Westerners, after British officers brought the game home from India.

Dressage means "training" in French, and was developed for the battlefield. The *haute école* (high school) created during the Renaissance was the highest form of dressage training, where horses were taught to execute leaps, stances, and manoeuvres designed to protect the mounted soldier.

The sport of show jumping evolved from fox-hunting, which involved jumping hedges and walls in pursuit of quarry. The first competitions were held in Ireland in the mid 1800s by the Royal Dublin Society.

Carriage driving has its origins in ancient Roman chariot racing. Today, there are several competitions that involve racing with wagons or carts. These include harness racing (one horse and a two-wheeled cart) and scurry racing (two ponies and a four-wheeled cart). Chuckwagon races (four horses and a four-wheeled cart) are a highlight of the Calgary Stampede – Canada's premier rodeo. Modern horse driving trials (one, two, or more horses and ponies and a carriage) are modelled on ridden eventing. They began in 1968, when the rules were formulated by HRH Prince Philip.

ORIGINS OF RIDING STYLES

While early riding involved hardly any equitation other than being able to sit astride one's horse and give rudimentary cues to control and guide, riding quickly developed into a more complex exercise. As the horse's role in our world became more varied, different riding styles evolved in various parts of the world, for diverse reasons.

ENGLISH RIDING

The style that is generally referred to as "English" or "Continental" riding is a versatile method that can be easily adapted to suit most situations, from a leisurely trail ride to a serious competition. Today's methods have evolved from blending old cavalry and hunting techniques with dressage and the classical equitation known as *haute école*, which is epitomized by the riders of the world-famous Spanish Riding School of Vienna and their Lippizaner horses.

This fusion is also well illustrated by the Cadre Noir – the elite cavalry regiment based at the École Nationale d'Equitation in Saumur, France. Their dressage displays are almost equally renowned, and they have produced some of France's top international competitors.

LIPPIZANER
In the capriole, the horse leaps into the air and kicks out at the apex of the jump.

Britain was historically less enthusiastic about dressage, preferring the bravado of hunting and jousting. But King Henry VIII was sufficiently intrigued to employ an Italian-trained horse master at Hampton Court. And William Cavendish, who was created Marquis of Newcastle by Charles I in 1628, was an influential horseman who set up an academy in Antwerp after being banished from England by Oliver Cromwell.

After World War I, horses became less of a military necessity, and leisure riding took off. The skills of the highly

CHARGE OF THE LIGHT BRIGADE
Soldiers trained in the cavalry played a large role in the Crimean War (1853–1856). The ill-advised "Charge of the Light Brigade" resulted in huge casualties of horses and men.

COWBOY AND CATTLE
Cow sense, the ability to read and react to bovine body language, is prized in a ranch horse.

knowledgeable military grooms were dying out, however, and it soon became apparent that specialists trained in horse care and riding were desperately needed. The military image that used to be associated with riding derives from the fact that in Britain, until the 1950s, cavalry schools were among the few places to offer this kind of training. A large number of ex-cavalry instructors have been influential in shaping the English riding style known today.

WESTERN RIDING

When the Spanish conquistadors landed in the New World in the 1500s, they brought with them their Iberian warhorses. Over many decades, as they settled into what is now Central and South America, the Spanish changed their battledress and weaponry to equipment, apparel, and a riding style that better suited the needs of a *vaquero* (herdsman). From the modified *bota* (boot), similar to today's cowboy boot, to the wide-brimmed hat, over the next two centuries the influence of the Spanish and Mexican ranchers was felt throughout the Americas.

When white colonists in North America starting moving west in the 1700s – into areas that would become Texas, Arizona, New Mexico, Colorado, and California – they observed the *vaqueros* with great interest. It was not just their clothes and equipment; it was the way they rode. Their horses were finely tuned to react to light commands, and they had great cow sense. At the end of the war between the United States and Mexico in 1848, the Americans began to integrate the ranching culture of the Hispanics with their own. These American ranchers were the first cowboys.

By the 1850s, the process of selecting horses with smooth gaits had begun. Horses had to be easy to ride – a bone-jarring trot or an exuberant canter was no good. So horses that had a slow, smooth jog and an easy lope were sought after, and later bred as stock horses. The American Quarter Horse, the Appaloosa, and the Paint Horse are all ideal stock horses.

UNDERSTANDING THE HORSE

POINTS OF THE HORSE

The relationship between the structure and function of a horse is referred to as his "conformation". A horse's conformation dictates whether he can do the particular work a human asks him to do. Like humans, horses are built differently and are good at different things.

KEY FEATURES

A horse's head should be in proportion to the rest of his body with a slender, arched neck well set into powerful, sloping shoulders. If he is thick through the throat he will have trouble working on the bit.

The body of a horse should be lean according to his breed. He should have well-sprung ribs for optimum lung capacity, a croup no higher than the withers, so that he can transfer weight to his hind end, and a deep, broad chest. The topline – from the neck over the back to the hindquarter muscles – is like a suspension bridge, which means that most of the weight of a horse's body is slung between the "pillars" of the front and back legs.

The legs are crucial to a horse's wellbeing. Any injury to a leg may not only mean an end to his career, but may be life-threatening. There are no muscles below the knees and hocks, but instead a complex series of tendons and ligaments. A horse has a "stay apparatus" that locks the joints in place so that he can sleep while standing.

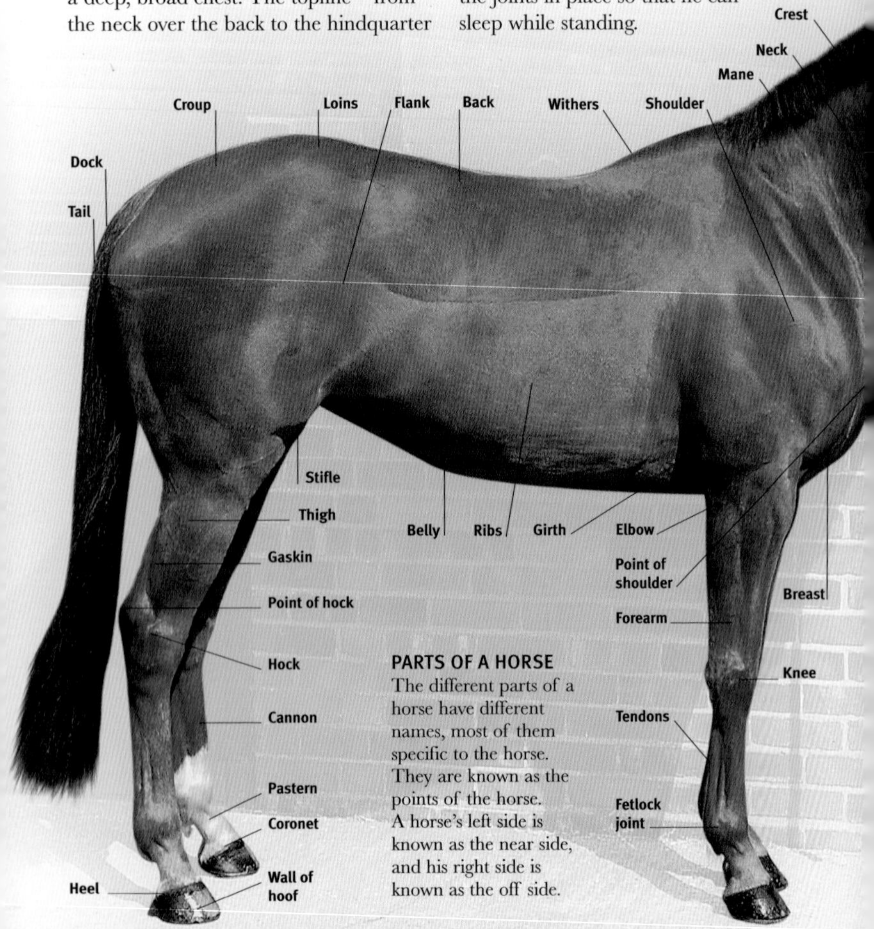

Crest
Neck
Mane
Croup
Loins
Flank
Back
Withers
Shoulder
Dock
Tail
Stifle
Thigh
Belly
Ribs
Girth
Elbow
Gaskin
Point of shoulder
Breast
Point of hock
Forearm
Hock
Knee
Cannon
Tendons
Pastern
Coronet
Fetlock joint
Heel
Wall of hoof

PARTS OF A HORSE
The different parts of a horse have different names, most of them specific to the horse. They are known as the points of the horse. A horse's left side is known as the near side, and his right side is known as the off side.

MEASURING UP

The traditional method for measuring a horse is in hands and inches, which comes from an old custom when horsemen would hold a hand horizontally and count the number of hand widths from wither to hoof. Today, the term "hand" stands for 4 inches (10 cm). Height is now also measured in metres.

A horse is an equine that stands more than 14 hands 2 inches (1.47 m). Anything less than that is considered to be a pony. A pony is not to be confused with a young horse, which is called a foal. A pony is a full-grown equine, but is simply smaller.

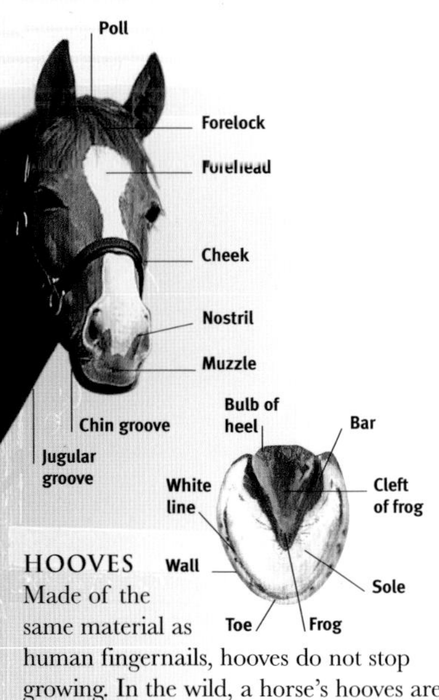

HOOVES

Made of the same material as human fingernails, hooves do not stop growing. In the wild, a horse's hooves are maintained naturally, wearing down as he travels over rough terrain. A domestic horse must have his hooves trimmed.

COAT COLOURS

BLACK
A black horse is completely black over the whole of his body and has a black mane and tail.

BAY
A bay has a reddish-brown body and head, with black lower legs and a black mane and tail.

BROWN
A brown horse has a mixture of brown and black hairs over his body and head, with black legs and a black mane and tail.

CHESTNUT
A chestnut horse can be any shade of copper, from bright to a rich, reddish-brown. His mane and tail are similar or paler.

PALOMINO
A palomino is golden-coloured with a much paler – sometimes even white – mane and tail.

ROAN
Roans have white hairs mixed with black (blue roan), bay (red roan), or chestnut (strawberry roan).

GREY
Grey horses vary from white to dark grey and can be plain, dappled (seen here), or flea-bitten.

SKEWBALD AND PIEBALD
A skewbald's coat has large areas of brown and white. A piebald's coat has large areas of black and white.

APPALOOSA
An appaloosa, or spotted, horse is grey with black or brown spots.

FACE AND LEG MARKINGS

SNIP
A flash of white between the nostrils; can go into the nostrils.

FRECKLED STRIPE
A vertical white mark down the face with small markings on it.

BLAZE
A wide white mark down the face, extending over the nose.

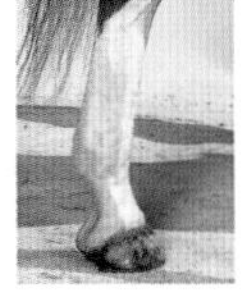
STOCKING
White extending from the hoof as far as the knee or hock.

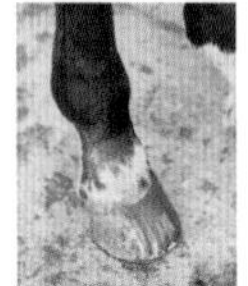
ERMINE
Small markings around a white coronet, especially black.

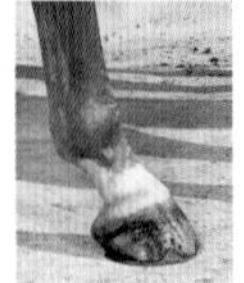
SOCK
White extending from the hoof up to the fetlock joint.

HORSES IN THE WILD

There is something majestic about a herd of horses in the wild, and it is humbling to see them on the move. Most horses living wild are actually feral, originating from once-domesticated stock. Instinct and genetics have honed them into creatures that can survive in the bleakest of conditions and flourish despite the many hardships they encounter.

WILD HORSES

We use the term "wild horse" quite often, but most modern horses that are living wild are the same species as the domesticated horse. The American Mustangs, the Australian Brumbies, Britain's New Forest Ponies, and the Camargue Horses of France are all feral horses. These horses can be captured and domesticated, and some even turn into successful riding and show horses.

The only true wild horse is Przewalski's horse (*Equus ferus*). It is named after a Russian explorer and naturalist who discovered it on the steppes of Mongolia in 1881. Mongolians refer to the horse as "takhi". Diminutive – standing around 13 hands (132 cm) – and bearing primitive features, such as dorsal and leg striping, a brush mane, and thin tail, this horse has never been domesticated.

Despite the fact that it has had strict legal protection in Asia since 1926, its numbers dwindled throughout the last century until there were none left in the wild. Luckily, when the wild horses were found in Mongolia, a few

PRZEWALSKI'S HORSE

Small groups of Przewalski's horses are being reintroduced to the steppes of Mongolia, and there are now about 100 of them in the wild.

EXTRA INFORMATION

WILD EQUINES

Zebras are wild members of the horse family. Some zebras have been tamed and live in captivity, but none have been domesticated. There are three known species of zebra: Grevy's (*Equus grevyi*), Mountain (*Equus zebra*), and Common or Plains (*Equus burchelli*), all from Africa. They are smaller than the horse, standing at 10 to 13 hands (102 to 132 cm). Each species has a unique pattern of black and white stripes, which hides them in the long grass where they live.

A Common, or Plains zebra

were brought to Europe, where they bred well in zoos and numbers grew. Due to an excellent captive breeding programme and a foundation that was established to save the animals from extinction, some horses have now been reintroduced into the wild.

There was once another wild relative of the horse as well as zebras. A desert creature closely related to the Plains zebra, the quagga (*Equus quagga*) lived in Africa. It had a tan body and stripes like a zebra, but only from nose to shoulder. Sadly, the quagga was hunted to extinction in the wild in the 1870s. There used to be some quaggas living in captivity in European zoos, but all of these died out in the 1880s.

SURVIVAL INSTINCTS

Equines have developed a strong set of instincts over thousands of years that have helped preserve the species that live in the wild. These instincts are also present in a domesticated horse.

The herd instinct is powerful in a horse. All horses will look to their herd or band leader for direction. In the wild, the real leader is usually one of the older, wiser mares. This dominant mare controls the movement of the other members of the herd. A stallion's role is to gather his herd, procreate, and keep watch for any rival stallions.

A horse is a prey animal in the wild, and one of his strongest instincts is the "flight or fight" trait. If a horse believes he is in danger, he will, like other prey animals, run. But if cornered with no means of escape, a horse will lash out and protect himself with teeth and hooves.

A horse reacts to another horse's body language, particularly if there is a perceived danger. If one horse determines that there is something treacherous from which he must flee, other horses will respond in the same way, running first and investigating later. An entire herd can be in motion in a fraction of a second after one takes flight.

TRAVELLING TOGETHER

The lead mare of this herd of wild horses is wearing a bell on a collar round her neck. This helps rangers to locate the herd because the other horses will follow where she leads.

THE NATURE OF HORSES

A horse is a social creature and loves the company of other horses. This desire to be with others is so strong that a horse that has lost his rider will gallop with the others on a racecourse or in a group out hacking. As a rule, a horse is not aggressive. Any arguments are usually about establishing or keeping a particular position in a group hierarchy.

LIVING IN A HERD

To isolate a horse from his own kind can be torturous for him, but this does not mean that horses always get along harmoniously. Among domesticated horses, stallions are usually kept away from mares and geldings (castrated male horses) because it is natural for them to collect mares and fight other males. Mares and geldings can be kept together, but this may lead to fights about leadership. Even in a group of only mares or only geldings, there will be horses that are dominant and they will always be reinforcing their dominance.

In a group's pecking order, the oldest, wisest horses are usually at the top and the younger, inexperienced horses at the bottom. When a new horse is introduced into a group, it can upset the balance of power and scuffles can ensue. Bickering takes the form of squeals, bared teeth, and even kicks. Usually, the new horse finds his place in the pecking order fairly quickly.

Horses enjoy interacting with each other and will stand head to tail, grooming each other with their teeth and lips and swatting flies off with their tails. They often develop lasting friendships and may pine for weeks for a friend who has been taken away.

UNNATURAL CONDITIONS

A horse is meant to roam up to 25 km (15½ miles) a day, foraging on grass and constantly processing his food. A modern riding horse, however, is often kept under conditions that are very artificial to his needs. He is housed in a small stable, sometimes for most of the day, and is fed one or two large, high-energy meals instead of being able to graze naturally for hours. And although a stable keeps a horse warm, dry, and clean, it is also isolating.

While a horse is one of the most adaptable creatures on earth, artificial living conditions can stress him. A lack of mental or physical stimulation can manifest itself in different ways, and a horse may find an undesirable outlet for his nervous energy. He may develop "stereotypies", more often called vices. A vice is a compulsive behaviour with which a horse occupies himself in order to cope with his surroundings. It is similar to the abnormal behaviour pattern one sometimes sees in zoo animals.

CONTENT PASTURE-MATES
Horses do not enjoy a solitary existence and are most at ease with another horse nearby.

HAPPY HORSES

A horse will remain happy when his owner is sympathetic to his nature and provides an environment that is as natural as possible. He should be allowed to graze in large pastures with other horses and brought into the stable only when necessary. But in metropolitan areas there is little room for fields, and in arid areas of the world, there is no green grass to enjoy. In these situations, to combat a horse's boredom, a handler should increase his exercise, increase his interaction with other horses, feed him smaller, more frequent meals, and even give him toys or mirrors for some interest.

Most horses can be considered creatures of habit, benefiting from a regular routine. When a horse's meals, training, and even time at liberty are planned out and kept to a daily schedule, it results in a fit, healthy equine partner.

FREE TO ROAM
Herds of tough horses known as "yeguas" can live according to their nature in enormous areas of the Patagonian steppe.

CHECK LIST

STABLE VICES

- **Wind-sucking** is when a horse latches on to a fence, stable door, or other horizontal object and gulps in air rhythmically.
- **Crib-biting** is when a horse chews away the wood as well as gulping in air.
- **Box walking** is when a horse walks round in circles inside his living quarters, wearing away a patch around the perimeter.
- **Weaving** is when a horse stands in front of his stable door and rocks from side to side.

THE THINKING HORSE

A horse is usually a very forgiving creature, and will tolerate the actions of an uneducated handler without too much reprisal. However, he has a tremendous memory – which can be both beneficial and detrimental to the rider or handler.

LONG MEMORY

The way a horse thinks is strongly influenced by his long memory. Both positive and negative past experiences have an affect on thinking and behaviour, which can be exploited through imprinting and training. A horse reacts well to praise and will easily learn that a pat or encouraging voice means he has done something correctly. Similarly, he will associate a past situation with the present. For example, a horse that refuses to load up into a horsebox may not be being obstinate or disobedient. He may be remembering that the last time he travelled in a box he was jostled around severely – maybe by a careless driver. Not wanting to repeat that unpleasant experience, he is understandably refusing to step into the box again.

TRIGGERING INSTINCTS
A horse box may seem like a dark cave to a horse, which may naturally trigger his fear instincts.

TRAINING TECHNIQUES

The majority of trainers who have been successful for a long period of time truly

EXTRA INFORMATION

NATURAL HORSEMANSHIP

The art of natural horsemanship has grown enormously in the last decade, but it is really nothing new. Xenophon, an Athenian soldier, wrote *Perihippikes (On the Art of Horsemanship)* around 400BCE. This could be considered the first book on natural horsemanship, due to its concern for the horse's welfare.

Natural horsemen study the nature and body language of horses and use equine psychology to teach them. Their training differs slightly, but most use the philosophy of communicating with a horse to make the "right answer" to the task easy and the "wrong answer" difficult. When a horse attempts to answer the question correctly, the trainer will reward. A horse is taught through the application of pressure in the form of a leg squeeze, a pull of a rein, or a tap with a whip. When a horse moves away from the pressure, it is released. This is the reward. The horse looks for the release of pressure to know that he has done the task correctly. The American horseman Pat Parelli is a founder of modern natural horsemanship.

Pat Parelli

understand the cognitive abilities of a horse and recognize how to exploit them. They understand that positive reinforcement handed out consistently makes training a horse much easier. In decades past, the idea of breaking a horse by force or violence was the norm. Now, when a horse is trained to carry a saddle and rider, the term often used is "starting" a horse instead of the old term "breaking in". Food can also be used for positive reinforcement, although this is used mostly for teaching tricks, not for training under saddle. A horse can even learn through clicker training, when a device is clicked to tell him he has behaved correctly.

An older, more experienced horse can also help with training. A "green" or inexperienced horse that has never crossed a stream or jumped a fence may often gain the confidence to do so by following a "schoolmaster" first.

A horse can be taught to override his instincts, especially his flight response to fright, through desensitization training. He is introduced to frightening situations and objects and is allowed to examine them until he finds the situation harmless. This is useful in the training of police horses, which have to remain calm in noisy situations that would normally be frightening for a horse.

MARE AND FOAL
A foal will take his cues from his mother. If she is relaxed and content, the foal will be calm too.

IMPRINT TRAINING

In a learning process that takes place within the first few hours of birth, a foal imprints on to his mother. In this process, he learns to recognize individuals, for example his mother, and his own species. Humans can use imprinting as a training technique. They handle the foal in subtle ways that mimic the real training he will have when he is older, so he will accept training and handling later in life.

THE HORSE'S SENSES

Because horses are prey animals, their senses have adapted for species preservation. Over the centuries, they have successfully developed into fleet-footed athletes with amazing self-preservation, not only surviving the centuries, but flourishing in the modern world.

SENSE OF SIGHT

A horse has an extraordinary field of vision, being able to see nearly all around his body. He cannot, however, see directly behind himself or below his nose, due to his eyes being on the sides of his head. He will turn his head to bring objects into focus that are out of his peripheral vision. A horse can differentiate between some colours, but sees them differently from us. Brightly coloured jumps, for example, translate into subtle reds, blues, and greys. Perhaps surprisingly, a horse sees very well in the dark, but introducing a light source at night will actually impair his vision. As with humans, a horse's eyesight worsens with age, and his eyes are subject to maladies similar to those of human eyes.

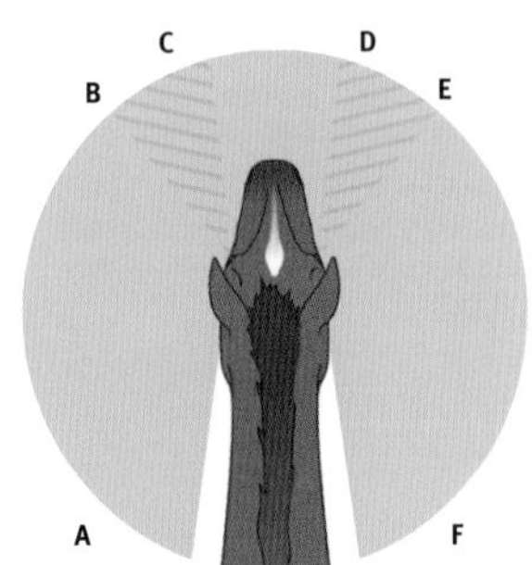

FIELD OF VISION
A horse can see nearly all around his body (A to F). He can see well in front of himself (C to D) but has two blind spots: right below his nose and directly behind him. He has excellent vision to the sides (B to C and D to E).

SENSE OF HEARING

A horse's sense of hearing is his most acute sense. He is able to hear many high-frequency sounds that humans cannot hear, and can pick up sounds from several kilometres away. Because of their acute hearing, loud noises or a cacophony of sounds will cause many horses distress. A horse can be voice-trained to recognize words and sounds, and will follow voice commands. He is also attuned to his handler's tone of voice.

EXTRA INFORMATION

RANGE OF MOVEMENT IN THE EARS

A horse uses his sense of hearing a great deal. He can swivel his ears independently nearly 180 degrees from front to back at a moment's notice. In this way he can funnel sounds coming from various directions more efficiently. Ear position also denotes a horse's mood (*see* p.37).

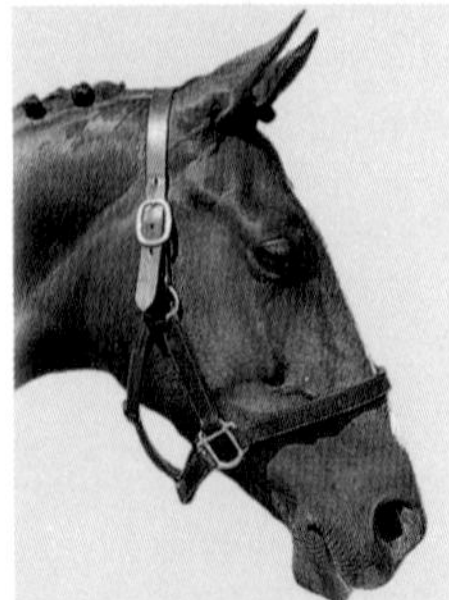

Ears pointing forwards

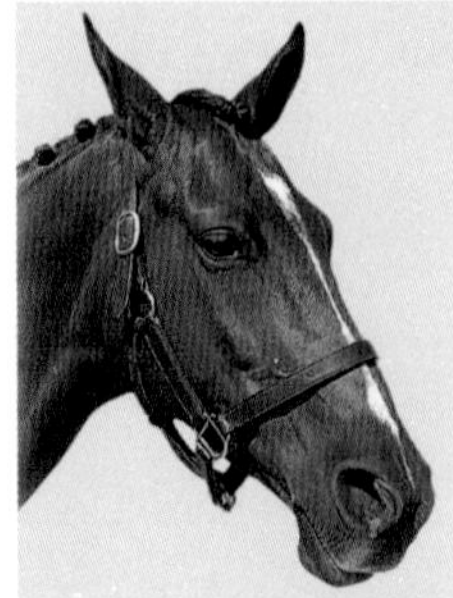

Ears pointing to the sides

Ears pointing backwards

SENSE OF TASTE

A horse's sense of taste develops depending upon how he is kept. For example, a racehorse is rarely fed treats, so he will not know automatically that apples, mints, sugar, molasses, and even carrots, are good to eat. Despite this, a horse has a discerning palate. He can tell dry, stemmy hay from hay full of flowers. He can even tell the difference between two types of water, which can be difficult for a handler when travelling with a horse. He will also go off his feed or refuse water if he finds the taste too foreign.

SENSE OF SMELL

Along with his sense of hearing, smell is very important to a horse's survival. He has a heightened sense of smell, and relies on it to help decipher whether someone approaching is friend or foe. He can smell water from a great distance and will be able to find his way back home by following scent, not by remembering the way. A stallion can determine whether a mare is in heat up to 8 km (5 miles) away, and a mare recognizes and bonds with her foals in the herd not by sight, but by smell.

HORSE BEHAVIOUR

FLEHMEN RESPONSE

A horse often makes this facial expression as a reaction to unusual smells or tastes in the environment. A stallion also does it when he is trying to locate a mare in heat. The horse curls his upper lip and raises his head in order to draw air across a specialized organ called the "vomeronasal" located in the roof of the mouth.

Horse performing the flehmen response

SENSE OF TOUCH

A horse is a thin-skinned, short-haired mammal, so he is very sensitive to touch, and one of the most blissful activities for him is to share mutual grooming. A horse can feel a fly land on his coat and flick it away simultaneously with a deft swing of the tail. And using his lips and whiskers, he will pull up grasses according to feel, not sight. A highly trained dressage horse can interpret the subtle weight shifts and leg aids of his rider. A horse that has to be kicked on constantly by his rider to make him move forwards, is not insensitive, however, but has instead been desensitized by over-use of the leg aid.

SENSITIVITY

A horse is sensitive to touch over his whole body, so he will be startled if you touch him with no warning.

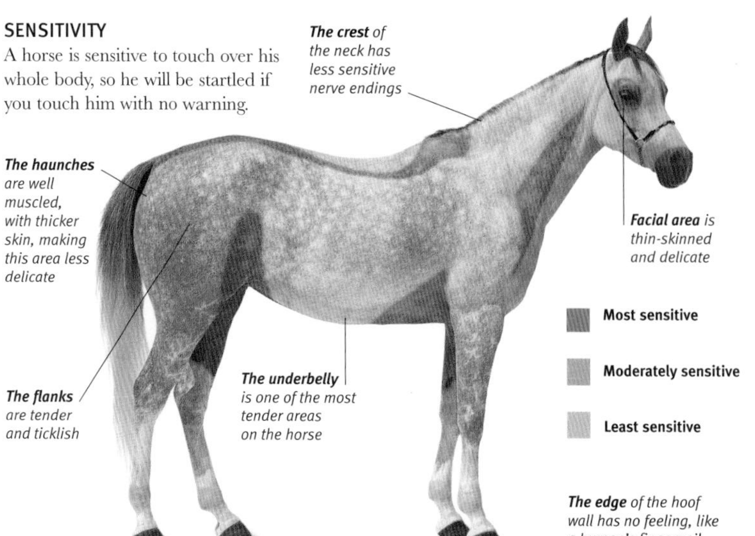

BODY LANGUAGE

A horse does not wag his tail or purr, but he still has plenty of ways in which to communicate how he feels. The signs may be subtle, but with a little experience, anyone can pick up on a horse's body language. Good horse handlers can interpret the smallest of signs.

AROUND THE EYES

A horse's pupils cannot widen, so eyes are a bit difficult to read. Usually, a horse has a soft expression around his eye. The area above the eye will show whether a horse is worried or angry. Some horses, when startled, will show the white area surrounding the eye.

MOUTH AND LIPS

A horse's mouth is very expressive. A droopy lower lip on an older horse often denotes a relaxed, content horse, and a horse that chews or licks without food present is being submissive or subordinate. A nuzzling lip shows affection, while a horse gnashing, grinding, or baring his teeth is showing irritation or anger.

FEET AND LEGS

A horse that is pawing the ground with a front foot is showing impatience. When he rests one hind foot, he is resting comfortably. But any horse that pulls a hind leg up and makes a jerking motion is very angry and threatening to kick.

READING BODY LANGUAGE

EMOTION	BODY LANGUAGE AND BEHAVIOUR
Contented	■ Relaxed neck and head position with hind leg resting and tail subtly swishing ■ Soft look in the eye ■ Ears flick to gather sound ■ Lower lip may droop down on an older horse
Interested	■ Head and neck elevated slightly ■ Ears forward ■ Nostrils subtly flared ■ Horse stands square or moves towards the object of interest ■ Eyes bright
Submissive	■ Horse lowers his head ■ He stands his ground but licks his lips or makes chewing motions ■ May shuffle his feet ■ Eyes alert ■ One ear points towards the dominant individual ■ Tail remains low
Aggressive	■ Horse humps his back slightly, lowers his neck, and may thrust out his head ■ May grind his teeth or even snap ■ He tightens his hindquarters, lashes his tail, and lays his ears flat against his head ■ Eyes have a sharp, assertive look
Excited	IN A STABLE ■ Horse may pace or wheel around ■ Raises his head significantly and arches his neck ■ Eyes widen and may show white ■ Nostrils flare ■ Horse may neigh or squeal ■ Tail will arch or even stand straight up IN A FIELD ■ Horse may gallop, buck, snake his head from side to side, slide to a stop, or prance ■ May snort after galloping ■ His heart rate is elevated
Angry or irritated	■ Horse looks at the source of irritation with a hard expression ■ May stamp his feet or paw the ground ■ Swishes his tail with vigour and lays back his ears ■ May grind his teeth or nip
Ill or depressed	■ Lacklustre eyes ■ Weak posture with low neck and motionless tail ■ Legs often splay out to hold the body up ■ Uninterested expression ■ Horse holds his ears neutrally or to the side ■ Breathing may change from normal
Fearful	■ Horse stops in his tracks, runs or leaps suddenly, and snorts ■ White ring around the eye ■ Nostrils flare ■ Head and neck raised ■ Heart rate increases ■ Breathing becomes rapid ■ Ears prick towards the frightening object

EAR POSITIONS

Some of the most expressive parts of a horse are his ears. If the ears are forward, a horse is interested in something in front of him. One ear flicked back while the other is forward means a horse is paying attention to something behind him – often the rider. Ears flattened low against the head denote an angry or irritated horse. Some horses will often hold their ears in a floppy sideways position, which is a sign of deep concentration and focus.

TAIL MOVEMENTS

Although a horse does not wag his tail, he can still express feelings with it. A horse that clamps his tail down indicates that he is tense or possibly not feeling very well. If he swings his tail softly he is relaxed and contented. A tail held high shows a horse in good spirits, but a horse that is lashing his tail back and forth is showing his displeasure.

ALERT AND HAPPY

A happy horse wears a confident expression that is easy to see, even by the untrained eye.

THE GAITS

Most horses have four natural gaits, also called paces. These are the steps of a horse, and the gaits common to all breeds are walk, trot, canter, and gallop. Some breeds naturally possess unique gaits, such as the Icelandic Horse's "tolt". A wild horse will walk most of the time, as it grazes, and will gallop only when escaping from danger.

THE WALK

This is the slowest gait and the one a horse uses most often. It is a four-beat gait, which means that there are four separate footfalls – left hind, left fore, right hind, then right fore. During the walk, a horse will always have three feet on the ground while one is lifted. A horse walks at about 3 km/h (2 mph).

Left hind going down

THE TROT

The trot is faster than the walk and has two beats to its rhythm. A horse moves his legs in diagonal pairs, with the left hind moving in tandem with the right fore, and the right hind moving in tandem with the left fore. A horse trots at about 10 km/h (6 mph).

Left hind and right fore together

THE CANTER

The canter, the second-fastest gait, has a rocking-chair motion due to its three beats: right fore, left hind, right hind and left fore together. A horse appears to have a skipping motion, and "leads" with either front leg, in this case the right (*see* p.151). A horse canters at about 27 km/h (17 mph).

Right fore on the ground

THE GALLOP

The gallop is a horse's fastest gait. It is very much like the canter, except that a horse will have four footfalls instead of three because the hind limb lands slightly before the forelimb with which it is paired in the canter. Racehorses, particularly sprinters, can reach speeds of more than 70 km/h (45 mph).

Right hind on the ground, then left hind followed by right fore

Left fore on the ground

EXTRA INFORMATION

LESSER-KNOWN GAITS

- The "tolt" is a gait performed by the Icelandic horse. It is a lateral four-beat gait and is often as fast as a canter.
- The "pace" is a lateral two-beat gait in which the legs move in unison on each side. Some breeds, such as the Standardbred, pace naturally.
- The "paso" is a four-beat lateral gait performed by the Peruvian Paso. Unlike other lateral gaits, the paso can be collected and extended.

Left fore on the ground

Right hind on the ground

Right fore going down

Left hind and right fore together

Right hind and left fore together

Left hind on the ground

Right hind and left fore on the ground

Right hind going down, followed by left hind

Right fore on the ground, left fore going down

Right hind on the ground, then left hind followed by right fore

HOW TO BEHAVE AROUND HORSES

Horses are not inherently mean or nasty, but because of their size and tendency to be nervous it is better to act with caution around them. Some horses enjoy interacting with people, while others prefer the company of their own kind. The more time you spend with your horse, the better you will understand his unique personality.

WORKING AROUND A HORSE

When you approach a horse, make your presence known in a quiet but deliberate way. Avoid jerky or sudden movements. A horse likes predictability, so approach with a quiet confidence.

Be very respectful of the power that is in the hindquarters when working around a horse. Stand close to him so that you are within an arm's reach at all times. A horse's kick can severely injure you, and staying closer reduces the distance to impact and therefore the power at impact. Do not duck under the neck or the belly, and be aware of where your feet are in relation to the horse's feet. It is easy for a horse to step on your foot accidentally if he absent-mindedly shifts his weight to another foot.

BEING IN CHARGE

Always take the role of herd leader, but do not confuse this with being over-dominant. Whether you are walking a

WALKING BEHIND A HORSE

When you walk behind a horse, place one hand on his hindquarters and give a little pat so that he knows that you are there. A horse generally kicks out in surprise, rather than anger.

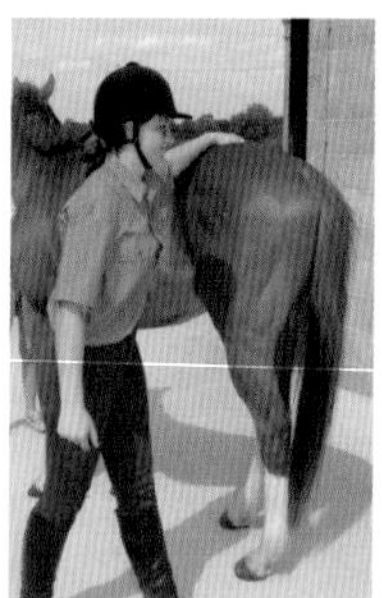

Place your hand

Begin to move round

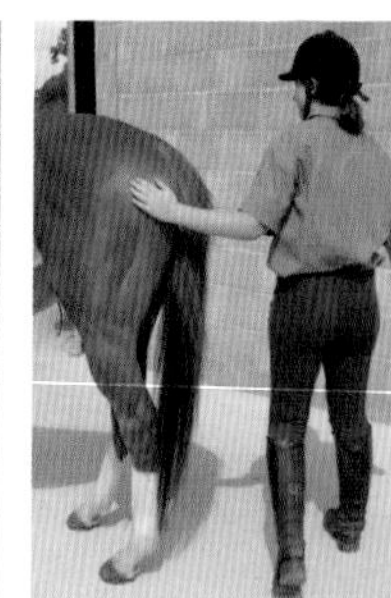

Maintain contact

DOS & DON'TS

- **Do** learn how to be with a horse. It will help to keep you both from getting injured.
- **Do** wear proper footwear that will protect your toes from being crushed should they be stepped on.
- **Do** be mindful of each horse's likes and dislikes. One horse may not like his ears being touched while another may not mind at all.
- **Don't** kneel by a horse, but squat instead. This will allow you to move away quickly if necessary.

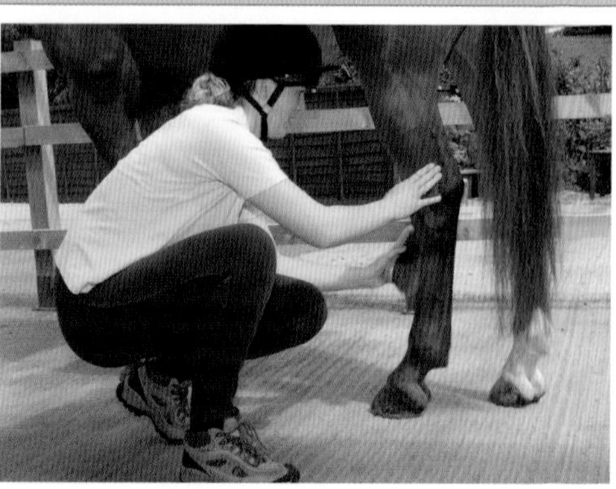

Squatting to look at a horse's hind leg

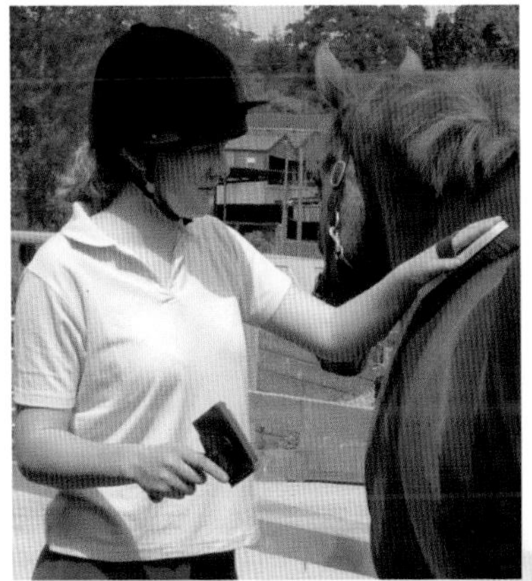

GETTING TO KNOW YOUR HORSE
Carrying out basic care tasks, such as grooming, will really help you get to know a horse. It is also a good time to look for any cuts, swellings, or skin problems.

horse forwards, or riding, or bathing him, you must be in charge. A bossy horse must be corrected so that he knows he has done something wrong.

When being led, a horse should follow you shoulder to shoulder. You should not have to drag him along, nor should he pull you. If he barges forwards, two sharp, hard tugs on the leadrope should be all that are needed to bring his attention back to you.

If he does the opposite, and shuffles along at a meandering pace, carry a long dressage whip (*see* p.132) in your left hand. When you have to slow down for the horse, reach back with your left arm held long and straight, flick your wrist, and tap his hindquarters with the whip. That should be enough to teach him that he must go at your pace, not the one he wants.

When you do have to correct a horse for being too bossy, or for ignoring your wishes, do so quickly and without anger. A horse is sensitive to human emotions but will not understand if you punish him for something he did earlier. He will only make the link between punishment and bad behaviour if you correct him immediately he does something wrong.

KNOWING SENSITIVE SPOTS

Observe a horse while you are grooming or tacking up. Note where he is extra sensitive to touch (*see* p.35) and avoid scrubbing him. If you reach a touchy spot, he might react by laying back his ears or making a nipping motion. Do not be afraid to speak to a horse while you are grooming. This will help him to know where you are.

TREATS AND REWARDS
Give treats from a flattened hand. It is better to give a horse treats when he is wearing a headcollar rather than a bridle with a bit in his mouth.

TACKING UP

ESSENTIAL EQUIPMENT

There is a vast array of riding equipment available, some items steeped in centuries of tradition, others based on the latest technology. While outfitting yourself and your horse, remember that the most innovative gadget on the market might not be necessary. Start with the basic tack and clothes and make sure they fit comfortably.

RIDING CLOTHES

To start riding, the essentials are a proper hat or helmet and safe footwear (*see* pp.49 and 72). You should wear a riding hat that meets the most recent safety standards of the country you live in (*see* p.53). It must fit correctly and the harness must be correctly adjusted too, otherwise the fit and safety are compromised.

You do not necessarily have to wear jodhpurs or breeches (*see* pp.48–49) for riding. Straight-cut jeans or other hard-wearing trousers are fine if you find them comfortable and they give you enough room to move, but you will find that jodhpurs and breeches are the most practical and durable. For everyday Western riding, long, flared jeans that cover the boots are best (*see* pp.72–73).

CARRYING A SADDLE
A saddle can be carried with the cantle against your side, or over your arm with the pommel towards your elbow.

It is practical to wear layers, and choose fabrics that are suitable for the activity and the weather; riding can range from hot, hard work in a lesson to being cold and windswept on a winter hack. Gloves are not essential but are useful to prevent your hands from being chafed as well as to keep them warm or to give better grip on wet or sweaty reins.

WESTERN SADDLE
Most Western riders use a specially elaborate saddle for competing in shows. This must fit the horse equally as well as his everyday saddle.

ENGLISH TACK

A horse that is going to be ridden needs a bridle, with a suitable bit, and a saddle (*see* pp.54–61). The main requirements for these are that they are well made, fit correctly, and are in good repair. This usually means they are made of strong, good-quality leather and are carefully maintained by cleaning with saddle soap. It is quite easy to fit a bridle, but a new saddle should always be fitted by a qualified saddler.

Most horses need only one type of bit, but some go better if their bit is changed occasionally, and some need a different bit for faster work.

A good pair of brushing boots (*see* p.63) provide leg protection for jumping and cross-country, and some horses need leg protection if they are clumsy. But do not be tempted to use an item of tack just because other people do – only use what your horse really needs.

WESTERN TACK

The basic essentials for Western riding are the same as for English riding – a saddle and a bridle (*see* pp.74–77). Always use the simplest bit that the horse responds to when doing any particular work.

There are various styles of saddle, but for any saddle to fit well and last, good workmanship and materials are crucial. The Western saddle is sturdy and solid, with thicker leather than its English counterpart. The girth, or cinch, can be made from a variety of materials including string and neoprene, and should be wide and comfortable around the horse's belly. Western saddles are traditionally used on top of woollen saddle blankets that are often colourful. These can be used on their own or placed over a plain wool pad that absorbs sweat and wicks moisture away from the back.

Like the saddle, the bridle should be made from strong, flexible leather with tight, even stitching, and buckles should be made from quality stainless steel rather than plated metal.

ENGLISH BRIDLE AND BIT
The bridle and bit help you control the horse's head. This English bridle features a flash noseband and a loose-ring snaffle bit. It is properly adjusted so that the horse is comfortable.

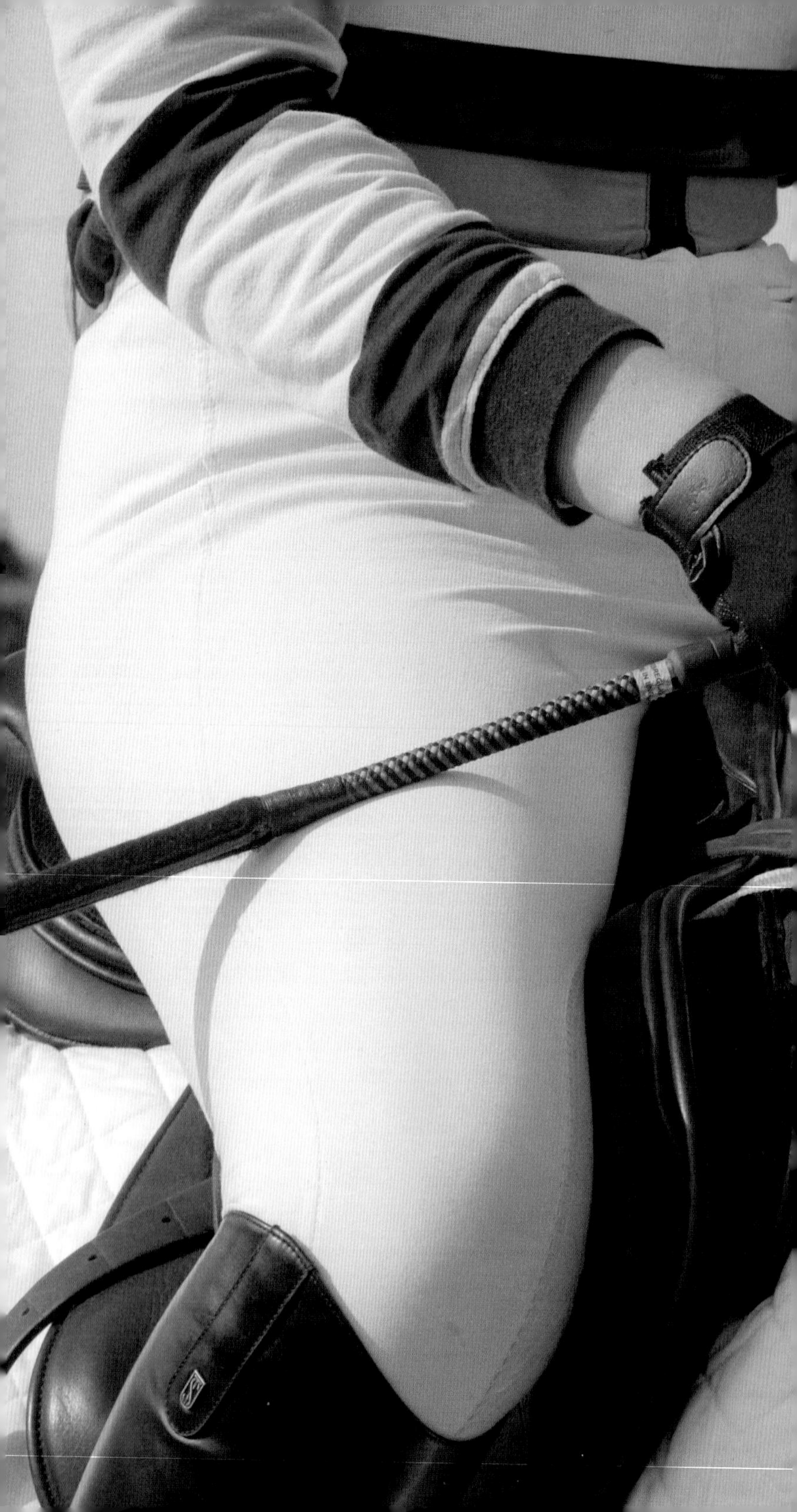

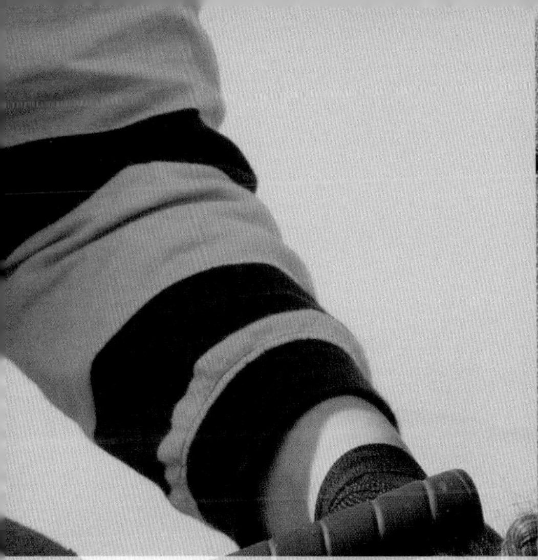

ENGLISH EQUIPMENT

English riding equipment has a more formal image than its Western equivalent. The most important aspects are that the tack is suitable for and fits the horse, and that the rider's clothes are safe and practical.

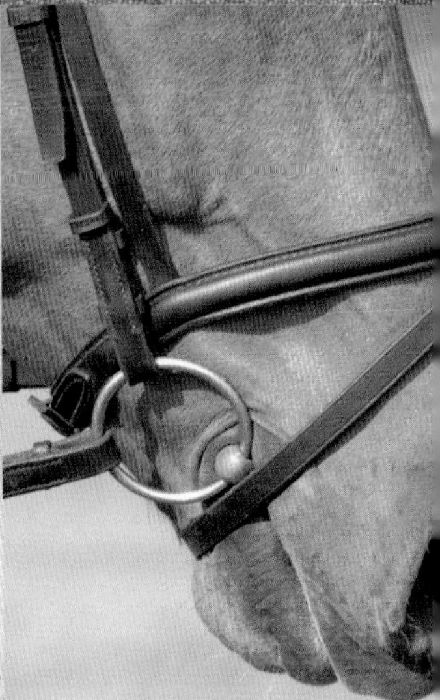

EVERYDAY RIDING CLOTHES

Comfort, safety, and practicality of clothing is paramount. You need freedom of movement, reinforcement on areas of hard wear, and some degree of waterproofing, windproofing, and temperature control as you may experience hot, cold, and wet conditions in a single ride. Avoid baggy clothes that will get in your way. Always wear a suitable hat and footwear.

SHIRTS AND TOPS

Most ordinary shirts and T-shirts will be fine for riding, provided they give you room to move freely and the fabric is comfortable. Cotton is a good fabric; microfibres are also ideal as they allow your skin to breathe and they dry quickly. Wear layers that wick moisture away from your skin. Avoid sleeveless or cropped tops – exposed skin leaves you vulnerable to horse bites and sunburn.

COATS AND JACKETS

Most casual riding coats are similar to the type you would buy for general outdoor use. The main difference is that they have a vent – an extra flap of fabric – at the back to allow more movement and prevent rain from dripping straight on to the saddle. Look for the most breathable fabric you can find; sometimes there is a compromise between this and waterproofing.

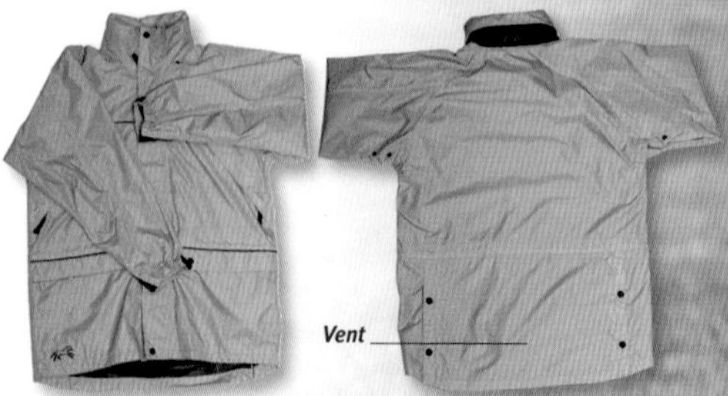

Vent

Front of coat **Rear of coat**

A GOOD RIDING COAT

Look for a coat with a waterproof, breathable outer layer and a rear vent, which can be fastened when you are off the horse if you wish.

PRACTICAL CLOTHES

Look for clothes that are practical – looking good is a bonus but safety must be your prime consideration.

A body-warmer *or gilet makes a smart, practical extra layer*

BREECHES AND JODHPURS

Close-fitting, stretchy jodhpurs (full length, usually worn with short boots) or breeches (slightly shorter and worn with long boots or half-chaps) are hard-wearing and practical. Most have reinforced knee patches, and some also have a reinforced seat. Jeans are fine but they often have an uncomfortable seam under the crotch and are not practical in wet weather; cotton moleskins can be a good alternative.

GLOVES

Gloves need to be close fitting, very flexible, and grip well. Look for reinforced palms and fingers, because these areas take a lot of wear. Synthetic fibres such as fleece and nylon are good. For summer, cotton gloves with pimples on the palms are ideal. String or leather gloves are very smart but not practical in all weathers.

Cotton gloves **Synthetic gloves**

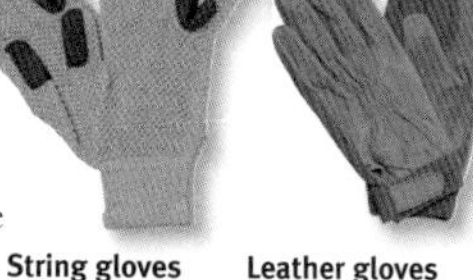

String gloves **Leather gloves**

HAND PROTECTION

Gloves protect your hands from chafing and can improve your grip on wet reins.

BOOTS AND CHAPS

Your boots or shoes must be made of tough material, preferably leather, to give your feet some protection. They must have a small heel to stop your foot slipping through the stirrup and an outer sole that runs the whole length of the boot. One of the most practical combinations for everyday riding is short jodhpur or paddock boots and half-chaps. Leather or suede half-chaps give the same protection as long boots.

Leather paddock boots

Half-chaps

Jodhpur boots

FOOT PROTECTION

Safe footwear reduces the risk of your feet getting stuck in the stirrups.

CLOTHES FOR COMPETITION

Competition clothing varies slightly according to the discipline and level, but the basic outfit consists of buff breeches, long boots, a shirt with tie or stock, a tweed, navy, or black jacket, gloves, and a navy or black hat. Being smart and well turned out is all part of the occasion; you and your horse should be a credit to each other.

DRESSED FOR THE OCCASION

Competition clothing involves a certain amount of etiquette, such as the colour of breeches or stock worn with a particular jacket. There are also rules designed for practicality and safety, for example, body protectors (*see* p.53) are compulsory in certain disciplines. You and your horse should always look smart, especially in showing and dressage.

BASIC OUTFIT

Good-quality woollen tweed is warm, breathable, waterproof, will last many years, and is suitable for most lower-level competitions. You should wear pale coloured breeches – fawn or buff – with a tweed jacket.

CROSS-COUNTRY OUTFIT

A body protector is mandatory for cross-country; wear a smart top, such as a rugby-type shirt of any colour, either under or over it. Body protectors come in a variety of colours and can be co-ordinated with your shirt and hat cover.

RIDER ACCESSORIES

STOCKS AND TIES

A stock is worn with an upright collar that has a loop to hold it. You wear a coloured stock or normal collar and tie with a tweed jacket, and a white stock with a black or navy jacket.

Coloured stock

Collar and tie

White stock

***A hat** should be black or navy and worn with the same colour jacket*

***Shirts often** come with detachable collars so they can be worn with a tie or a stock*

***Gloves must** be worn for dressage. White looks stylish and is worn at higher levels, but when you start out, black or brown gloves are acceptable*

***Breeches worn** with a navy or black jacket should be pale buff or white*

***Boots must** be black or brown and it is usual for adults to wear long boots*

***Spurs are** required at the higher levels of dressage*

DRESSAGE OUTFIT

This rider is dressed smartly for a dressage competition. She is wearing a show jacket, which can be made of a synthetic or wool-mix material. Her hat matches the jacket, and a neatly fastened stock, plain white shirt, gloves, pale breeches, and polished boots complete the outfit.

HATS AND BODY PROTECTORS

A riding hat is one of the most important items of equipment for the rider. It must be in good condition and conform to the latest official safety standards set by your country or the discipline in which you are competing. The safety standards also cover the style of the harness and a reputable retailer should be able to advise you on size and fit.

AVOIDING SERIOUS INJURY

There is nothing that can protect you completely, but you can take steps to minimize injury. Hats and body protectors are designed to protect your vital internal organs; they work by absorbing the shock of a fall and helping to distribute the impact. In cross-section, the cushioning material looks rather like polystyrene with air bubbles in it. Impact causes the material to compress, so it is important to replace your hat or body protector if it has taken a hard blow – whether from a fall, from being dropped on a hard surface, or from being kicked. For this reason, these items should be carefully looked after although you should replace them about every five years even if they have not had a blow.

A hat *and its safety harness must be correctly fitted*

A body *protector must be measured to fit you*

A shirt *can be worn under or over a body protector*

LEGAL REQUIREMENTS

In Britain, it is illegal for any rider aged 14 or under to ride on the road without an approved hat. Laws may be updated, so make sure you are aware of any changes.

HATS AND HARNESSES

An undamaged, well-fitting hat and harness that conforms to current legal safety standards is essential for every rider at all times. The regions that have standards are Britain, Europe, USA, Australia, and New Zealand. Current safety standards do not allow harnesses with chin-cups.

ACHIEVING A GOOD FIT

Both the hat and its harness must be correctly fitted. Buy your hat from an approved retailer who can advise you.

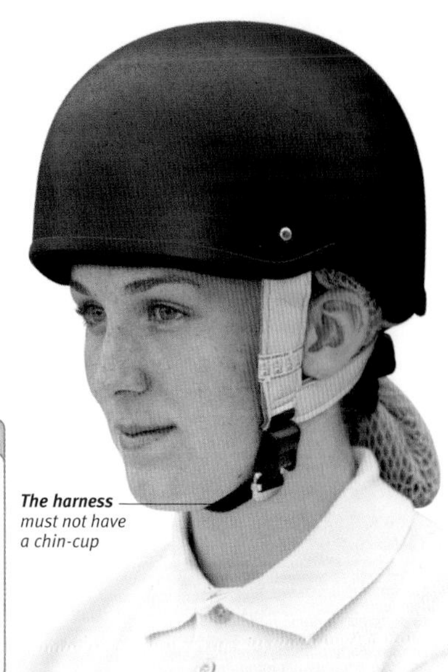

The harness *must not have a chin-cup*

RIDER ACCESSORIES

HAT COVERS

Coloured silks are worn for cross-country, but a black or navy velvet suits more formal occasions. A fluorescent hat cover is ideal for riding out, or hacking, on the road

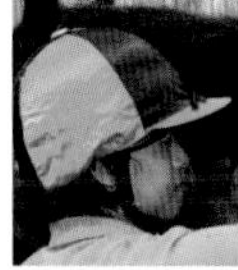

Coloured silk

EQUIPMENT TYPES

VENTILATED HAT

A lightweight hat that is popular with riders for jumping and endurance.

Lightweight ventilated hat

VELVET-COVERED HAT

A smart hat with a leather harness that is suitable for many types of riding.

Velvet-covered hat

CARBON-FIBRE STRIP HAT

A style of hat with a carbon-fibre central strip that is popular among show jumpers.

Hat with a carbon-fibre strip

BODY PROTECTORS

Three levels of protection are available: level 1 (black label) for jockeys only; level 2 (brown label) for basic needs; and level 3 (purple label) for normal riding, jumping, and working with horses. Shoulder protectors may be integral to or separate from the body protector.

CORRECT FIT

Both the front and back of a body protector must fit correctly. Take advice from a trained retailer and, if you grow or change shape significantly, have the fit checked.

Front view

Back view

SADDLES

The majority of saddles are based around a structure called the tree. Usually made of wood, it is the tree that determines the size and width of the saddle – while the filling around it can be adjusted to some extent, it is the tree that must fit the horse. The filling, or flocking, is usually made of wool but inflated air panels can also be used.

GENERAL-PURPOSE SADDLE

Unless a horse is regularly ridden in a specialist discipline, he is likely to have only one saddle – a general-purpose model, which is shaped between the dressage and jumping styles (*see* pp.56–57) and is suitable for most types of riding. The tree can be sprung or rigid. The sprung variety, with a strip of flexible steel built into each side of the wooden structure, generally feels more comfortable to the rider, but provided the fit is good and the rider's weight is evenly distributed, it makes little difference to the horse.

FROM THE SIDE

When you place the saddle on the horse, the cantle should be slightly higher than the pommel so that the deepest part of the seat is positioned centrally.

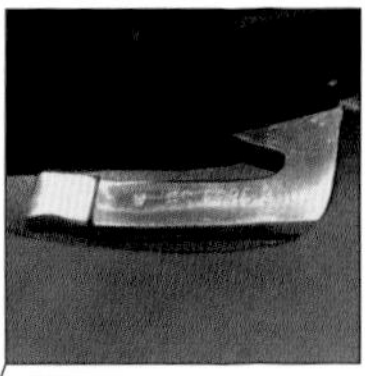

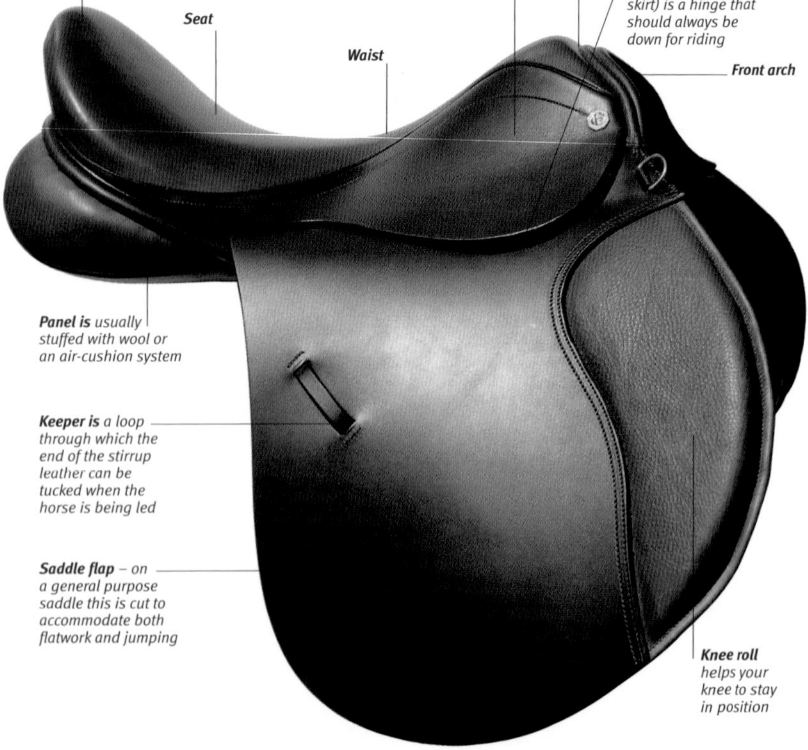

Cantle

Seat

Waist

***Skirt covers** the stirrup buckles*

Pommel

***Stirrup bar** (under the skirt) is a hinge that should always be down for riding*

Front arch

***Panel is** usually stuffed with wool or an air-cushion system*

***Keeper is** a loop through which the end of the stirrup leather can be tucked when the horse is being led*

***Saddle flap** – on a general purpose saddle this is cut to accommodate both flatwork and jumping*

***Knee roll** helps your knee to stay in position*

UNDERNEATH

It is easy to forget to look after the underneath of the saddle. Clean it regularly and check for signs of wear; keep the leather supple but do not oil it too often (*see* p.93).

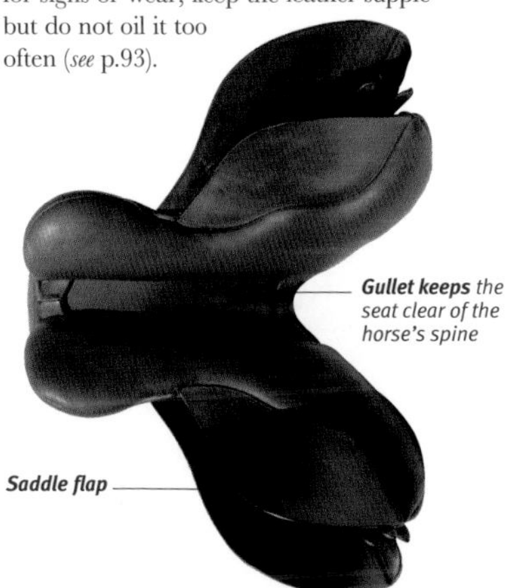

FROM THE BACK

When you look at a tacked-up horse from behind, with a rider in the saddle, you should be able to see a clear gap between the horse's spine and the saddle all the way through.

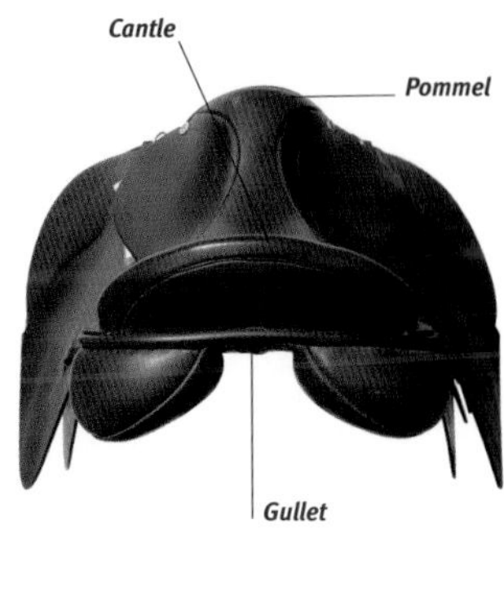

ASSEMBLED SADDLE

Thread each stirrup leather through the hole in the top of a stirrup iron, then buckle it. Slide the part of the leather that is just above the buckle on to the stirrup bar. Push it fully across, then pull the back of the leather down so that the buckle is snug against the bar. The end of the leather should not be put through the keeper while you are riding. The girth is buckled to two of the three girth straps located under the flap on each side of the saddle.

PREPARE THE GIRTH

Place the girth across the saddle so that you can quickly attach it when the saddle is on the horse's back.

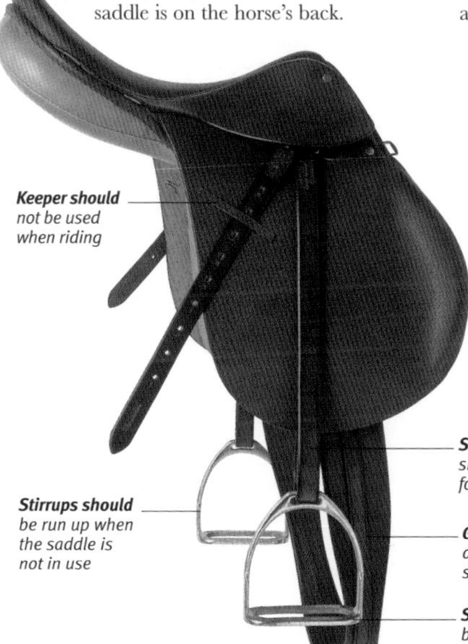

UNDER THE SADDLE FLAP

More of the saddle's structure, such as the points of the tree and the girth strap attachments, can be seen under the flaps.

***Point pocket** covers the point of the tree, which should match the shape of the horse*

***Buckle guard** protects the flap from wear*

Knee roll

***Girth straps** attach to the saddle by webbing strips: two straps on one strip, one on another. For safety reasons, always buckle the girth to two straps that are not fixed to the same piece of webbing*

TYPES OF SADDLE

Riders who seriously pursue a specific discipline will eventually need a more specialized design than a general-purpose saddle. Specific designs are available for jumping, dressage, and different showing categories. Saddles used for cross-country are often based on a very lightweight racing design that gives the rider maximum contact with the horse and ensures that the horse carries no unnecessary weight. Many riders prefer not to use large, padded thigh rolls or knee blocks. These might seem to offer greater stability but some people feel that if the horse falls, they can hold the rider in place for too long and prevent him from being thrown clear.

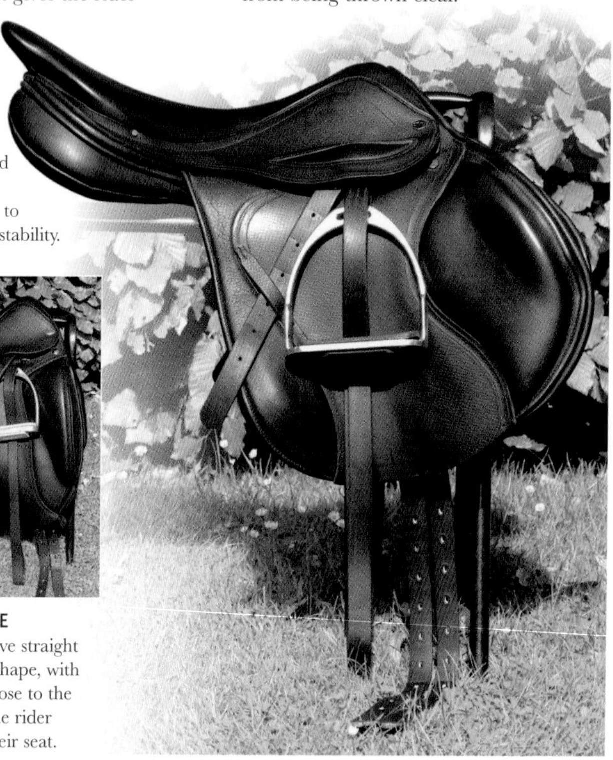

JUMPING SADDLE

Jumping saddles have a relatively flat seat. The flaps are forward-cut, and the knee and thigh blocks are designed to increase the rider's stability.

DRESSAGE SADDLE

Dressage saddles have straight flaps and a deeper shape, with the balance point close to the pommel, to allow the rider maximum use of their seat.

TYPES OF GIRTH

Usually made of leather or synthetic fabric, this crucial piece of equipment is the only way to secure the saddle on the horse, so it must be kept in good condition – as must the girth straps on the saddle. Some have an elasticated panel that affords the horse more room to move and breathe, but be careful of over-tightening them (*see* p.67).

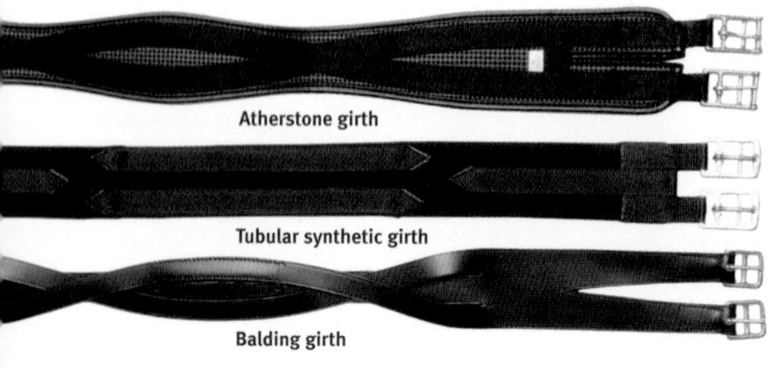

GIRTH SHAPES

Some girths are narrower behind the horse's elbow to reduce the likelihood of rubbing. "Balding" and "Atherstone" girths are similar in shape, but the Balding has three straps that cross over, while an Atherstone is made of a single piece.

STIRRUPS AND TREADS

The most common types of stirrup are the tall, narrow "fillis iron" and the wider "hunting iron", which has rounder sides. Most people put rubber treads in the base for grip. Technically, it is always correct to use treads on fillis irons but only correct on hunting irons if you wear leather-soled boots. Safety stirrups are designed to release the feet quickly in a fall.

STIRRUP LEATHER

Good-quality stirrup leathers are essential. Synthetic alternatives are not as strong as real leather.

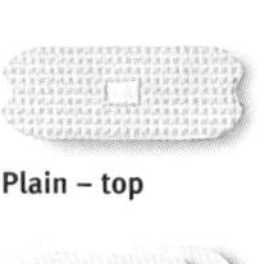

Plain – top

Plain – underneath

Safety – top

Safety – underneath

TYPES OF TREAD

The plain and safety styles are shown above. Treads are removable and are inexpensive to replace when they wear out.

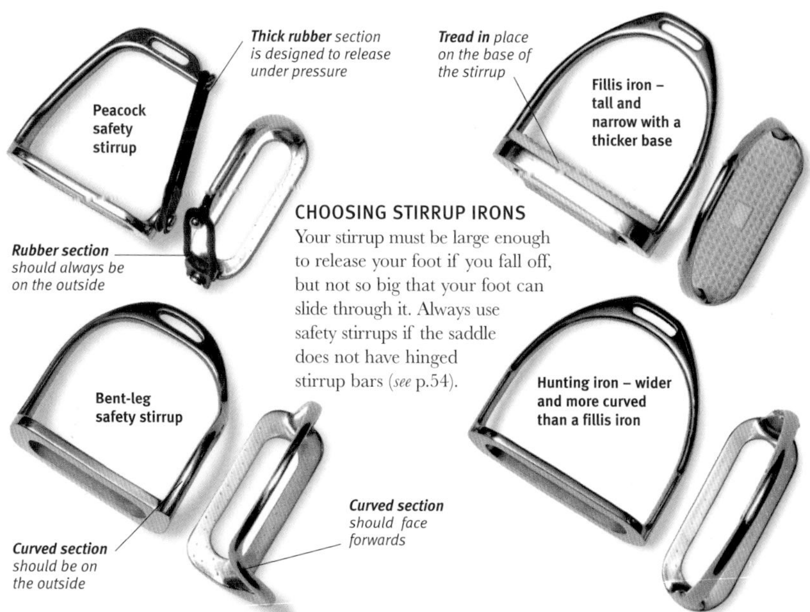

CHOOSING STIRRUP IRONS

Your stirrup must be large enough to release your foot if you fall off, but not so big that your foot can slide through it. Always use safety stirrups if the saddle does not have hinged stirrup bars (*see* p.54).

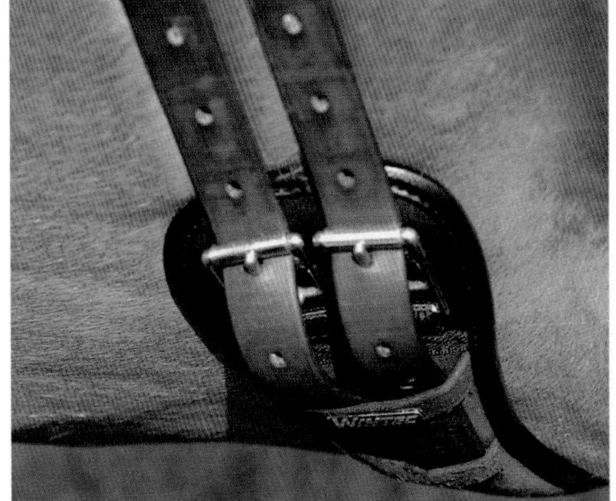

Buckles on a dressage girth

DRESSAGE GIRTH

Also known as a "Lonsdale" girth, a dressage girth is short and designed for use with the extra-long straps of a dressage saddle. It buckles lower down so that the rider's leg can lie absolutely flat against the flap of the saddle.

Dressage girth in place

BRIDLES AND BITS

A bridle should always be used when a horse is being ridden, as it offers the greatest degree of control – riding with just a headcollar or halter is not safe. When you choose which type of bit and noseband your horse will wear, always seek advice from someone more experienced, as both items can do considerable damage if wrongly used or fitted.

BRIDLES

As long as it is well made, correctly fitted, and properly looked after, a bridle made of good-quality leather will last many years and be comfortable for the horse. Good leather is very strong but has the added safety feature that it will break under great pressure. This might sound strange, but if a horse becomes caught up on something, release is often the safest option, so the bridle needs to be breakable. Washable, synthetic bridles are available but may not be as durable, safe, or comfortable in the long term.

The headpiece and throatlash are made from one piece of leather. The headpiece connects to the bit via the cheekpieces, and the throatlash helps to stop the bridle from slipping over the ears. The browband stops the headpiece from slipping backwards. A noseband is not essential but is generally used in some form. The cheekpieces, noseband, and throatlash are usually attached with buckles, while the bit and reins are attached with buckles or billets.

Reins are *looped through the throatlash for storage*

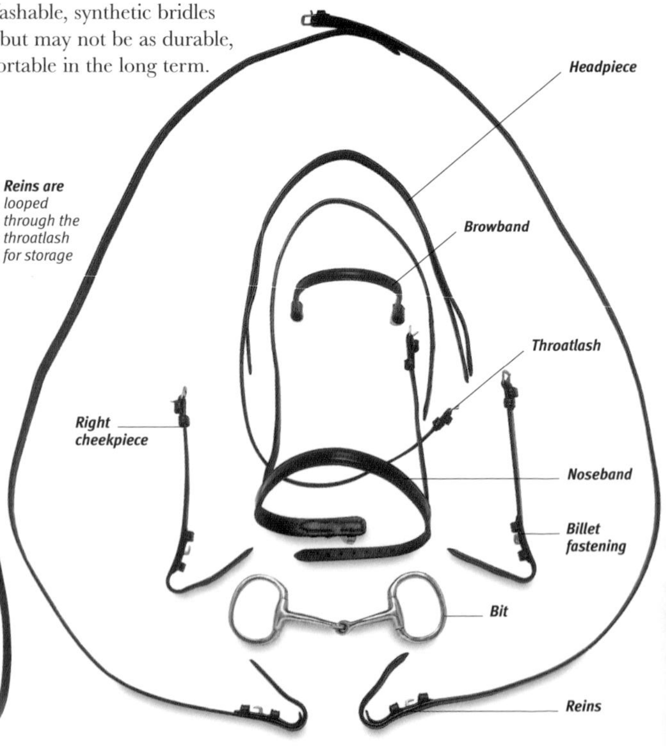

Headpiece

Browband

Throatlash

Right cheekpiece

Noseband

Billet fastening

Bit

Reins

A BRIDLE IN STORAGE

When a bridle is not in use, hang the headpiece on a large bracket with the browband facing forwards. Thread the throatlash through the reins and buckle it. Put the noseband around the cheekpieces and into its keepers.

A BRIDLE IN PIECES

The first time you take a bridle apart, lay it out to see how the parts fit together. To assemble it, thread the noseband and headpiece through the browband then attach the cheekpieces, bit, and reins, making sure nothing is twisted.

SNAFFLE BRIDLE

The term "snaffle bridle" applies to a bridle that has only one bit attached, usually some form of snaffle or pelham (*see* pp.60–61). It can be used with different nosebands – such as the basic cavesson, flash, or drop (*see* p.60) – or with no noseband at all. On all bridles, buckle fastenings face outwards and billet fastenings face inwards.

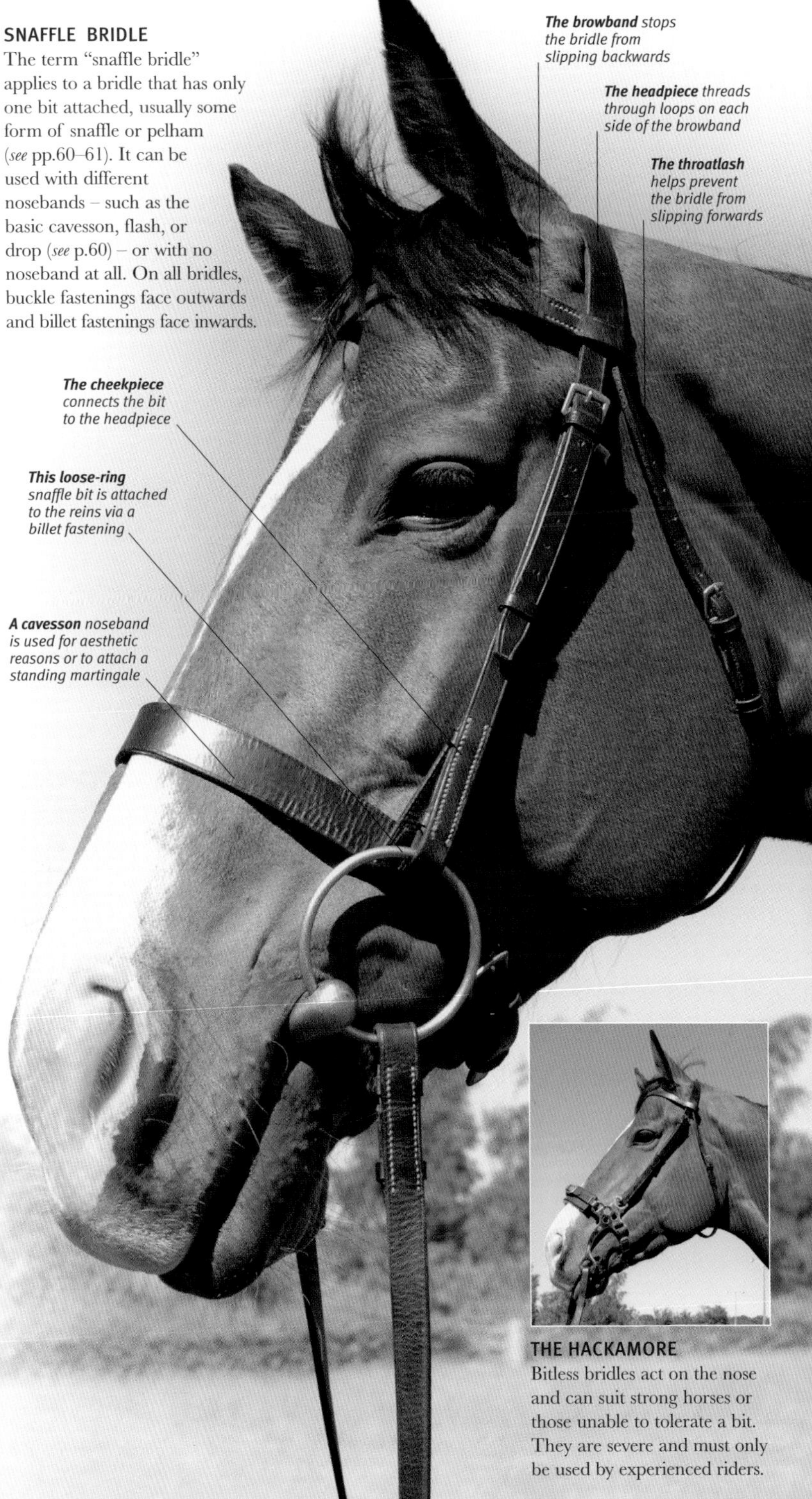

THE HACKAMORE

Bitless bridles act on the nose and can suit strong horses or those unable to tolerate a bit. They are severe and must only be used by experienced riders.

TYPES OF NOSEBAND

The basic noseband is the cavesson (*see* p.59). This offers no control in its own right, but is the point where a standing martingale is attached to the bridle. A horse's nose is very sensitive – there is more of the nostrils than the part you see at the muzzle – so nosebands other than cavessons should be used with great care and only when really needed.

A drop noseband can be used for a horse that resists the bit by opening his mouth, crossing his jaw, or pulling his tongue over the bit. A grakle works in a similar way but over a wider area, and its lower strap is less likely to interfere with the horse's breathing than a drop noseband. A flash noseband is basically a cavesson with a separate piece attached at the front that works as a drop noseband.

DROP NOSEBAND
The front of a drop noseband fastens four fingers width above the nostrils. The back fits below the bit rings in the chin groove.

GRAKLE NOSEBAND
A grakle has two straps that cross over a pad on the bridge of the horse's nose. One fits below the bit and one above.

FLASH NOSEBAND
The top of a flash noseband fits like a cavesson. The lower strap passes below the bit and must be clear of the nostrils.

TYPES OF BIT

Each type of bit works slightly differently, by putting pressure on one or more areas of the horse's mouth, lips, tongue, and head. There are many types, and most are based on two designs – the snaffle, which acts only on the mouth, and the curb, which acts on the poll and is most often seen as the second bit in a double bridle or in forms such as the pelham. Both can be straight-bar or jointed; the single-jointed type has a "nutcracker" action that can be severe, while the double-jointed snaffle design is milder.

Correct fitting is crucial. The mouthpiece should protrude about 5 mm (¼ in) each side of the mouth. A straight bar bit should hang against the corners without wrinkling them; a jointed bit should make the horse "smile" but not create wrinkles.

BIT MATERIALS

Various types of steel, plastic, and rubber are used to make bits. Good quality is essential so that they do not break or chafe. Check their condition regularly.

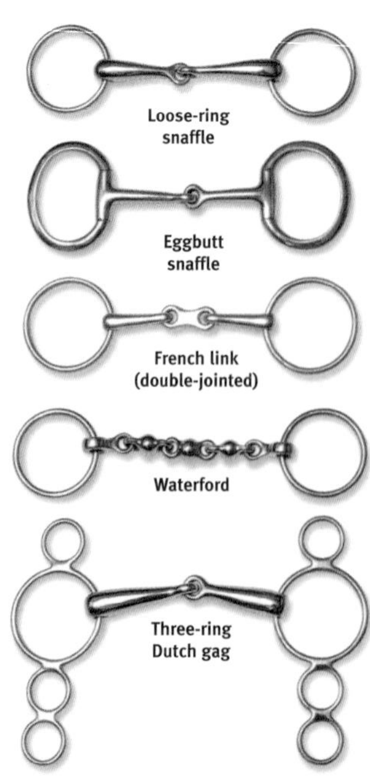

MARTINGALES

The types of martingale most often used are the running and standing martingales. They give extra control and should not be used just for aesthetic reasons. Both comprise a long strap that attaches at one end to the girth and at the other end to the reins or noseband.

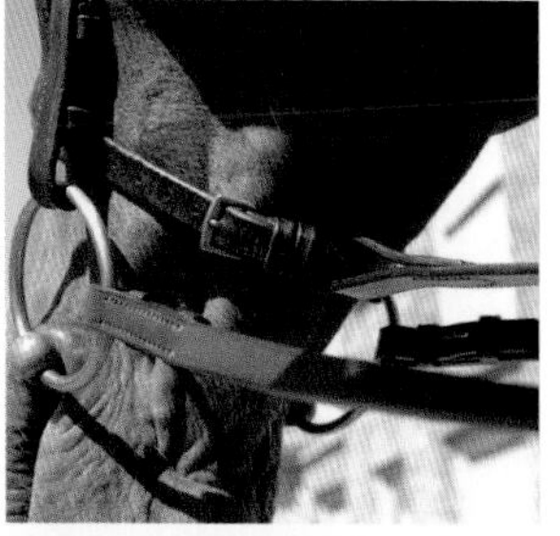

STANDING MARTINGALE

A standing martingale helps you to control a horse by stopping him from raising his head too high, and can be used on a horse that tosses his head. It has a single strap fixed to a cavesson noseband.

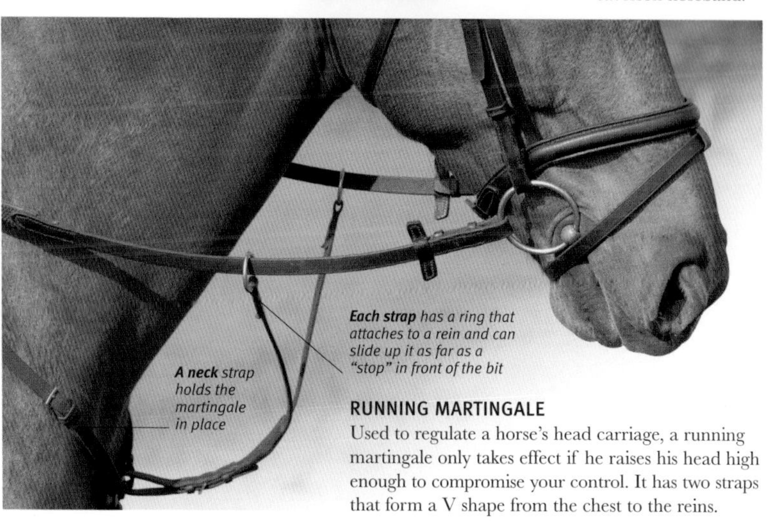

RUNNING MARTINGALE

Used to regulate a horse's head carriage, a running martingale only takes effect if he raises his head high enough to compromise your control. It has two straps that form a V shape from the chest to the reins.

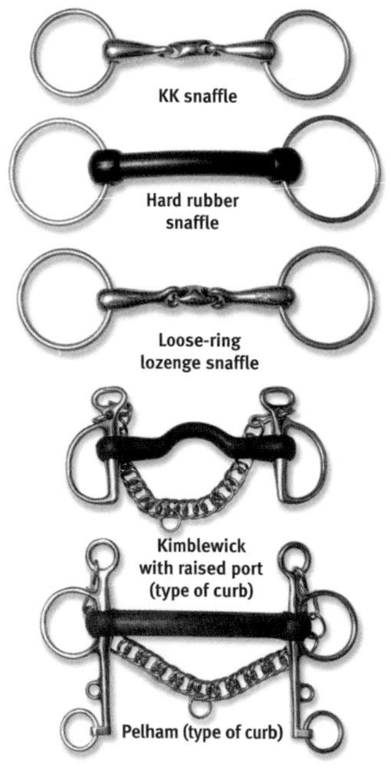

EQUIPMENT TYPES

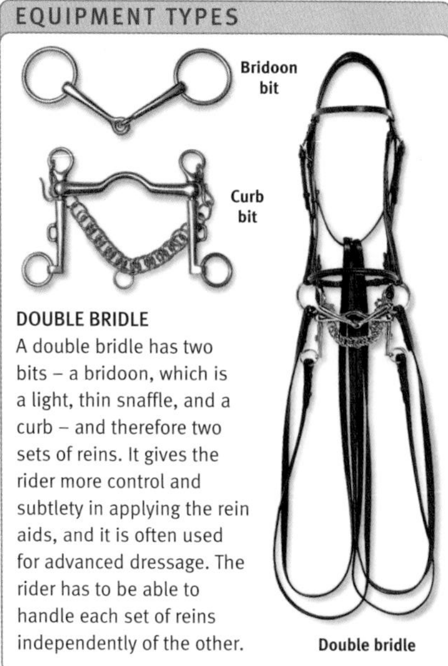

DOUBLE BRIDLE

A double bridle has two bits – a bridoon, which is a light, thin snaffle, and a curb – and therefore two sets of reins. It gives the rider more control and subtlety in applying the rein aids, and it is often used for advanced dressage. The rider has to be able to handle each set of reins independently of the other.

HORSE PROTECTION

Beyond the basic essentials of a saddle and bridle, there is a range of special items of tack that can help protect the horse from discomfort and injury. Saddle pads, boots, and bandages all have specific uses, but it is important to remember that they should not be used to compensate for poorly fitting tack or careless riding.

COMFORT AND SAFETY

Just as the saddle and bridle must fit correctly and be suitable for the horse and the type of riding, so must other pieces of equipment. Items such as numnahs and boots are not fashion accessories – each has a purpose and can cause or mask damage if used wrongly, so do not be tempted to use them just because other people do. However, there are times when a few basic items will make all the difference.

JUMPING PROTECTION

It is sensible to put protective boots on the horse for show jumping and cross-country situations where he is likely to knock his legs or risk an over-reach.

***Saddle cloths** can provide extra shock absorption for the horse's back*

UNDER THE SADDLE

Most riders use a numnah or saddle cloth to keep sweat and dirt off the saddle. Cotton or wool are the best fabrics. A numnah should be shaped to pull right up into the gullet of the saddle.

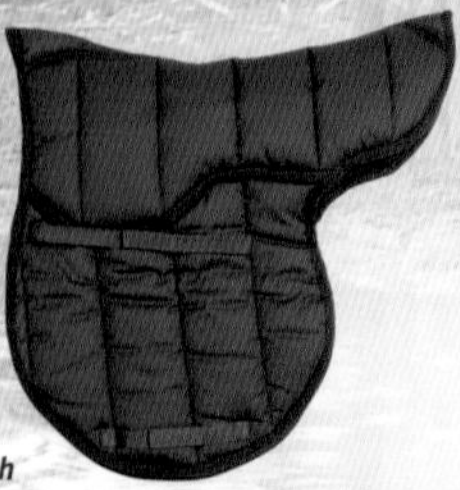

Numnah

EQUIPMENT TYPES

SADDLE PADS

Back pads give extra shock absorption under the whole saddle, while wither pads are used at the front only. These can be useful if a horse's weight fluctuates and affects the fit of the saddle.

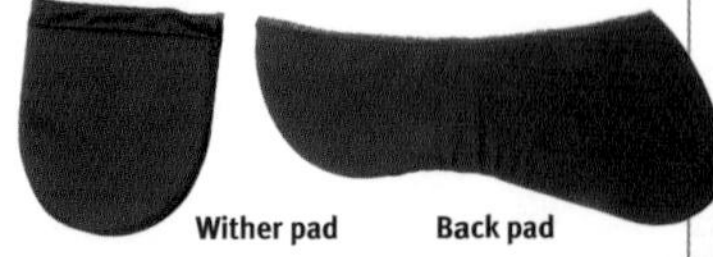

Wither pad **Back pad**

BRUSHING AND OVER-REACHING

Horses that move correctly should not need boots for daily work. But those prone to "brushing" one leg with the opposite hoof, treading on their own heels, known as "over-reaching", or any horse doing unusually hard or fast work might need some protection.

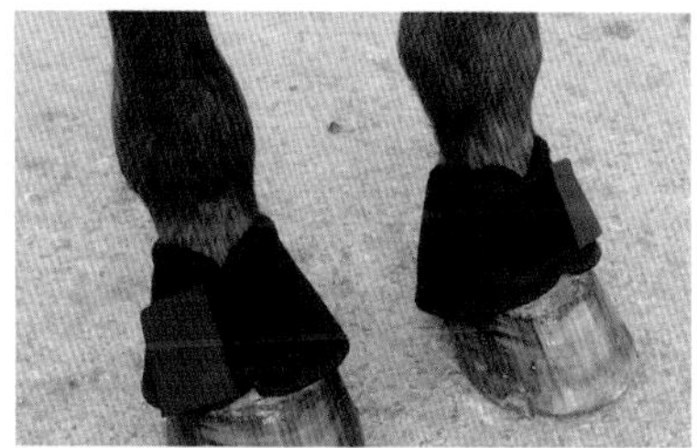

OVER-REACH BOOTS

Most cross-country riders use over-reach boots to reduce the risk of injury. The basic "bell boot" style is designed to slip on over the hoof but can be fiddly to put on and tend to flip off. A design with tough Velcro fastenings, as shown above, is easier to use.

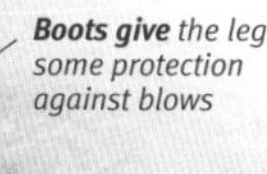

Boots give *the legs some protection against blows*

TIPS AND TECHNIQUES

PUTTING ON EXERCISE BANDAGES

Exercise bandages are used for protection or tendon support. They are thinner than stable bandages and sometimes slightly stretchy, so be careful not to wrap them too tightly. They start below the knee, finish above the fetlock, and are always worn over padding. **Step 1** Wrap the padding round the leg. Start the bandage diagonally with the top corner protruding, then make the turn just below the top of the padding. **Step 2** Fold the corner under the next turn and bandage down the leg. **Step 3** Bandage to the top of the fetlock and back up, then tie securely. **Step 4** Ensure that the finished bandage does not restrict the horse's movement.

1 **Start at the top**

2 **Bandage down the leg**

3 **Tie securely**

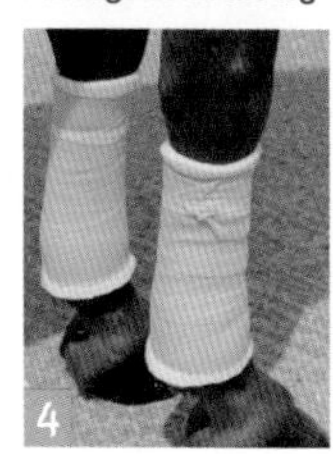

4 **Finished bandages**

PUTTING ON BRUSHING BOOTS

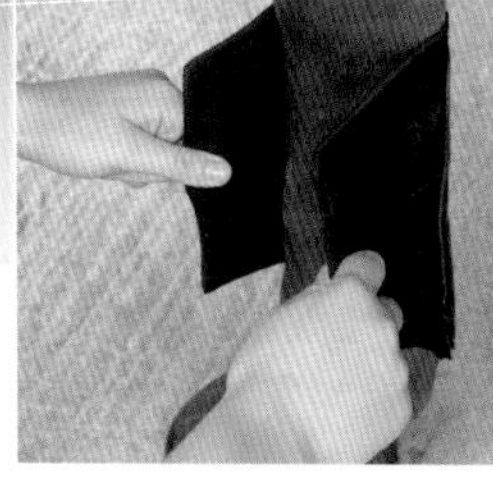

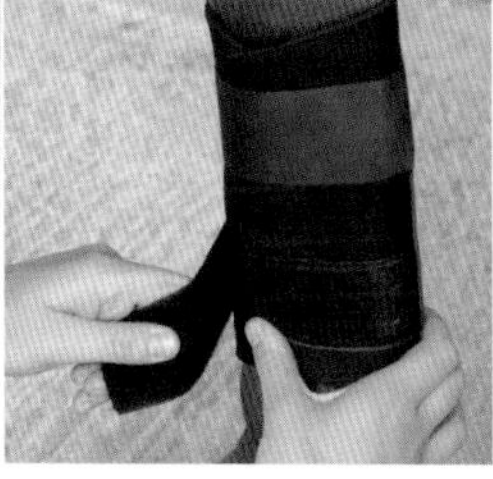

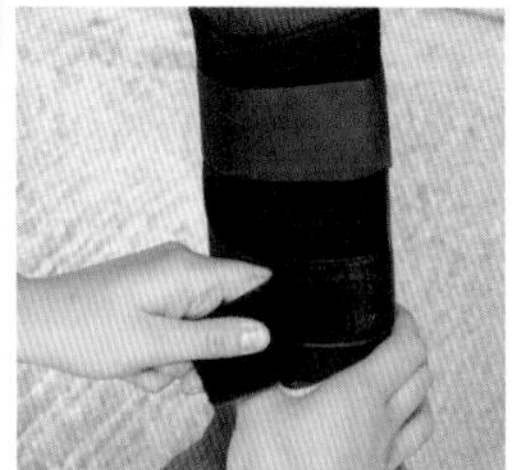

1 POSITION THE BOOT A brushing boot fits between the knee and the fetlock. Position it a bit high and slide it down into place so that the hair lies smoothly underneath. Most boots are shaped to make fitting easy.

2 FASTEN THE BOOT Do up the top straps first. The free ends should go towards the rear. (For boots with double closure, the underneath straps go from front to back, and the top ones from back to front.)

3 CHECK THE FIT Make sure the boot is correctly fitted and adjust as necessary. Brushing boots should fit snugly so that they do not slip down, spin round the leg, or interfere with the horse's movement.

PUTTING ON A HEADCOLLAR

Headcollars are used for leading and tying up a horse and are usually made of either leather or a synthetic fabric, such as webbing. They consist of a headpiece, throat strap, and noseband connected by cheek straps. When tying up a tacked-up horse, always put a headcollar and leadrope over the bridle. Do not tie up using the reins.

***If there** is a leadrope attached to the headcollar, tuck it over the horse's neck or keep hold of it. Do not trail it on the ground*

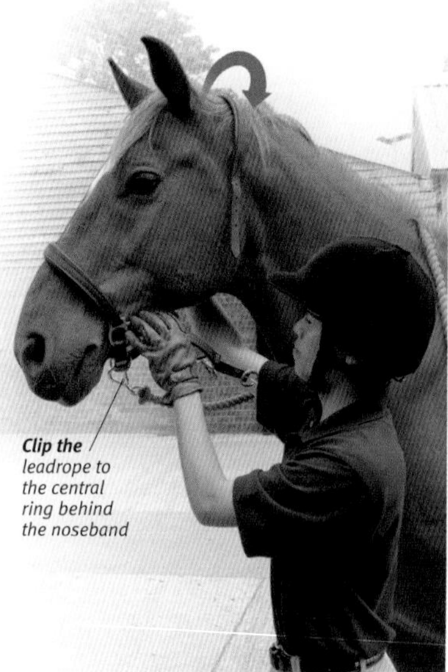

***Clip the** leadrope to the central ring behind the noseband*

1 SLIP ON THE NOSEBAND Start by unfastening the buckle on the headpiece. Standing on the horse's near side (his left side), hold the noseband in both hands and slide it carefully over the horse's nose.

2 BRING OVER THE HEADPIECE Hold the noseband with your left hand and take the headpiece in your right hand. Bring it up as far as you can, then push the end of the headpiece over the horse's head, behind his ears.

TIPS AND TECHNIQUES

CATCHING A RELUCTANT HORSE
Hang the headcollar and leadrope over your shoulder and approach the horse towards his shoulder so that he can see you. If he is reluctant to be caught, hide the headcollar behind you and offer him a carrot, which he can have as a reward once the headcollar is on. If a horse is often difficult to catch, let him associate it with pleasures, such as feeding, as well as work.

Offer a titbit

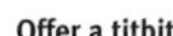

Fasten the headcollar

EQUIPMENT TYPES

HEADCOLLARS

In the UK, leather and webbing headcollars have mostly replaced halters (*see* p.77) as they distribute the pressure placed on the horse's head more evenly. However, strong webbing headcollars are not safe for travel (*see* p.270) or turnout as they are less likely than leather to break under pressure – if a horse gets caught up on something he must be able to escape to avoid injury.

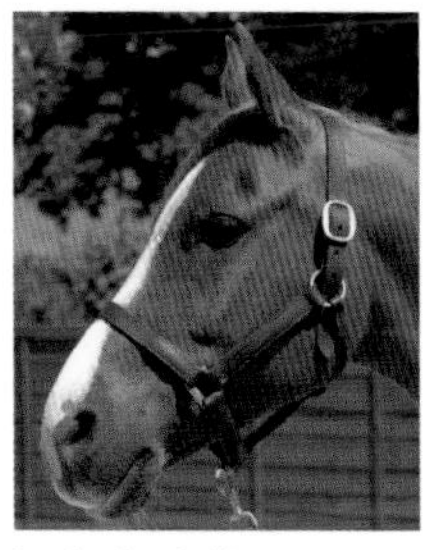

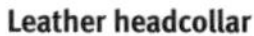

Leather headcollar

Webbing headcollar

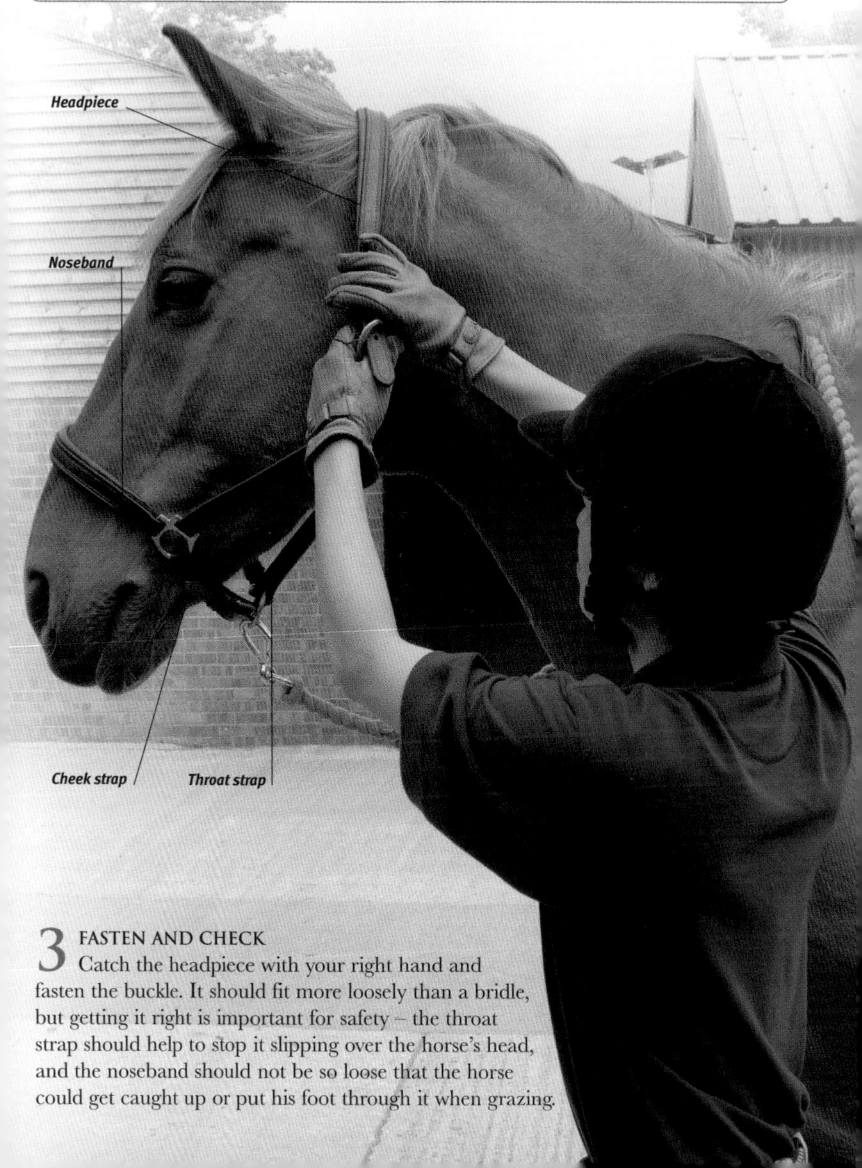

Headpiece

Noseband

Cheek strap

Throat strap

3 FASTEN AND CHECK

Catch the headpiece with your right hand and fasten the buckle. It should fit more loosely than a bridle, but getting it right is important for safety – the throat strap should help to stop it slipping over the horse's head, and the noseband should not be so loose that the horse could get caught up or put his foot through it when grazing.

PUTTING ON A SADDLE

Before you put on a saddle, check that both stirrups are run up, and put the girth across the saddle so it is out of the way but can be fastened immediately. Make sure the horse's back and belly are clean and the coat is lying smoothly. Practise putting on a saddle without anything underneath so that you can see exactly where it should sit.

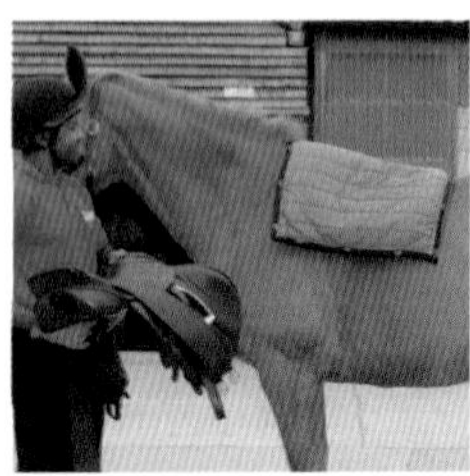

1 PLACE NUMNAH The saddle is usually put on from the near side. If using a numnah, this can be put on first or with the saddle. Place it slightly too far forward, over the withers, so that when you slide the saddle back it smooths out the hair.

2 PLACE SADDLE Holding the front arch in your left hand and the cantle in your right, gently lift the saddle on top of the numnah. Pull the numnah up into the gullet and slide both back into place together, with the pommel resting just behind the withers.

Lift up *the numnah into the front arch and at the cantle, so that there is always an air channel between the saddle and the horse's spine*

TECHNIQUES

ADDING A RUNNING MARTINGALE

If your horse wears a martingale, place the neckstrap over his head with the buckle on the near side. **Step 1** When you reach under the horse for the girth, slip it through the loop on the end of the martingale. **Step 2** After putting on the bridle, unfasten the reins at the central buckle and pass each rein through a ring of the martingale, then re-fasten the reins.

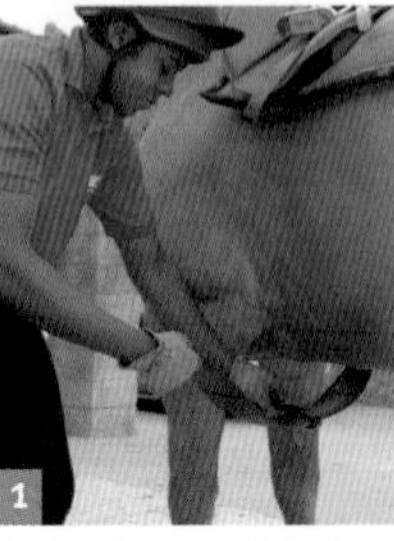

1 **Put the girth through the loop**

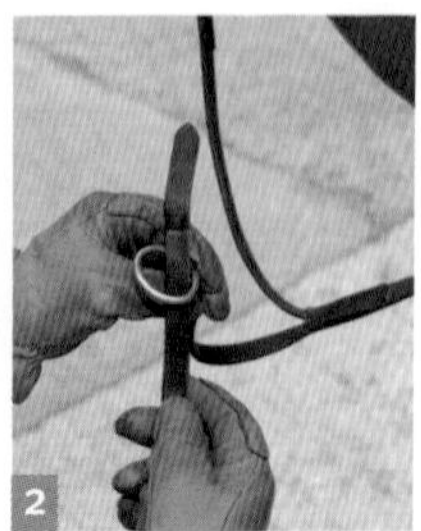

2 **Pass the reins through the rings**

3 REACH FOR GIRTH

Let the girth hang down from its buckles on the off side, then reach under the horse's belly for it from the near side. Make sure the numnah and saddle panels are lying flat on both sides.

***The buckles** on one end must be fastened on the same hole and both sides should be as even as possible*

4 FASTEN GIRTH

Attach the girth to the first strap plus the second or third (*see* p.55), making sure that nothing is twisted. Fasten it loosely at first and check that there is one hand's width between the girth and the horse's elbow.

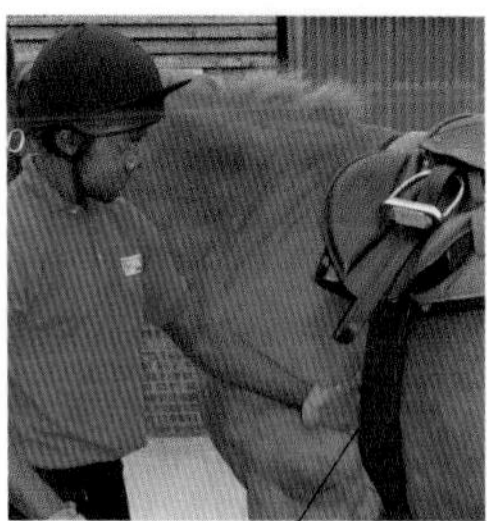

***For riding**, you should just be able to insert your fingers flat under the girth, enough to smooth down the coat*

5 CHECK FIT

Fasten the girth so that it holds the saddle on. If you are not riding straight away, leave it loose until you are ready. Tighten it fully before you mount and smooth the skin underneath.

TAKING OFF A SADDLE

As soon as you have dismounted, run up the stirrups, which stops them from hitting the horse's back as you take off the saddle, and loosen the girth. If the horse is sweaty or hot, do not remove the saddle straight away, to prevent sores on his back – your weight on the horse's back will have slowed his circulation and it might need a few minutes to come back to normal.

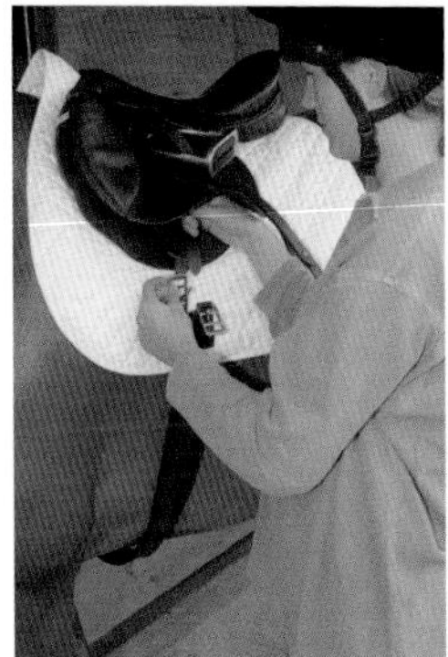

1 UNDO THE GIRTH

To remove the saddle, unfasten the girth on the near side and let it drop down gently, releasing it from the martingale if necessary.

2 LIFT UP THE GIRTH

Go round to the off side of the horse. Place the girth lightly over the saddle, with the underside up so that any mud does not transfer on to the seat.

3 SLIDE THE SADDLE

On the near side, hold the front arch of the saddle, and numnah if there is one, in your left hand and the cantle in your right, and slide it off towards you.

PUTTING ON A BRIDLE

Before you put on the bridle, check that it is correctly assembled. Undo the noseband and release the reins from the throatlash (*see* pp.58–59). Put it on from the horse's near side and get into the habit of doing everything correctly and safely. If the horse must be tied up again after tacking up, put the headcollar on over the bridle.

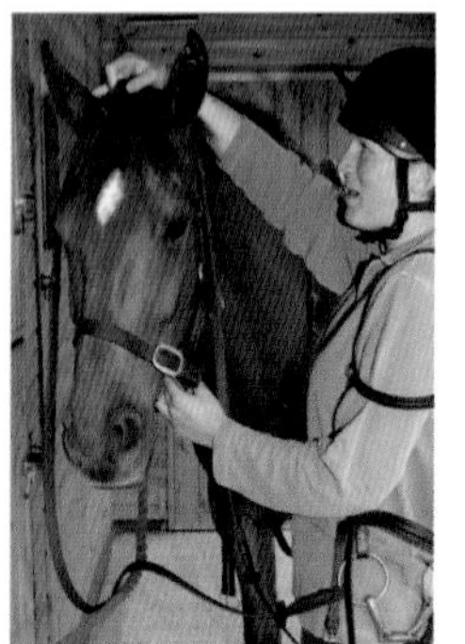

1 REMOVE HEADCOLLAR
With the bridle hanging over your left shoulder, slip the reins over the horse's head and down his neck. Undo and remove the headcollar and hang it up safely nearby.

Hold the *cheekpieces together just below the browband*

2 PUT IN BIT
Hold the bridle in your right hand and bring it round the horse's head from underneath. Rest the bit on the thumb and first finger of your left hand. Bring it up to the horse's mouth and gently encourage him to accept it.

Never try *to force the bit into the horse's mouth*

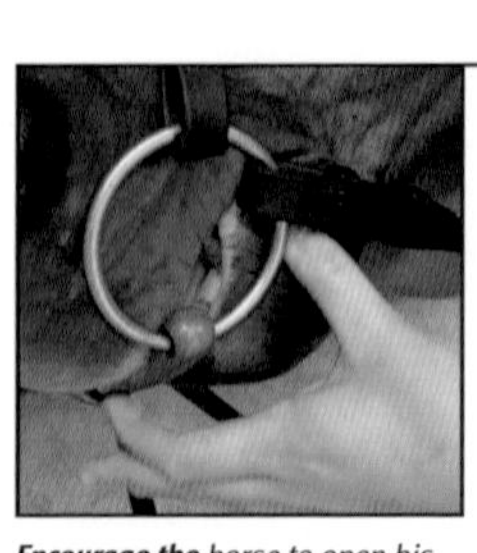

Encourage the *horse to open his mouth for the bit by pressing your thumb gently into the corners of his lips. There are no teeth here, but you should still be careful*

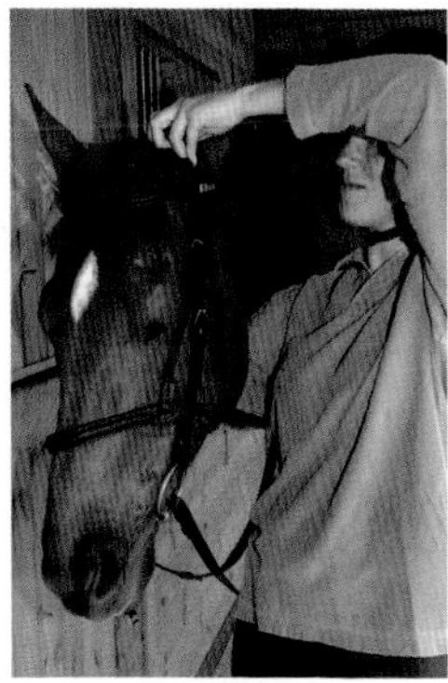

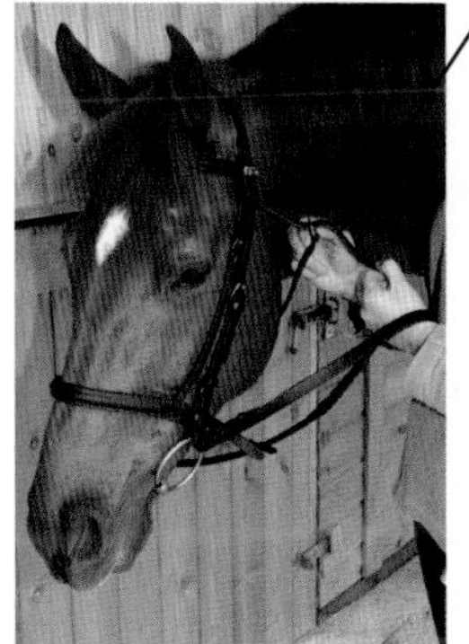

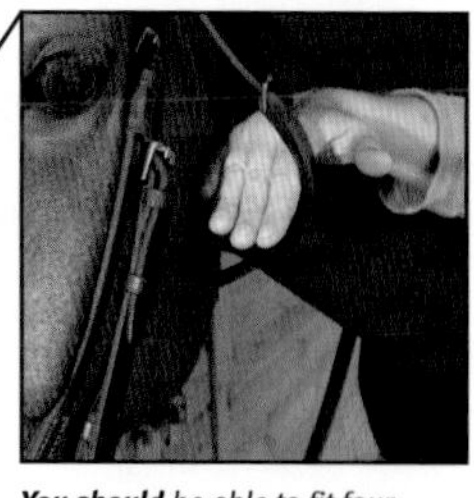

You should be able to fit four fingers sideways between the throatlash and the horse's cheek – tight enough to help stop the bridle from slipping over his head, but not so tight as to interfere with his movement or breathing

3 PULL EARS THROUGH As the horse takes the bit, bring the bridle up so that the bit lies in the corners of his mouth. Bring the headpiece over his ears, gently pulling each ear through. Pull the forelock over the browband and make sure that no hairs are caught under it.

4 FASTEN THROATLASH Reach under the horse's head for the throatlash. Make sure it is not twisted, then bring it through to the near side and fasten the buckle.

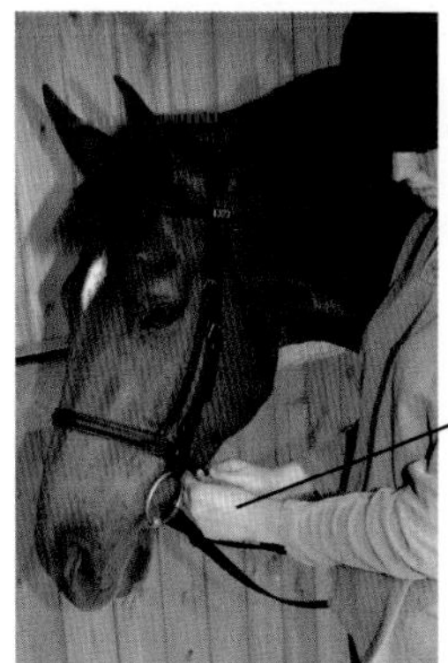

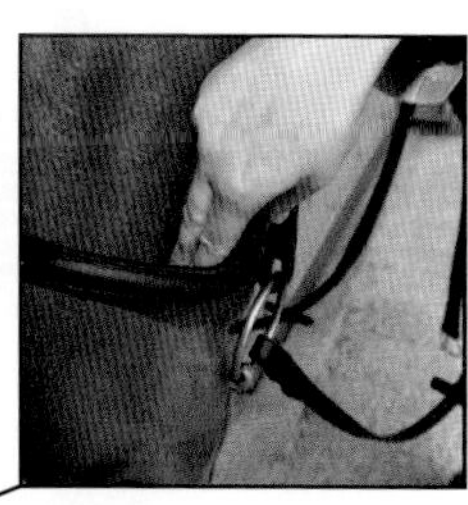

You should be able to fit two fingers sideways between a cavesson noseband and the horse's face

5 FASTEN NOSEBAND Stand in front of the horse and check the bridle is straight. Make any necessary adjustments then fasten the noseband under the horse's chin.

TAKING OFF A BRIDLE

If you are untacking in the stable, face the horse to the door so that you do not have to pass his hind legs to get out. If you are going to put a headcollar on, have it ready to hand and, once the bridle is off, keep the reins over the horse's neck until you have fastened the headcollar. Never pull the bit out of the horse's mouth. Instead, support the bridle so that he can drop the bit without banging his teeth.

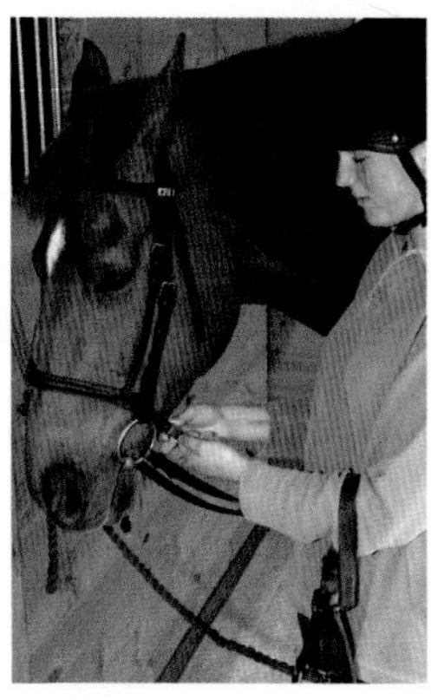

1 UNDO THE STRAPS Keep the reins over the horse's neck. Undo the noseband and throatlash from the near side.

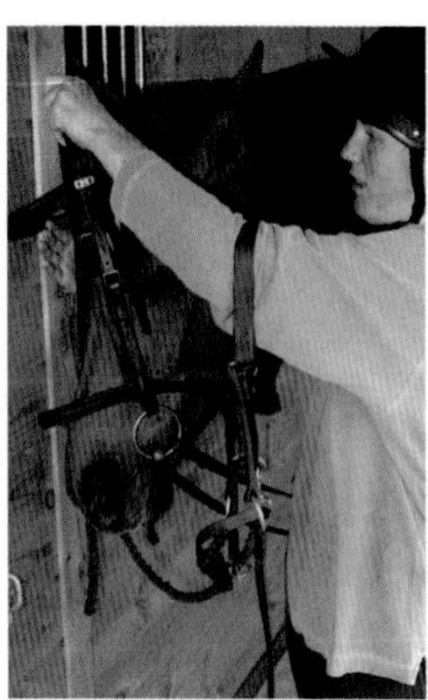

2 PULL OVER THE EARS Hold the bridle by the headpiece and pull it gently over the horse's ears, letting him drop the bit.

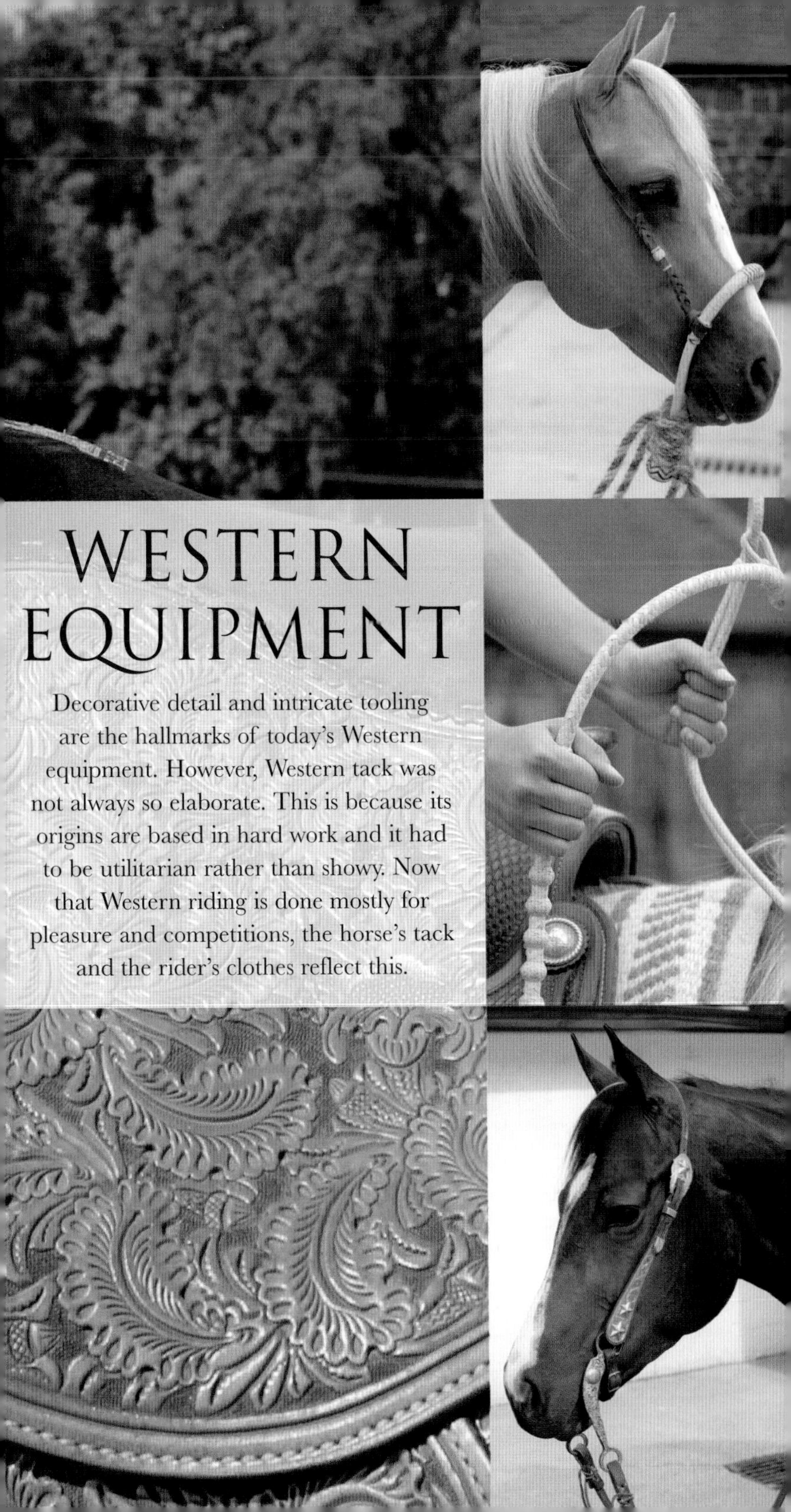

WESTERN EQUIPMENT

Decorative detail and intricate tooling are the hallmarks of today's Western equipment. However, Western tack was not always so elaborate. This is because its origins are based in hard work and it had to be utilitarian rather than showy. Now that Western riding is done mostly for pleasure and competitions, the horse's tack and the rider's clothes reflect this.

WESTERN CLOTHES

Since Western riding originated from a working discipline, there is no set "uniform". When riding for pleasure, people wear clothes that are utilitarian and functional yet still reflect an Old West style. In shows, however, riders are expected to show individuality and flair.

HEAD GEAR

The Western hat is a staple of the wardrobe. It has a wide brim to shield the rider's eyes from the sun and. is made from fur felt or straw to absorb sweat. However, the hat offers no protection against head injuries. Many Western riders opt for a new style of trail-riding helmet similar to English helmets.

STRAW HAT
A good straw hat is made of tightly woven, slender fibres so that the hat keeps its shape.

FUR FELT HAT
Most fur felt hats are made of rabbit fur that has been treated to make it durable.

RIDING BOOTS

Most Western riders wear "roper" boots, which are sturdy and protect your feet when working around a horse. They have a round toe and can be pull-on or lace-up. They also have heels, which prevent the feet sliding through the stirrups and getting caught, which is dangerous if you fall off.

Pull-on roper boots

Lace-up roper boots

JEANS AND SHIRTS

The majority of riders wear jeans, and the cowboy-cut style is the most popular. Cowboy-cut jeans have a higher rise at the waist than normal, a little more room through the thigh to accommodate the leg position in the saddle, and a larger flare at the bottom so that the hems of the jeans slide easily over riding boots. Also, the seam along the inner leg is flat to prevent it chafing the leg in the saddle. Stretch-blend denims are often used for added comfort.

Riders normally wear long-sleeved cotton shirts, although everything from sweaters to T-shirts are appropriate depending on the weather. Long sleeves help to protect the rider from the sun's harmful rays and from overhanging branches or brush on the trail.

DOS AND DON'TS

- **Don't ride** without a hat, and consider wearing a helmet even when riding in a sand-school. Like all equine activities, Western riding has its share of risks.
- **Do wear** a lightweight vented helmet when you are riding out. This should fasten with a secure harness around the ears and under the chin and will protect your skull in the event of a fall.
- **Do wear** a safety helmet when you participate in fast-paced events, such as barrel racing and pole bending.

Riders wearing helmets

SHOW CLOTHES

Different classes and events have their own style, but in general, show apparel tends to be flamboyant, with patterned shirts and silver buckles. Riders often co-ordinate their outfit with the colour of their horse's coat.

DRESS TO IMPRESS
In competition, aim for a unique look that does not detract from your riding skills or the horse.

***Shirt should** be long-sleeved and light in colour to reflect the sun's rays*

***Cowboy-cut** jeans traditionally have a higher rise at the waist*

FULL CHAPS
Chaps were designed to protect the rider's legs from brush, ropes, and fences. They should fit high on the hips and tight down the legs. Western chaps are long so that they cover the boots when the rider is mounted.

CASUAL GEAR
Clothes must be comfortable – too tight and they will restrict; too loose and they will chafe.

WESTERN SADDLES

An all-purpose Western saddle weighs about 18 kg (40 lb). The basic structure is the "tree", comprising the cantle, the bars, and the swell (pommel), which is covered with leather – often rawhide for strength and flexibility. Western saddles are made in three "bar widths": quarter-horse, semi-quarter horse, and full-quarter horse.

INVESTING IN A SADDLE

Competitors can spend thousands of pounds on a custom-made show saddle, but this does not mean that in order to ride Western you must make this significant investment. Western saddles come in various styles for various types of riding, but an all-purpose working saddle, which is plainer and cheaper than other types, is perfectly adequate for beginners and for those not wanting to enter shows. Even more affordable are synthetic saddles, which are lighter weight too. No matter what the decoration or the price tag, a good saddle combines quality workmanship and materials.

ALL-PURPOSE SADDLE

An all-purpose saddle is a good choice if you do not wish to compete.

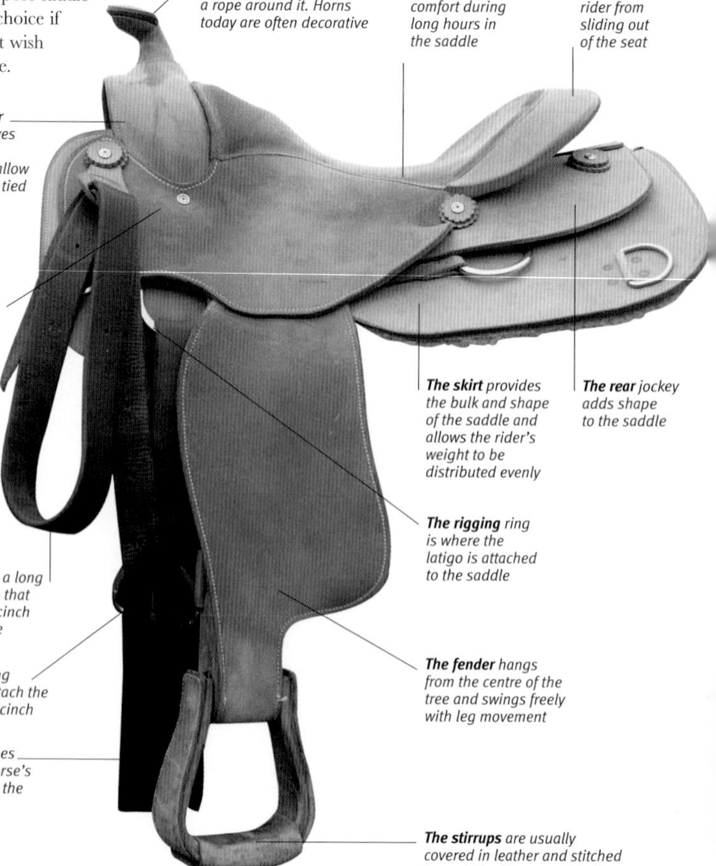

***The horn** developed from the cowboy's need to wrap a rope around it. Horns today are often decorative*

***The seat** is designed for comfort during long hours in the saddle*

***The cantle** prevents the rider from sliding out of the seat*

***The swell**, or pommel, gives the saddle strength to allow a rope to be tied to the horn*

***The front** jockey gives the saddle some shape*

***The skirt** provides the bulk and shape of the saddle and allows the rider's weight to be distributed evenly*

***The rear** jockey adds shape to the saddle*

***The rigging** ring is where the latigo is attached to the saddle*

***The latigo** is a long leather strap that secures the cinch to the saddle*

***The cinch** ring is used to attach the latigo to the cinch*

***The fender** hangs from the centre of the tree and swings freely with leg movement*

***The cinch** goes under the horse's belly to keep the saddle on*

***The stirrups** are usually covered in leather and stitched in rawhide. They are wide for stability and comfort*

***The latigo** hanger allows the rider to put the long end of the latigo up and in front of the leg*

***The breastcollar** stops the saddle from slipping back, although this one is more ornamental than functional*

***The rigging** ring varies from saddle to saddle*

PLEASURE SADDLE
Made with a variety of horn, swell, seat, and skirt styles according to the needs of the rider, pleasure saddles are usually fairly plain. Although some have decorative features, they are usually machine-pressed with designs to cover imperfections in the leather.

SHOW SADDLE
One of the most beautiful aspects of the Western show saddle is the intricate leather tooling. Many are decorated with silverwork.

ENDURANCE TRAIL SADDLE
Lighter than a traditional Western saddle, an endurance saddle allows the horse more freedom of movement and is very comfortable to sit in.

WESTERN BRIDLES

There is a variety of styles of bridle used in Western riding. They are adjustable but come in pony, Arab, and horse sizes. Some styles are used for specific riding disciplines, others are used according to the experience and temperament of the horse.

WESTERN HEADSTALLS

In Western riding, the main part of the bridle is known as the headstall and is usually made of leather. For schooling and everyday riding, the Western headstall is the most popular.

Most headstalls are used with split reins. These consist of two separate straps, but unlike English reins they are not fastened together at the ends. They can be held in two hands and bridged over the horse's neck, or in one hand held above the saddle horn (*see* p.220).

SNAFFLE BIT

A Western horse is often ridden in a snaffle bit for schooling or hacking out. As in English riding, the snaffle does not work by leverage, but by applying direct pressure against the sides of the horse's mouth and across the tongue. The most common snaffle bit used for Western riding is an O-ring, or loose-ring, snaffle, with a jointed mouthpiece.

***Ear loop** goes around one of the horse's ears*

***Cheek piece** is adjustable to allow the bit to hang correctly in the horse's mouth*

***O-ring** snaffle is a basic bit used for schooling and everyday riding*

WESTERN HEADSTALL

A basic Western headstall does not have a noseband and also eliminates the browband, instead opting for ear loops that encircle the ears independently.

SIDE-PULL BRIDLE
With a noseband and another strap under the jowls, the side-pull bridle applies pressure on each side of the horse's face when the reins are pulled.

BRIDLE WITH CURB BIT
A curb bit places pressure not only on the horse's mouth, but also on the tongue, the roof of the mouth, the chin groove, and the poll.

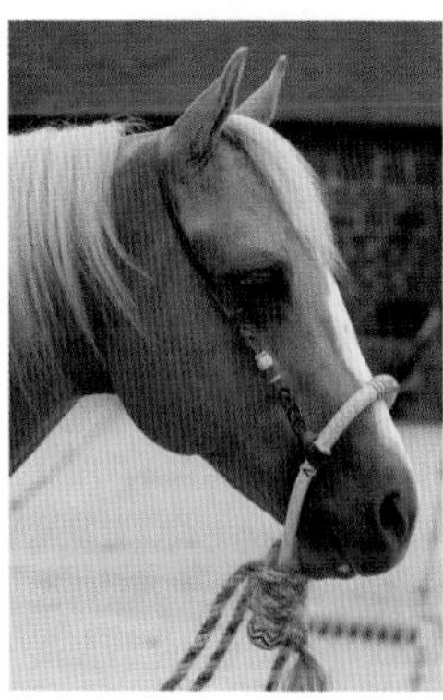

BOSAL AND MECATE
The combination of a bosal and mecate works as a bitless bridle. The bosal works on the bridge of the nose more than the chin groove.

TYPES OF BRIDLE

A side-pull bridle, which does not have a bit, is often used when training Western horses. The headstall fits close to the head and has reins fixed directly to the sides. It works on direct pressure, meaning that the rider pulls the hand in the direction he or she wants to go and the horse will follow.

When a horse is fully trained, he will be ridden in a bridle with a curb bit. He is called a "bridle horse" and will respond to the slightest neck-reining aids. A curb usually has a rounded peak in the middle of the mouthpiece known as a "port". Some ports are low, allowing the horse more tongue room, while some are quite high, putting pressure on the horse's palate. In the hands of an inexperienced rider, a curb can be too severe for a horse as it only takes a light aid for the horse to respond.

A bosal (pronounced boh-*sahl*) is a braided, rawhide noseband fixed to a headstall. The noseband is teardrop shaped and ends in a heel knot under the horse's chin. A mecate (pronounced meh-*kah*-tay) is a heavy rope that is tied to the heel knot to form reins or a leadrope. A rider will ride two handed with a bosal and mecate, and the horse can feel his rider pick up the reins by the shift of the bosal.

The mechanical hackamore, known as just a hackamore in English tack (*see* p.59), is a bitless bridle that is used one or two-handed in Western riding. It usually has cheeks and applies pressure to the horse's poll, chin, and nose. It gives the rider powerful control of a horse and is therefore often seen on strong horses in speed events or on the trail.

EQUIPMENT TYPES

ROPE HALTER
While most Western handlers use headcollars to lead a horse (*see* pp.64–65), some like to use a Western rope halter. It gives them a little more control by applying pressure on the horse's head and nose. The halter is secured with a quick-release knot on the cheek. The top portion should lie directly behind the ears, and the noseband should be two fingers width below the cheekbone.

Horse wearing a rope halter

PUTTING ON A SADDLE

A Western saddle is heavy and unwieldy, so familiarize yourself with its size and weight before heaving it on to a horse. It is best to practise swinging the saddle up and over a barrel or fence before attempting to saddle a horse. Hook the off-side stirrup and cinch around the horn so that they do not get caught underneath the saddle.

1 PLACE SADDLE PAD Stand on the near side and place the saddle blanket well in front of the horse's withers, then slide it into position just behind the withers' peak.

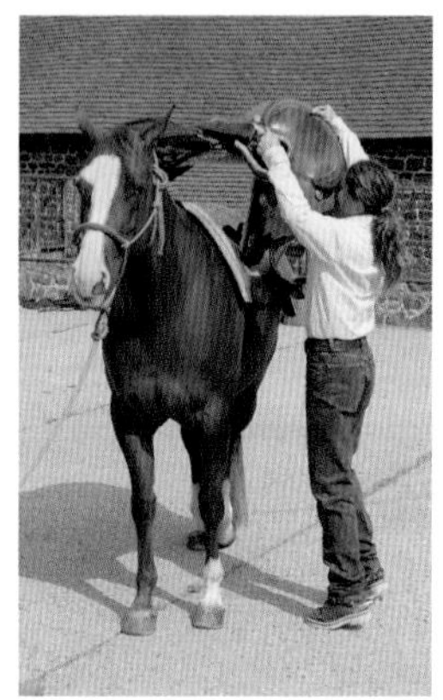

2 PLACE SADDLE With one hand under the pommel and one on the skirt, hold the saddle at hip height. Swing it to the right then gently up on to the horse's back.

3 FIX STIRRUPS Let down the cinch and unhook the stirrup on the off side. Hook the near-side stirrup over the horn of the saddle while you fasten the cinch.

4 REACH FOR CINCH Reach under the horse's belly and take hold of the end of the cinch, bringing it to the near side.

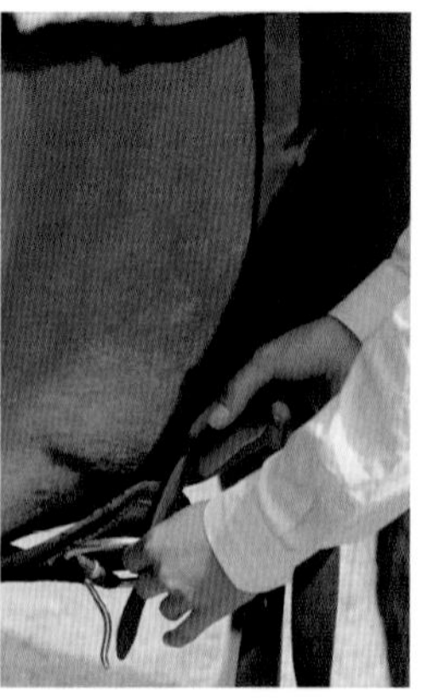

5 THREAD LATIGO Next, take the latigo and thread it through the cinch ring, or buckle.

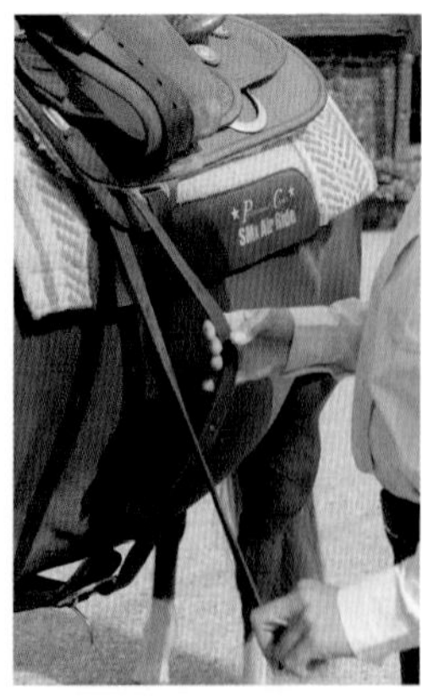

6 SECURE LATIGO Pull up the latigo and thread it through the rigging ring, then through the cinch ring again.

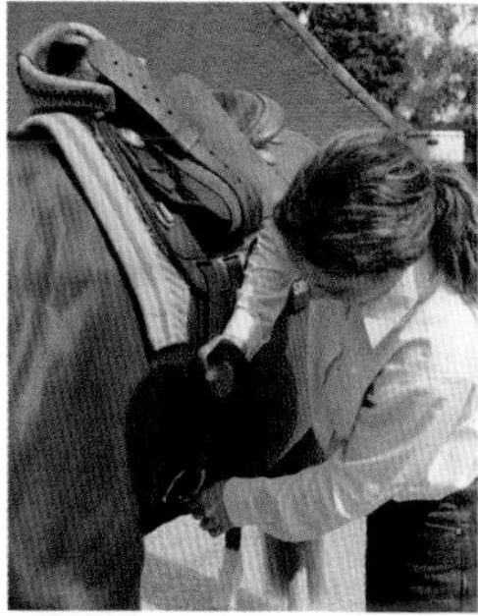

7 BUCKLE CINCH
Pull the latigo tight and fasten the cinch ring. You should be able to slide your hand between the cinch and the horse. (A Western saddle is difficult to adjust when you are on the horse, so check the cinch before mounting.)

8 FINISH OFF
Finally, thread the end of the latigo through the rigging ring once more.

TAKING OFF A SADDLE

The steps for removing the saddle are the same as for putting on – but in reverse order. It is easier to remove than put on, since you do not need to lift it, but remember that it is very heavy. You will need to make a few adjustments so that when you pull the saddle off with the saddle blanket, you do not hit the horse with any loose straps, buckles, or stirrups.

1 PUT UP LATIGO
Unfasten the latigo and arrange it in a loose bundle. Wrap its end round it then thread this through the rigging to secure the latigo to the saddle.

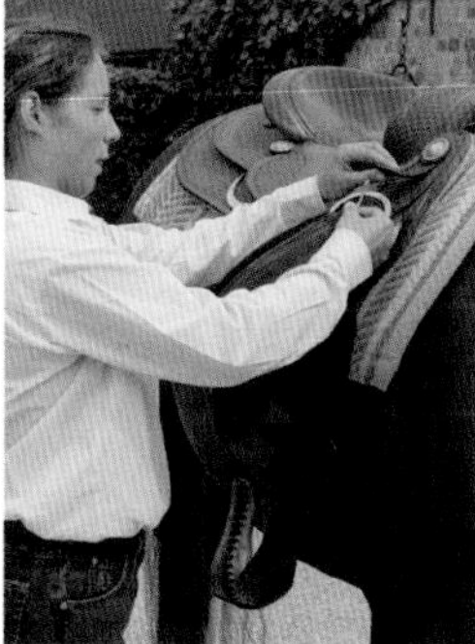

2 PUT UP CINCH
On the off side, put up the cinch by hooking the cinch ring securely to the saddle.

3 REMOVE SADDLE
Take the saddle off from the near side. Place your arms underneath the saddle blanket. Lift it slightly and pull it and the saddle towards you.

PUTTING ON A BRIDLE

Care must be taken that tack is not only fitted properly, but goes on without causing the horse discomfort. You should stand on the near side to put on a bridle, and because the Western headstall is relatively simple, this procedure is fairly easy to master.

1 HOLD THE BRIDLE Hold the reins in your left hand. Hold the headstall in your right hand and pass it under the horse's chin to rest on his nose.

2 OFFER THE BIT Lay the reins across the horse's neck, then grasp the bit's mouthpiece in your left hand, keeping any curb strap separate.

3 OPEN THE MOUTH Put your left hand flat in front of the horse's mouth, then work your thumb into the corner until he opens his mouth.

4 DRAW UP THE HEADSTALL Try not to bang the horse's teeth with the metal as you insert the bit into his mouth and draw up the headstall.

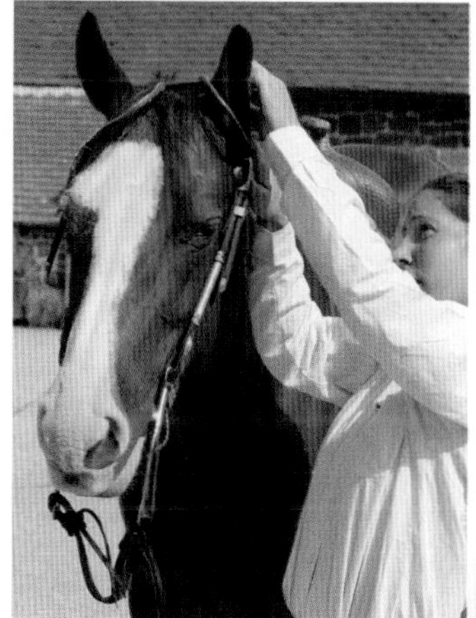

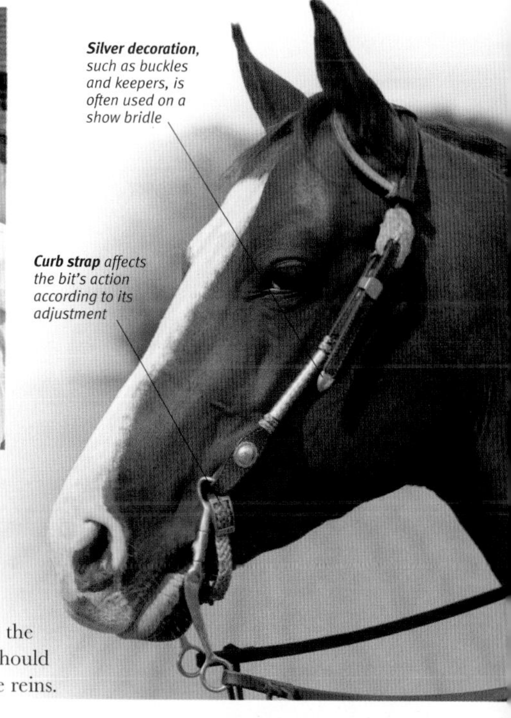

5 PLACE OVER THE EARS
Bring the headstall over the horse's ears and gently push his ears into the ear loops.

6 CHECK THE FIT
The bit should only just wrinkle the corners of the mouth. A curb strap should have no effect until the rider pulls the reins.

TAKING OFF A BRIDLE

Remove the bridle from the near side. This is easier than putting it on, because most horses will drop the bit from their mouths when you lower the headstall. Some handlers, in their haste, may pull the headstall off too quickly, causing the bit to knock against the horse's teeth. After a time, this may cause a horse to become "head shy" or difficult to bridle. But if you remove the headstall from behind the ears smoothly and slowly, the horse will comply and drop the bit. If there is a throatlash, as on an English-style bridle (*see* pp.58–59), make sure you unfasten this before you remove the headstall.

1 LIFT THE HEADSTALL
Unfasten the throatlash, if there is one, before taking off the bridle. Lift the top of the headstall slightly, ease it over the horse's ears, then stop.

2 FREE THE BIT
Allow the horse to drop the bit in his own time. This will usually happen straight away, but give the horse the time he needs regardless.

LOOKING AFTER A HORSE

A HORSE'S NEEDS

Horses need care and attention on a regular basis. A well-performed routine, in which the horse is fed, watered, groomed, and exercised at set intervals, is the basic requirement. In addition, their hooves need regular attention from the farrier and it is your responsibility to look out for anything that might develop into a problem.

PROVIDE GOOD CONDITIONS

Whether the horse is stabled or field-kept, in work or resting, it is your duty to provide optimum conditions. All horses appreciate routine and some like attention more than others, but most do not like to be cuddled or fussed over any more than necessary.

A stabled horse will need rugs (*see* pp.94–95) in the winter; a field-kept horse will probably need a turnout rug, but some are tough and grow thick coats that, provided they get plenty of nutrition, will give all the warmth and protection they need. These care requirements will vary depending on the type of horse and where and how he is kept, and it is up to you to work out what each one needs. When you have ridden a horse, especially if he has worked hard, you must make him comfortable and see to his needs before your own.

Exercise is important – a horse cannot remain standing in his stable for long periods of time. At the very least he will become bored and difficult to manage; at worst, it can lead to health problems. If a stabled horse cannot be ridden he should be turned out in a field, even if only for a short time, or given some other form of exercise, such as lungeing.

EXERCISE AND FREEDOM
Horses need space to move around, let off steam, and have a roll. Regular turnout in a field is the best way to provide all this.

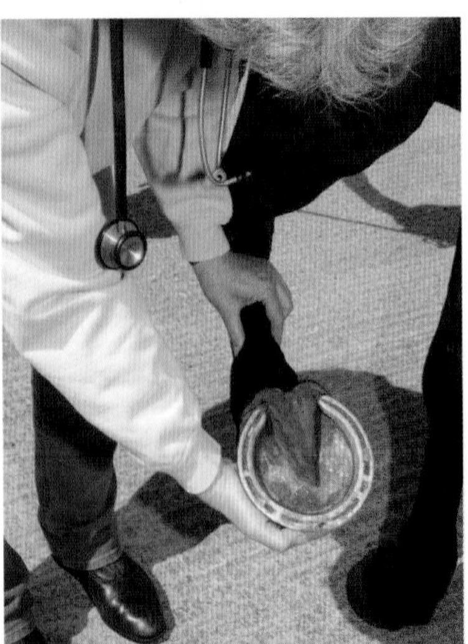

CHECK REGULARLY

Wherever and however a horse is kept, he needs to be checked over every day for injuries and have his feet picked out and his shoes checked (*see* pp.90–91), as well as being fed and watered. Stabling overnight and turning out during the day is a practical solution, especially if you cannot ride every day; you only need to muck out once a day and can give feed and hay in the morning and evening. A horse that is stabled all the time will need to be mucked out at least twice a day and fed at least three times, while a field-kept horse must be checked once or twice a day. Look him over for injury, pick out his feet, check his water supply and check the field fences are secure.

VETERINARY CARE
When you need to call the vet, bring the horse into a stable or enclosed area and clean him up so the vet can see him properly.

CHECK LIST

BASIC REQUIREMENTS

- Good living conditions, plenty of water and forage with extra feed according to his needs, and feet and general health looked after.
- A routine he can understand and a handler he trusts and respects.
- The companionship of horses or other large animals such as cattle.
- Shelter from bad weather, be it a stable or field shelter, a large hedge, and/or a suitable rug.

GOOD TACK

Each horse should have his own saddle and bridle, adjusted to fit and kept in good condition.

GIVE HIM SOME COMPANY

Horses are herd animals; they like company and do not like being kept on their own. This is why it is necessary to train them to be ridden both alone and in company, as their natural instinct is to observe the herd hierarchy with one horse as "boss" in a group. The rider or handler effectively takes over the role of boss mare and the horse has to know he can trust and depend on you to feed him and keep him out of danger. Know when to encourage your horse with praise, and always be patient in the way you deal with him.

Try to keep a horse somewhere with other horses or livestock. Horses kept in a happy environment, where they understand the hierarchy, will be easier to handle than lonely, stressed horses. There have been extreme cases in which racehorses were said not to travel anywhere without their favourite companion – be it a sheep or a chicken!

LEADING AND TYING UP

Most of us will need to lead a horse at some time – to or from the field, around the yard, to trot up for the vet, or in and out of a horsebox, for example. A headcollar is safe for most situations at home, but on the road or at a show you will have more control using a bridle.

LEADING A HORSE

You usually lead a horse from his left, or near side, although he should be happy to be led from either side. Stand just in front of the horse's shoulder, holding the lead rope near his head with your right hand. Hold the slack of the rope in your left hand: never wrap it round you because you will be injured if the horse pulls away.

FROM A STABLE
Make sure there is enough space for both you and the horse to get through the door. Do not let him barge out or push you over.

SHOULDER TO SHOULDER
Leading from next to the horse's shoulder gives you the best control. From this position you can easily control his pace.

Hold the *slack of the rope in your left hand*

Never wrap *the rope round your hand as it could crush your fingers if the horse pulls hard*

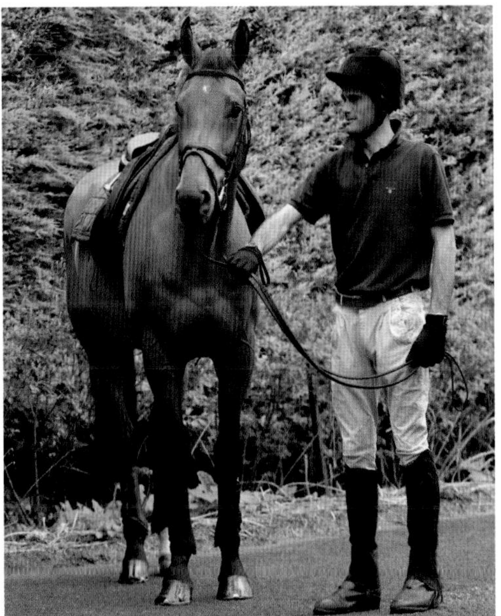

LEADING IN A BRIDLE
Bring the reins over the horse's head. Hold them near his chin with your right hand, separating the two reins with one finger. Hold the slack of the reins in the other hand.

TYING UP A HORSE

The only safe knot for tying up a horse is a quick-release knot. In an emergency, you can quickly pull the end to release the horse. Always tie the lead rope to a piece of breakable string attached to a metal ring on the wall so that, should the horse pull back in fright, the string will break before any serious damage is done.

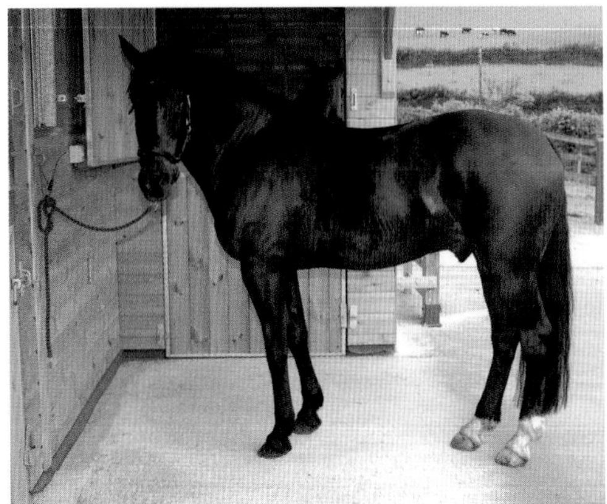

SAFELY TIED UP
The structure to which you tie the string must be strong enough not to give way if the horse pulls back. The lead rope must be just long enough to allow the horse some movement.

TECHNIQUES

TYING A QUICK-RELEASE KNOT IN A LEAD ROPE
For clarity, a quick-release knot is shown here tied to a ring. In practice, you must always tie the lead rope to a loop of string attached to the ring. **Step 1** Pass the working end through the tie-string and bring it round in front of the rope to make a loop. **Step 2** Make a second loop in the working end and pass it through the first. **Step 3** Pull the second loop to secure the knot. Thread the end of the rope loosely through this loop to stop the horse untying himself.

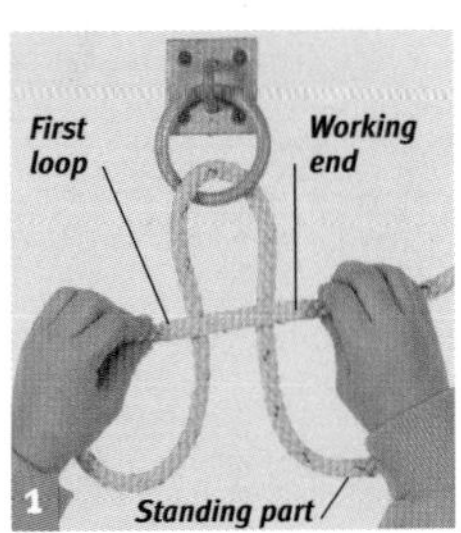

Make a loop

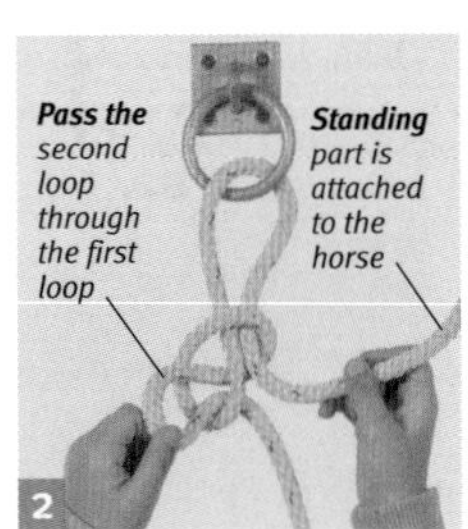

Make a second loop

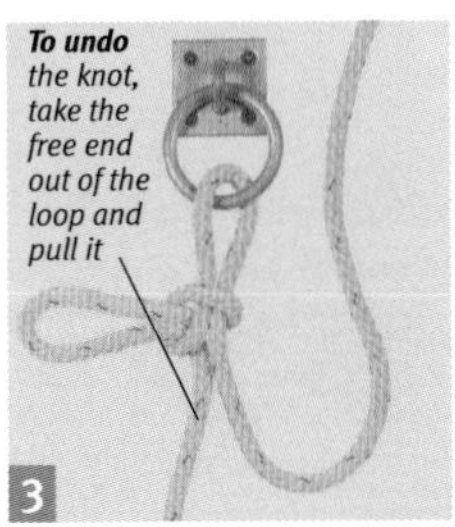

Finished knot

GROOMING

Regular grooming is essential unless the horse or pony lives out all the time, in which case you should just remove mud and stains before you ride. The feet should be picked out at least once a day, and the eyes and nostrils should be wiped with a clean sponge. Avoid washing mud off too often as this makes the horse susceptible to skin irritations.

THE GROOMING KIT

A few basic items are indispensable, and will last a long time if you keep them clean and dry when they are not in use. Ideally, each kit should only be used for one horse, although this is not always practical in large yards. To groom a horse, tie him up somewhere safe and well-ventilated so that the dust does not get into either your nose or his.

DANDY BRUSH
Use a dandy brush, with its long stiff bristles, to remove dried mud from horses with thick coats. It is unsuitable for thin-skinned horses.

BODY BRUSH
To remove dust and scurf from the coat, use a body brush, which has shorter, softer bristles. It can also be used gently on the mane and tail.

RUBBER CURRY COMB
A rubber curry comb can be used to loosen mud from the coat or to "strap" – a grooming action that boosts muscles and circulation.

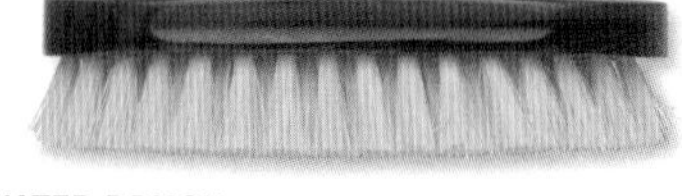

WATER BRUSH
Use a damp water brush to smooth the mane and tail, or to scrub mud off the hooves. The bristles are too coarse for the coat.

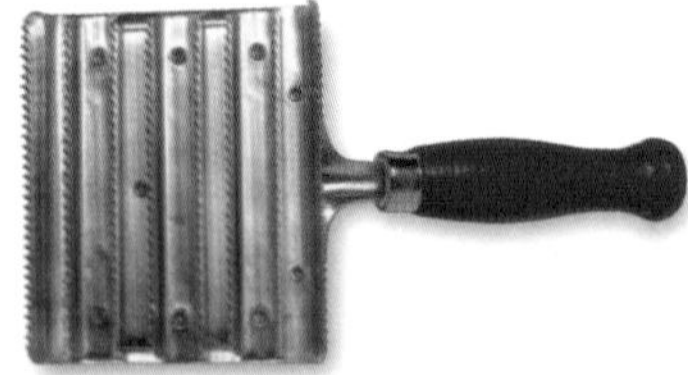

METAL CURRY COMB
Do not use a metal curry comb directly on the horse's coat. It should be used only to remove dirt and dust from the body brush.

HOOF OIL
Use hoof oil if you want to improve the appearance of hooves for a special occasion. Hoof oil is sometimes thought to moisturize the hooves, but in general its effect is purely cosmetic.

EXTRA INFORMATION

WHY GROOMING IS NECESSARY
Regular grooming keeps a horse's skin and coat clean and healthy. It boosts the muscle tone, circulation, and lymphatic system. However, horses living out should not be groomed too much. They need the grease in their coat to protect them from bad weather.

HOOFPICK
A vital piece of equipment, a hoofpick should be used at least once a day to remove mud and stones from the hooves.

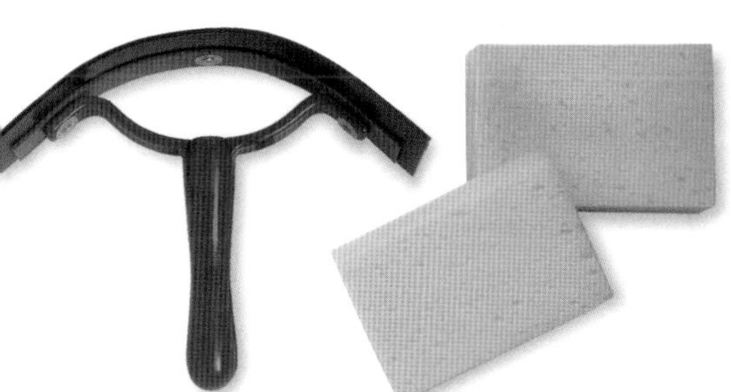

TECHNIQUES

CLEANING A BODY BRUSH

Clean the body brush every few strokes. Briskly pull a metal curry comb through it so that the dust flies away from you, not towards you.

Using a metal curry comb

SWEAT SCRAPER

A sweat scraper is an important tool used to remove sweat and water from a horse's coat so that he dries as quickly as possible.

SPONGES

One sponge should be used to clean the eyes and nostrils, the other for cleaning the dock area and removing coat stains.

GROOMING A HORSE

You should always ride out looking clean and tidy, but for a stabled horse it is also worth grooming when you return, because more scurf will come out when the horse is warm. Grooming does not only involve brushing – it includes picking out the feet and wiping the eyes, nose, and dock.

BRUSHING THE BODY

Start at the poll on the near side, with the body brush in your left hand. Use your body weight to make bold, circular strokes, following the direction of the hair.

BRUSHING THE FACE

Use a soft body brush to brush the face. Work around the headcollar or briefly untie the horse and fasten the headcollar around his neck. Hold his head steady with your free hand.

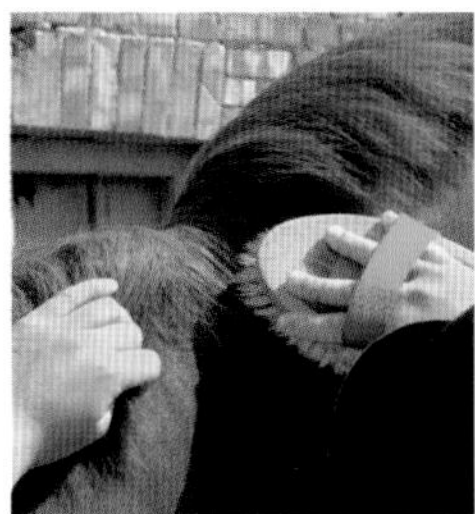

BRUSHING THE MANE

Brush the mane before the neck. Push the mane to the far side and groom the crest, then smooth it back and work through it a lock at a time, starting at the poll.

BRUSHING THE TAIL

Stand to one side of the horse. Hold up each lock so that when you work through the ends you do not pull the roots. Untangle any knots with your fingers to avoid breaking the hairs.

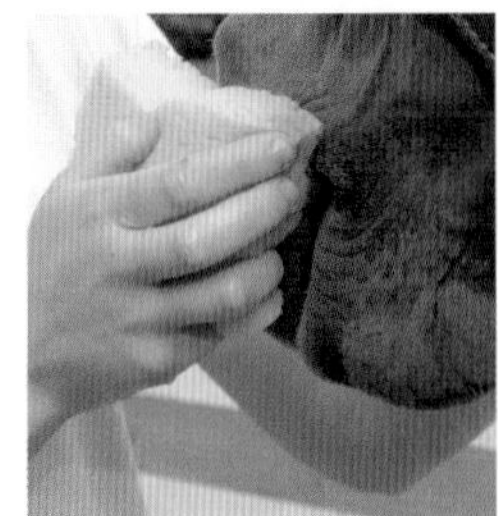

SPONGING THE FACE

Remove debris from around the eyes, nostrils, and lips with a clean, damp sponge. Work gently and carefully, especially around the eyes, and use only plain water.

LOOKING AFTER THE FEET

The part of the hoof you see when the foot is on the ground is called the wall. Like fingernails, it is mostly made up of dead matter although it is constantly growing, and it protects a highly sensitive structure that includes tendons and bones. In the centre of the sole is the spongy, V-shaped frog, which acts as a shock absorber.

LIFTING A FRONT FOOT

A well-behaved horse should pick up his feet willingly. To lift the near fore, stand with your left shoulder to the horse's left shoulder. As you reach down, bend your knees, keep your back straight, and keep your head away from the horse's foot. Reverse the procedure for the off fore.

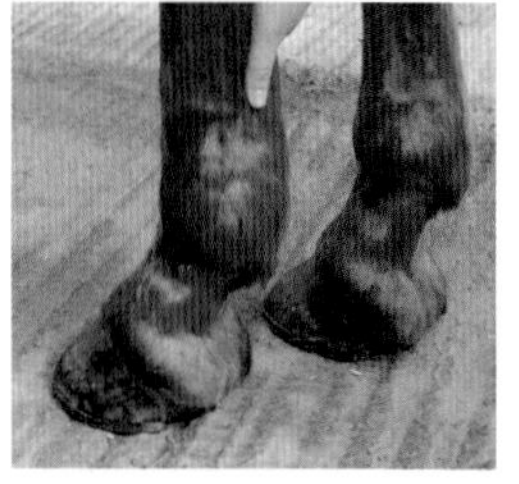

1 MOVE HAND DOWN Place your left hand firmly at the top of the leg, and in one smooth movement, run it down the outside to the knee. Transfer it to the inside and continue running it down to the fetlock joint.

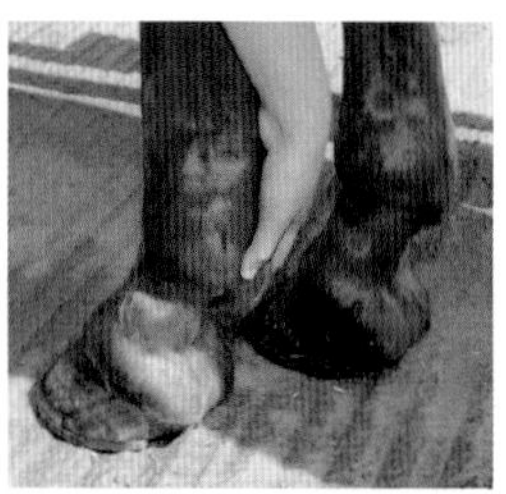

2 CUP THE FETLOCK When your hand reaches the fetlock joint, squeeze it gently, or put slight pressure on the inside of the leg, and say "up" so that the horse picks up the foot.

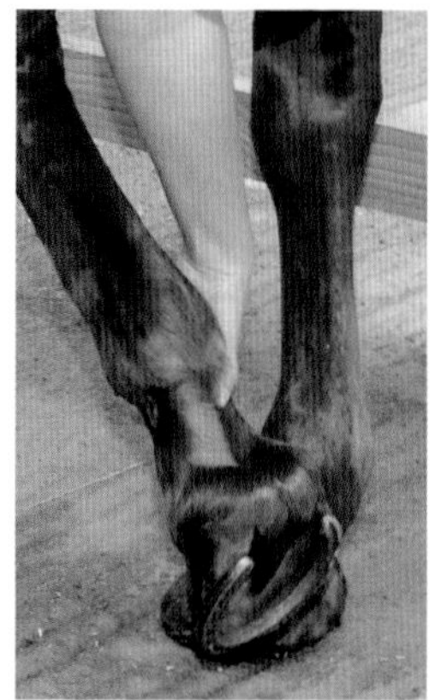

3 CATCH THE FOOT The horse should lift his foot and carry most of the weight. If he does not lift it, lean on his shoulder so that he puts more weight on the opposite leg, then try again. As he lifts his foot, catch it with your fingers.

LIFTING A HIND FOOT

Stand with your shoulder to the horse's quarters. Speak to him and put your nearest hand firmly on the quarters without tickling him, so that he knows you are there. Encourage the horse to lift his foot for you by using your voice and, if necessary, a little pressure on the inside of the fetlock. Do not lift the foot higher or further back than necessary. Keep your face out of kicking range.

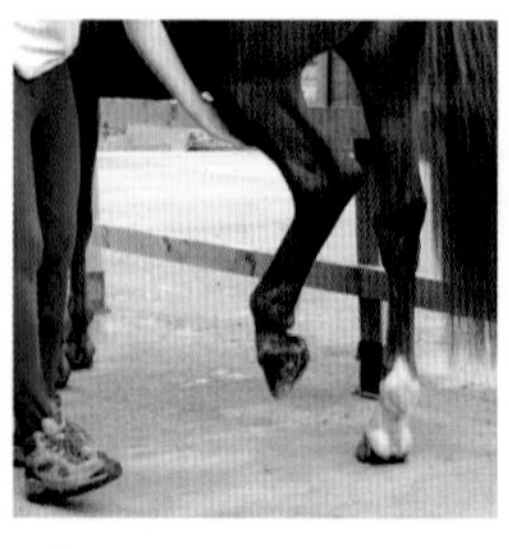

1 RUN HAND DOWN Move your hand down the outside or back of the leg, then without taking your hand off, transfer it to the inside and run it down to the fetlock.

2 CUP THE HOOF When the horse lifts his foot, cup the hoof in your hand, holding it firmly enough to keep it still while making him support his own weight.

EXTRA INFORMATION

TYPES OF SHOE

Most horses are shod for riding, but some can work without shoes, or with front shoes only. Unshod horses still need to have their feet regularly trimmed. There are various types of shoe, and each should be suitable for the foot that carries it. The most common is the hunter shoe, which has a groove called a "fuller" to increase grip. A simple, plain shoe gives less grip. Egg bar and heart bar shoes give extra support for certain medical conditions. Shoeing and trimming must only be done by a qualified farrier.

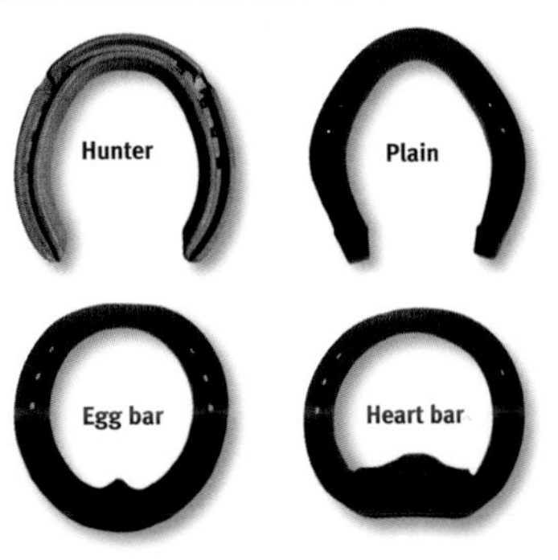

PICKING OUT A FOOT

A horse's feet need to be picked out at least once a day to remove mud, stones, and any other debris. At the same time, you should check that the feet are healthy and there are no wounds. Running your hand down each leg to pick up the foot is also a good opportunity to feel the horse's joints and tendons and check for swellings or soreness.

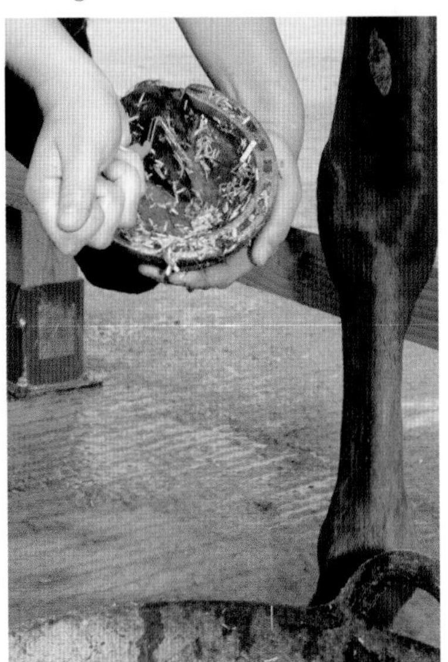

1 USE THE HOOFPICK
Hold the hoofpick in your free hand and use it from heel to toe on each side, always pointing it downwards. Get all the debris out from around the frog and shoe but never use the hoofpick on the frog itself – use your fingers for this area.

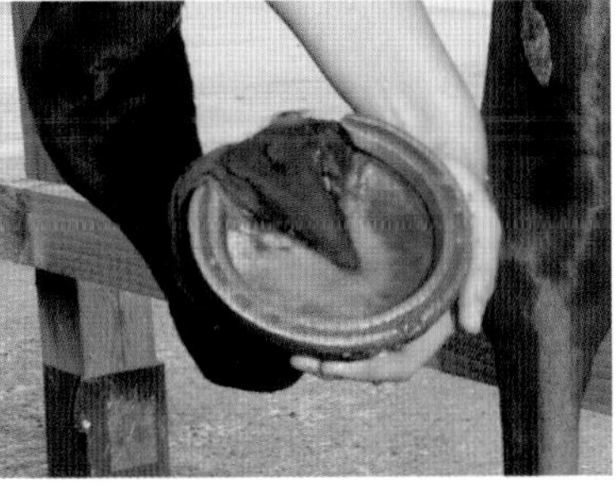

2 THE CLEAN FOOT
There should be no mud or stones lodged around the frog or under the shoe. The sole and frog should be clean so that you can check their condition. Some "flaking" of the frog is quite normal but too much can indicate a problem.

DOS & DON'TS

- **Do oil** a hoof by dipping a brush in the hoof oil and covering the surface area of the hooves from coronet to toe and heels.
- **Don't oil** the hooves too often – oil will not cure anything and might cause further problems.
- **Do improve** hoof condition through the horse's diet and take advice from a farrier.
- **Don't oil** the frog as it needs to breathe.

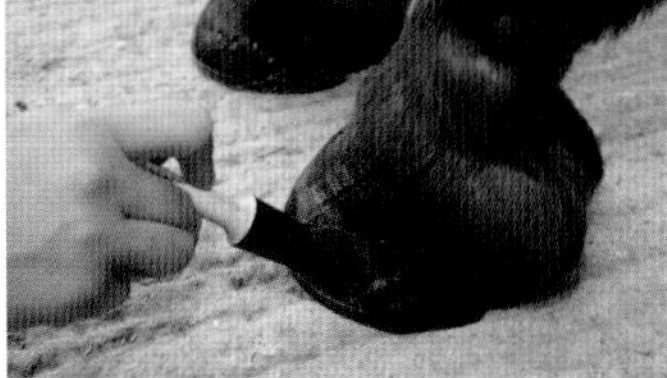

Oiling a hoof

AFTER RIDING

When you come in from a ride, there is a routine you should follow for taking care of the horse's needs, from checking his feet for stones and removing sweat from his body, to organizing his rugs, feed, and turnout. This need not take long but must come before your own needs.

COME HOME COOL
One of the golden rules of riding is that you should never bring a horse home hot and sweaty. Walking the last few kilometres or so of a hack is good for the horse's training – associating going home with going fast can lead to behavioural problems – and will help him cool off and relax.

CARING FOR THE HORSE

If the horse has become particularly hot and sweaty, walk him home then dismount and lead him around with the girth loosened before you untack. When you take off the saddle, pat his back briskly to help restore circulation. A wet horse will need to be dried and any sweat marks removed. Hot horses might appreciate a quick wash down if the weather allows, but they must be dried thoroughly.

Do not put a stable or turnout rug straight on a wet horse – use a cooler (*see* p.95) or, in cold weather, a sweat rug over a layer of clean straw. To prevent colic, do not feed the horse until he is cool. It is usually fine to offer him a haynet (*see* pp.98–99) and a short drink of water with the chill taken off.

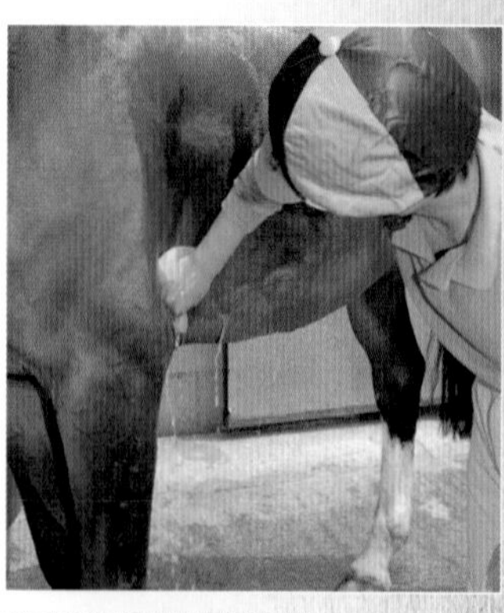

SPONGE SWEATY AREAS
Dry sweat is uncomfortable for the horse, and if he is turned out, can lead to scalding and attract flies. You can either leave sweat to dry and brush it off, or if the weather is warm enough you can sponge it off and remove excess water with a sweat scraper.

CHECK FOR STONES

Always pick out the horse's feet when you return from a ride, in case he has picked up a stone. Check that there is no injury to the sole or frog. Run your hands down his tendons to check for heat and bumps.

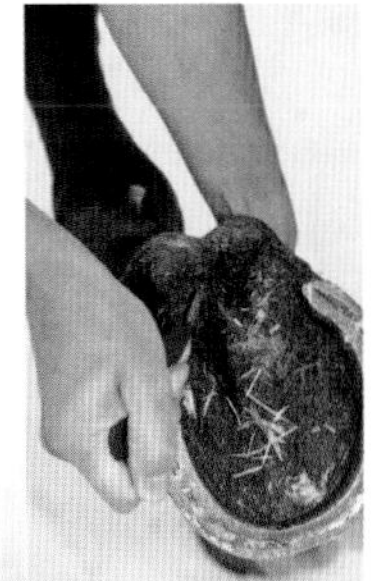

TIPS AND TECHNIQUES

CLEANING TACK

Tack should be cleaned after every ride. You need a sponge, saddle soap, and water. Too much water makes leather deteriorate, so wring out your sponge well. **Step 1** Clean all the metal parts with water. You can dunk the bit in the bucket, but do not dunk the leather. **Step 2** Hang up the bridle and wipe off dirt and sweat, undoing the buckles and cleaning those too. Place the saddle on a saddle horse or rail and do the same. **Step 3** Rub a barely damp sponge over the saddle soap and work well into the leather parts of the bridle and saddle – one application should be enough.

1 **Rinse metal parts but do not wet the leather**

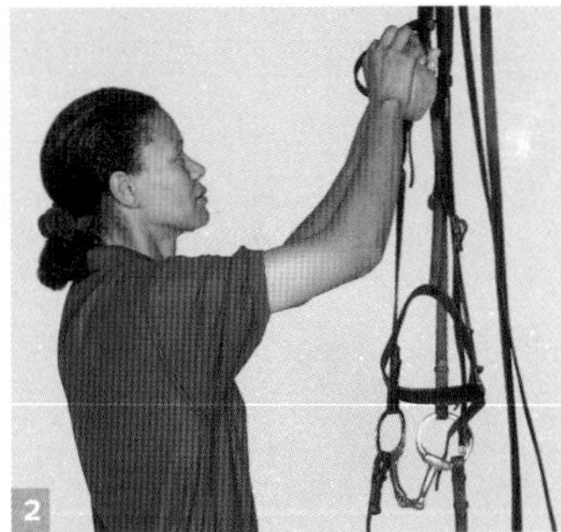

2 **Wash off dirt and sweat with a damp sponge**

3 **Rub in a small amount of saddle soap**

PUTTING ON A RUG

The rug is a large item – for a horse over 15 hands (1.5 m) it is likely to be more than 1.8 m (6 ft) long – so you need to handle it carefully to avoid frightening the horse or getting caught up. Before putting it on, make sure the inside is dry and there is no mud or sweat that could cause abrasion or infection. Folding the rug in half before putting it on or taking it off makes the task easier and safer.

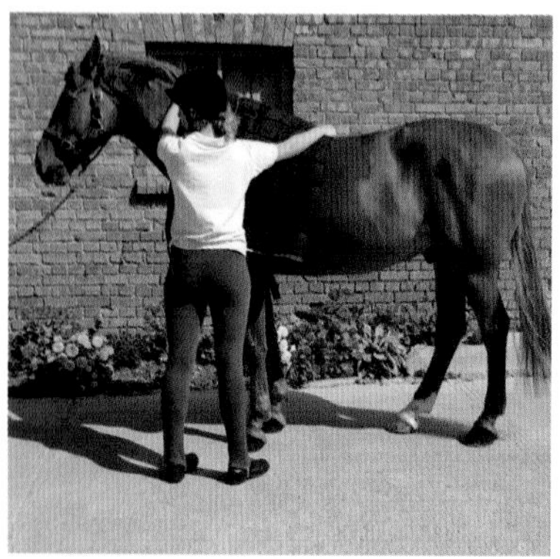

1 **POSITION FOLDED RUG** Fold the rug in half, tail end up to front end so that the lining of the back half faces upwards. Place it – do not throw it – on the horse with the front end well in front of his withers.

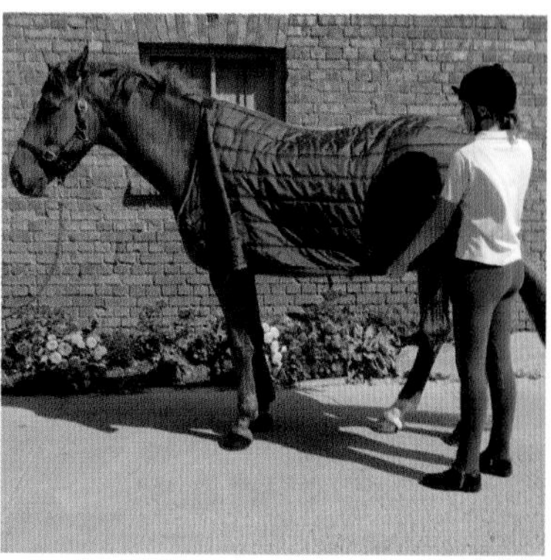

2 **UNFOLD RUG** Unfold the rug from front to back so that it covers the whole horse. Make sure it is straight and hangs down evenly on both sides. Release all the straps, making sure they are not twisted or knotted.

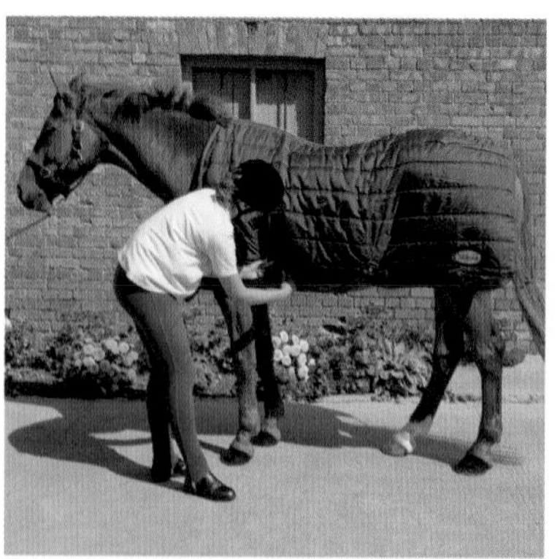

3 **FASTEN SURCINGLES** Most rugs have two straps called "surcingles" that pass under the horse's belly. It is important to fasten each one diagonally so that they cross over underneath the horse.

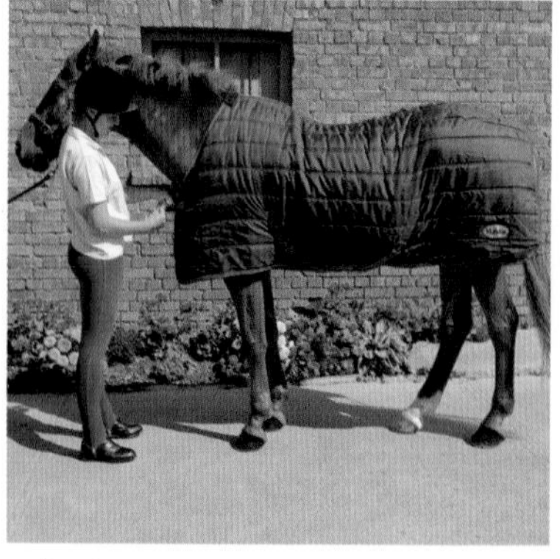

4 **FASTEN CHEST STRAPS** Most rugs have two buckles or Velcro straps at the chest. Fasten these so that they fit snugly – the rug should allow the horse to move freely but stay on securely without rubbing him.

TAKING OFF A RUG

Make sure that the horse is tied up safely or being held. Once the rug is off, hang it up to dry or air, or fold it tidily. Do not leave it on the floor.

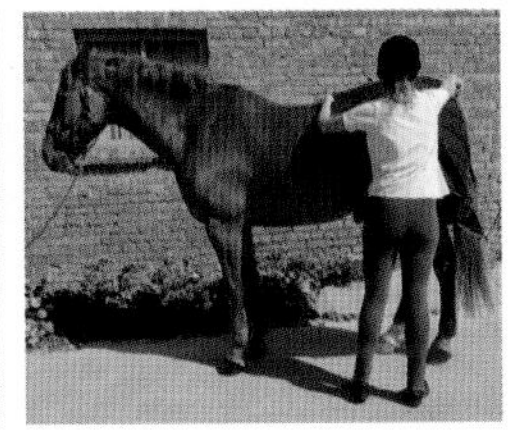

1 UNBUCKLE STRAPS Undo the straps, knot the surcingles loosely, then fold the rug front to back.

2 SLIDE OFF Stand safely to one side of the horse and slide the rug off sideways. Do not pull it off from behind.

TECHNIQUES

FASTENING LEG STRAPS
If a rug has hind leg straps, pass one strap round the inside of the leg and fasten it on the same side. Loop the second strap through it and fasten it the same way.

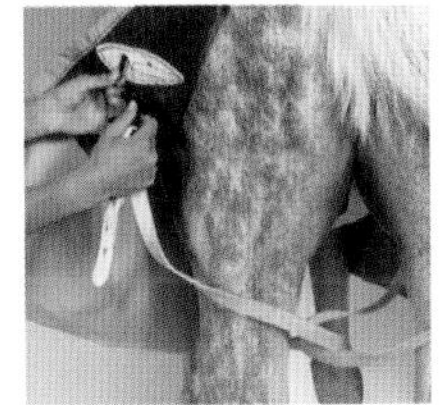

Crossed leg straps

EXTRA INFORMATION

TYPES OF RUG
Turnout rugs have a tough, waterproof outer shell with a quilted or fleece lining. Many have a flap to cover the top of the tail. Stable rugs for night use usually have a quilted cotton or nylon outer with a duvet-style filling; for daytime use, a woollen or fleece rug is ideal. Cooler rugs wick away sweat and moisture while keeping the horse warm. Exercise rugs keep the loins of horses warm in very cold weather.

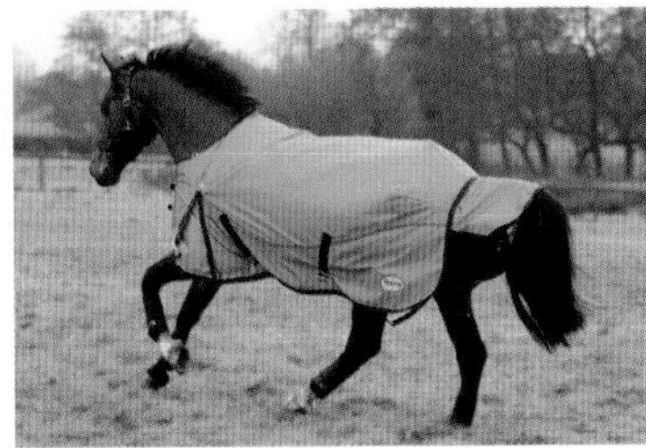

Turnout rug

Stable rug

Fleece day rug

Cooler rug

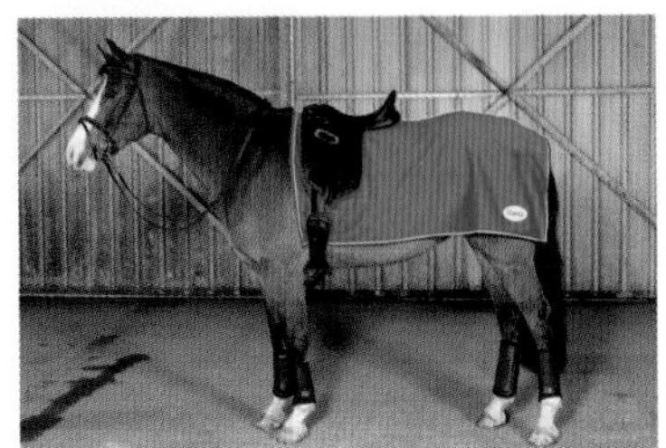

Exercise rug

BASIC FIRST-AID

There will be times when you have to treat minor wounds yourself or decide whether to call the vet. It is easy to be misled by something that seems minor – for example, an innocuous-looking wound can become serious if it is near a joint or becomes infected. If there is any doubt in your mind, seek expert advice.

KEEPING A HORSE HEALTHY

Once you are familiar with horses, you will be able to assess their overall condition quickly. There are plenty of general indicators (*see* p.97) but each horse will have his own characteristics. It is a good idea to get to know a horse's normal pulse rate, but only take his temperature if you think he is really sick. A suitable diet for the type of horse, the work he does, and the way he is kept is the key to good health. A regular worming routine is important, and the horse's teeth should be checked by a vet or horse dentist once or twice a year. If you are worried about anything always consult a vet.

TAKING THE TEMPERATURE

Grease a thermometer and put it gently into the rectum, standing to one side and holding the tail out of the way. Hold the thermometer firmly, as the muscles can contract and pull it in. A horse's normal temperature is 37–38°C (100–101°F). If it is above 39°C, call the vet.

CHECKING THE PULSE

The pulse can be taken at the median artery inside the foreleg or at the facial artery under the jaw, where it is often easier to find. The resting pulse should be 36 to 42 beats per minute – it will rise after exercise, but should settle within about 15 minutes.

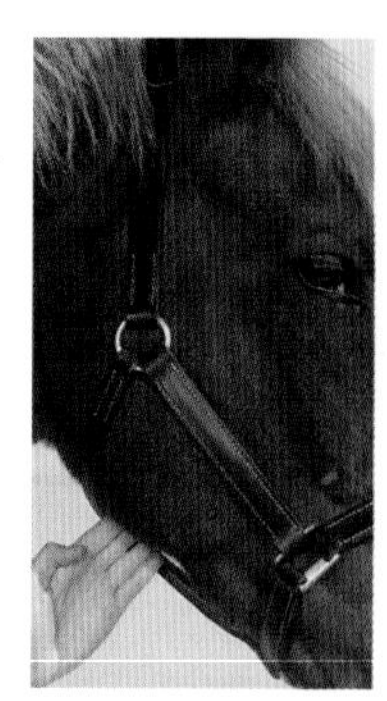

COMMON HORSE INJURIES

INJURY	CAUSE	ACTION
Clean cut	These can have a wide variety of causes. It is important to learn to recognize what you can and cannot treat without help and to know when complications are likely.	Follow steps on p.97 for cleaning a cut. If in any doubt call the vet.
Laceration	This type of wound is easily picked up in a field. It may not be clean and may need stitching. Even if the horse is not in pain, this could be a complicated injury.	Call the vet. Clean area with water or weak saline solution while waiting.
Puncture	Usually occurring in the foot, this type of wound is nasty and will cause lameness. Heat and swelling can appear in the pastern and fetlock before the foot itself.	Call the vet. Clean area with water or weak saline solution while waiting.
Bruising	Often hard to diagnose, this occurs where the horse receives a blow. Swellings and haematomas may appear slowly, and a bone may have been chipped or fractured.	Call the vet.

DEALING WITH LEG PROBLEMS

Horses' legs are vulnerable to injury and skin infections. Lameness or an unusual stance of the front feet can be signs of serious problems. They should be investigated immediately, and the horse should not be worked.

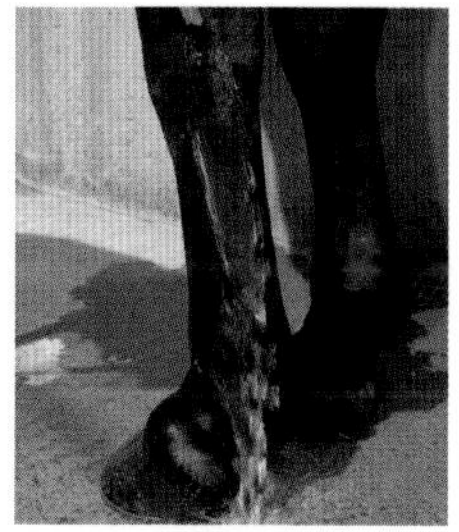

HOSING A LEG
If hosing is necessary, stand the horse quietly and apply a gentle stream of water. Hold the hose close to the horse's leg.

The padding *should always stick out at the top and the bottom of the bandage*

The bandage *should reach to just above the pastern*

STABLE BANDAGE
Thick, soft stable bandages are always used over a large piece of padding to help keep the pressure even.

CLEANING A CUT

If the horse's tetanus vaccinations are up to date, you can often treat minor cuts yourself. It is vital to make sure that the wound is clean and to keep the edges moist for a few days. Call the vet if you are unsure.

1 STOP THE BLEEDING
Apply pressure to stop any bleeding. (Do not panic if there is a lot of blood unless it is pumping, which means an artery is cut. In this case, call the vet quickly and apply pressure until he arrives.)

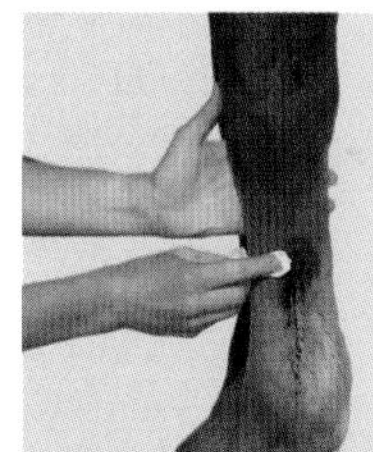

2 CLEAN THE WOUND
Flush out any debris using a hosepipe or squeeze a large piece of cotton wool soaked in weak saline solution over the cut. Avoid strong antiseptics – they could do more harm than good.

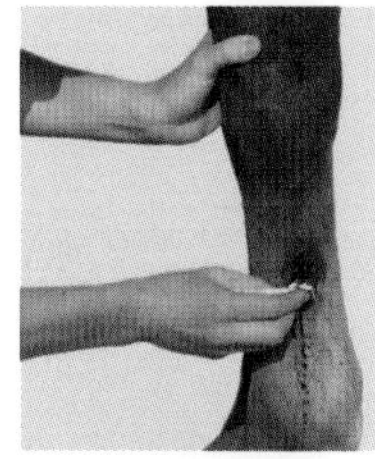

3 CHECK THE AREA
Clean the surrounding skin and check for any other wounds. Keeping a minor wound soft and clean is usually enough to bring out any debris inside, but your vet will decide whether further treatment is needed.

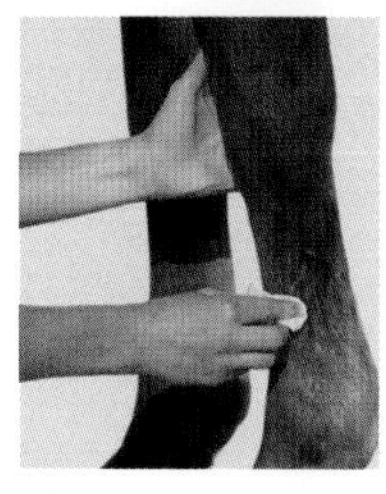

CHECK LIST

SIGNS OF GOOD HEALTH

- Horse is comfortable when taking weight squarely on all four feet; resting a leg is normal for some horses, but note if it is unusual for your horse.
- Not lame when moved.
- Alert – ears pricked and head up unless resting.
- Eyes bright and clear.
- No wounds or swellings.
- Coat sleek and lying flat.
- Body fleshed out but not fat; ribs not visible but evident to a light touch.
- Eating normally and chewing well.
- Drinking normally.
- Temperature, pulse, and respiration normal; average respiration is 8 to 15 breaths per minute.
- Droppings regular; should break on hitting the ground, although consistency can vary according to diet.
- Urine quite thick and either colourless or pale yellow.

A VET'S VISIT

- Have the horse ready in plenty of time and make sure that areas the vet will need to see are clean.
- Try to provide good light and a flat area where the horse can be trotted up.
- Ask the vet to give the horse a general check-over at annual booster time.

Trotting up for the vet

FEEDING

Horses have a complex digestive system that is vulnerable to problems, some of which can be fatal. It is important to follow the basic rules of feeding little but often, not exercising after hard feed, and not giving a large feed or too much cold water to a hot or tired horse. Each horse should also be fed according to his type, temperament, and work load.

HORSES GRAZING IN A FIELD
Fresh grass is the most digestible form of fibre, but good quality hay or haylage is the next best thing.

PROVIDE FOOD AND WATER

The most important things for a horse are access to fibre – in the form of grass or hay – and clean water; these provide the essential ingredients to keep his digestive system functioning. Fibre should make up at least two-thirds of the daily food intake for most horses and some, especially ponies and those not in work, can exist very well without hard feed (i.e. grain). Stabled horses should be given plenty of hay or haylage at frequent, regular intervals.

A constant supply of clean water is vital, and horses usually drink sensibly, according to their needs. After hard work, offer small amounts of water with the chill taken off.

FEED ACCORDING TO NEEDS

Each horse must be fed according to his individual needs at the time. The exact amount, and the ratio of hard feed to hay, will depend on his work load and temperament, whether he is stabled or field-kept, and whether he naturally keeps on weight. If he is doing little or no work, most of his ration will be grass or hay, with about 15 per cent as hard feed divided into two feeds a day. In light work –

RULES FOR FEEDING

FEEDING RULE	REASON
Water	Supply ad lib except during strenuous exercise, when intake should be regulated.
Feed according to need	Work out how much feed the horse needs, according to size, then adapt the ratio of hay to hard feed taking into account the individual horse's needs.
Use only good-quality feed	Poor-quality, musty, or mouldy feed or hay is not only less nutritious, it can also be harmful and cause the horse to develop allergies.
Feed little and often	Horses have very small stomachs, which cannot hold a lot of food. They need to be able to graze or pick at hay for much of the time and should be fed as near to the same times each day as possible.
Do not chop and change the food	Try to stick to the same products, but if you have to change the feed, do so gradually. This includes grass – for example, a horse that has been stabled all winter should be grazed for a while each day before being turned out completely.

usually defined as being ridden for up to an hour a day, including some schooling – the hard feed would increase to about 25 per cent, and splitting it into three feeds a day is a good idea.

Only increase the hard feed you give a horse in line with an increase in his exercise. The more hard feed in the diet, the more crucial the balance between feed and exercise. If a horse that has been in work is suddenly rested, for example due to injury, it is very important to cut the hard feed and make up the difference with hay, because too much unused protein in the blood can lead to serious illness.

CHOOSE A SUITABLE FEED

There is a wide range of different feed products available, and it is best to find one or two that suit your horse and stick to them – do not keep changing. Like us, horses need proteins, carbohydrates, vitamins, and minerals. These can be obtained from "straight" feeds, such as oats, or "compound" feeds, which include cubes and ready-made muesli-style mixes, as well as from hay.

COARSE MIX
Mixes often feature oats, wheat, and pulses along with other forms of fibre and minerals.

PELLETS
Like mixes, pellets are available in a variety of energy levels. They are more fibrous than mixes.

OATS
The traditional energy feed, nutritious oats can be fed whole, rolled, or "bruised".

BARLEY
An alternative to oats, barley must be soaked or "bruised" to make it digestible.

HAY
Meadow hay and seed hay must smell sweet and be of good quality.

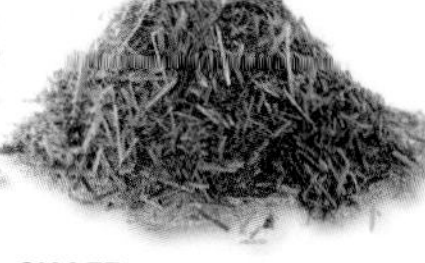

CHAFF
This is chopped hay mixed with oat straw, alfalfa or molasses.

HAYLAGE
A cross between hay and silage, haylage varies in energy content.

ALFALFA
Horses love alfalfa but it is rich in protein, so do not feed too much.

DOS AND DON'TS

- **Do use** good-quality hay.
- **Do use** haylage within a few days of opening the bag, before it starts to ferment.
- **Do be** careful with meadow hay. It often has other plants in it, many of which are fine, but weeds indicate poor pasture and can be harmful when dry. Ragwort is a fatal poison.

TIPS AND TECHNIQUES

HANGING A HAYNET
Step 1 Open the net fully and stuff in the hay. Make sure there is no string inside. Pull the drawstring tight. **Step 2** Thread the string through a metal ring and tie it to the net with a quick-release knot (*see* p.87). The net should be level with the horse's chest when empty. **Step 3** Tuck the end of the string through the loop of the knot.

1 Stuff the hay into the net

2 Tie a quick-release knot

3 Tuck in the end

LEARNING TO RIDE

GETTING STARTED

Learning to ride should be a combination of fun and effort. It is a great way to enjoy outdoor life and see the countryside, with the added bonus of helping to keep you toned and supple. People with natural athleticism, balance, and co-ordination have an advantage, but you do not need to be especially strong or sporty to ride a horse. At first, as with any new sport, you will probably discover muscles you hardly knew existed – but you will soon begin to feel the benefits.

RIDING HORSES

Part of the skill of riding lies in developing a "feel" for the horse. Horses are willing creatures and are keen to do what you ask them. A good rider learns to understand the signals a horse gives through his behaviour and temperament. You will gradually learn how best to combine empathy and firmness in order to handle these powerful animals successfully.

RIDING OUT
Enjoying the great outdoors on horseback is a unique and potentially sociable experience.

Riding can be sociable or solitary, depending on your preference and experience. Horses, however well trained, can be unpredictable, so you need to be prepared for setbacks – including falls. A positive attitude is important. There is so much to learn – from taking command of and working with the horse to accepting what equestrians refer to, with more than a hint of irony, as "the ups and downs of the sport".

LEARNING SAFELY

You might have already had a go at riding on a casual basis, such as on a pony trek or on a friend's horse. This is great fun, but when you decide to learn properly it is important to learn the correct methods and the reasons behind them. Once you start to take control of the horse yourself you need to be aware of the risks and pitfalls, although there is no need to let them put you off. The importance of safety around horses should never be underestimated and if you learn the correct way from the start, you will soon see that it is

WHAT TO EXPECT

IMPROVING YOUR BALANCE
Lunge lessons enable you to ride safely without reins and stirrups. You can concentrate on your position and learn to move with the motion of the horse while someone else controls him. This helps you to gain the confidence to ride primarily through balance rather than by hanging on to the horse's mouth, and prepares you for riding outside the confines of the sand-school.

Having a lesson on the lunge

founded on good sense and will enable you to have plenty of fun without taking any unnecessary risks.

You can have lessons in a group or on a one-to-one basis. Your first lesson will be based around learning to mount and dismount, how to sit in the saddle, hold the reins, and ask the horse to walk forwards, turn, and stop. It should take place in an enclosed area known as a manège or, more commonly, sand-school. You will also learn how to adjust your stirrups to the correct length and tighten the horse's girth. These basics are not very exciting but they are essential, and a good instructor will introduce some activity as soon as possible to make the lesson more interesting.

If this is your first close encounter with a horse, the feeling of sitting astride him can be both exhilarating and daunting. You will soon see the sense of learning in a controlled environment. With a little patience, it should not be long before you can experience the great outdoors on horseback, and basic horsemanship skills will help you enjoy it all the more.

IN CONTROL
Being in control of a horse – especially in open spaces – is a skill that takes practice and courage.

TYPES OF RIDING

Whether it is a holiday trek or trail ride, a tailor-made riding holiday, weekly lessons at your local riding school, or something more ambitious, there's a riding activity to suit most tastes and skill levels. You can treat it as a leisure pastime or a serious competitive discipline, and use it to relax or to further your equestrian ambitions.

RIDING STYLES

Riding is a popular holiday activity and most people have heard of trekking, trail riding, and the main competitive disciplines. But the words "hacking" and "schooling", which are used frequently in this book, might be less familiar. A hack is a short ride out in the countryside, while schooling usually refers to the suppling exercises used to help keep horses fit. Once you are truly bitten by the riding bug, terms like these will become as much a part of your life as walking and running.

For many people, riding conjures up images of jumping – either in glamorous show jumping competitions, adrenaline-fuelled cross-country, or jump racing. For others, a leisurely ride in beautiful countryside or a riding holiday through dramatic scenery comes to mind. The wide range of specialist holidays now available means you can ride almost anywhere, from cattle ranches in the United States or Australia to the forests and fjords of Scandinavia or the vertiginous passes of the Spanish Sierra Nevada. For those who love to watch others demonstrate their skills, there are frenetic polo matches played on ice in St Moritz or in the high altitudes of Ladakh, dressage displays in which divas make their horses dance before your eyes, or the thrills and spills of a three-day event such as Badminton or Burghley. Whatever type of riding you are interested in, there is bound to be somewhere you can learn for yourself.

WESTERN STYLE
Synonymous with a relaxed, practical approach, Western riding is a popular choice.

You can learn just enough to enjoy a riding holiday or delve deeper and realize that, with horses, it is quite possible to keep learning all your life. It might take years to emulate the professionals, but it is hard to become bored when every horse is different and no situation is ever entirely predictable. There are many facets to horsemanship, both ridden and unmounted, and the beauty of equestrianism is that there are so many ways to enjoy it.

TOP LEVEL DRESSAGE
Former Olympic eventing gold medallist, New Zealander Blyth Tait performs a harmonious dressage test on Welton Envoy at the Lexington Horse Trials, 2000.

RIDING ON THE FLAT

Riding "on the flat" means that there is no jumping involved but, while this can be less demanding physically, it is still challenging and requires skill. Many people decide to specialize in dressage, which is done purely on the flat. It demonstrates control and obedience, and ranges from the most basic level to the advanced movements that look so impressive. Western disciplines such as reining, which has a growing following in Europe, are also purely flatwork. The skills and techniques used in reining are quite different from dressage, and it can be a terrific alternative to English riding.

RIDING HOLIDAYS
A vast choice of riding holidays is available the world over to suit a wide level of experience.

JUMPING

Most riders learn jumping to some degree – it is not the sole territory of specialists and can be done in the manège or out in the country. In an enclosed manège, you are most likely to jump coloured fences similar to those used at show jumping competitions, which can be adapted to suit your ability. Out in the countryside, you might come across streams or ditches, logs, and "fixed" cross-country type fences. Jumping is a useful skill to have, but if you do not enjoy it you are not alone – many people prefer to ride only on the flat. However, remember there might be occasions when you have to negotiate a log or small stream across the path when out hacking.

Show jumping and cross-country jumping can be done at all levels, from small beginner fences to the much more challenging obstacles at professional level.

SHOW JUMPING
The jumps used in riding schools or at show jumping competitions are easy to adjust in both height and width to suit the ability of horse and rider.

WORKING TOGETHER

Like people, horses show a preference for different types of work, and this is something you will gradually learn to judge. If you ride one horse on a regular basis, or are considering buying your own, it is very important that you are well matched.

RIDING ON THE BEACH
Horses, like riders, need fun and variety to keep them interested. The beach is a magical place to ride for both horse and human.

TRAINING A HORSE

Riding school horses will be well trained already. But as you become more experienced, you will probably have the opportunity to ride less educated horses and have lessons that teach you and your mount at the same time. The chance to ride a young horse in its early stages of training, supervised by an instructor or someone suitably experienced, is a fantastic way to learn more about how horses behave. Contributing to a horse's development in this way can be hugely rewarding; there is a long learning process involved that starts from their earliest days and must be done carefully and skillfully to produce a well-mannered horse.

The way a youngster is handled on the ground, even before he is ridden, will shape his attitude to being ridden for the rest of his life. It is said that a bad horse is made, not born that way. The early stages of training are crucial, as this is when the horse learns to co-operate with humans. He will only do this willingly if he is comfortable and happy.

RIDING SCHOOLS AND INSTRUCTORS

It is important to choose a riding establishment where the horses, instructors, and equipment are all of a suitable standard and the latest health and safety regulations are followed. This might sound a bit formal but the more you learn, the more you will see the sense in it, and a good instructor can make the learning process great fun. It simply is not worth compromising on safety.

RIDING SCHOOLS

Establishments vary enormously, from formal training schools to approved trekking and activity centres. You can also enhance your learning through riding clubs such as Rural Riders and the Pony Club, which caters for anyone up to the age of 25 and runs activities throughout the world. It can also be helpful to watch the professionals in action, either at competitions or by attending "clinics" and watching videos.

Where you take your lessons will depend on where you live, the type of riding you want to learn, your age, and what the local establishments can offer. There is plenty to be learned at a trekking centre, for example, but if you want to study serious equitation you will need to go somewhere that has a good manège and other facilities.

GROUP LESSONS
Learning as part of a group means you get less individual attention from the instructor, but you will benefit from watching other people.

Many countries have approval schemes for riding schools. A centre that has official approval is likely to adhere to up-to-date safety standards and be fully insured, which is important.

Learning to ride is also about learning to care for the horse, and this can be done wherever the horses are. Most riding schools offer horse and stable management lessons as well as riding, so that you can learn about the whole picture. Riding skills and horse care go hand in hand and the combination of the two is known as horsemanship.

INSTRUCTORS

For those riding privately owned horses there are freelance instructors who will teach at different venues, including private premises. National equestrian federations can usually provide a list of qualified, registered instructors. Some instructors advertize in the local press while others rely mainly on word-of-mouth recommendations.

As well as having a recognized qualification or a proven track-record, a good instructor should be friendly and confident with both horses and people. Personalities and skill levels can be factors in your choice. Some instructors, for example, might be excellent at teaching beginners, while others might prefer to concentrate on advanced riders.

WHAT TO EXPECT

WELL-RUN YARD

When you visit a stable yard or riding school with a view to having lessons, the most important factor is whether the horses look content and well cared-for. The place does not have to be pristine, but a clean, tidy, and efficient environment – with happy horses and people – is important.

A busy riding-school yard

BOOKING A LESSON

Finding somewhere to learn can be easy or difficult, depending on where you live. Try looking in the telephone directory, on the internet, or asking your local saddler for a recommendation – word of mouth is always a good method of research. Then take a look at the place, talk to the people, and see if you like it.

When you book a lesson, you will probably be asked some quite personal questions about your size, weight, and riding ability. Be honest – the instructor needs this information to match you with the right horse and, unless you are booking a solo lesson, the right group. It may be best to have your first few lessons on a one-to-one basis, while you master the basics of getting on and off, walking forwards, turning, and halting. But if you prefer the camaraderie of a group lesson, it can be just as effective. Learning in a group teaches you how horses behave around each other.

PRIVATE LESSONS

One-to-one tuition gives you the instructor's undivided attention, but means you have to work even harder.

BALANCE AND STABILITY

Riding is all about balance, and even the bravest person can feel quite vulnerable perched high up on a horse. Movements are often carried out while apparently sitting quite still, so great co-ordination is required and your body must always be in a good, relaxed posture. Any tension in you will be felt instantly by the horse, causing him at best to misunderstand your aids and, at worst, physical pain.

PERFECTLY POISED

The techniques used to communicate with the horse have been developed to ensure that neither your own, nor the horse's body is placed under undue strain. In the basic riding position, anyone looking at you should be able to draw an imaginary straight line through your shoulder, hip, and heel on each side (*see* pp.130–131 and 222–223). This is the optimum position for poise and stability on the flat – you are able to use your seat and legs independently of each other, as and where required by each movement. Riders balance on their seat bones, with most of the power and energy coming from the hips, seat, and lower back. This is easier to understand if you are familiar with the "ki" or "centre" concept taught in marshal arts, or the Alexander Technique for posture. Skiers will also have an idea of how to balance their body over bent knees, and will have used many of the same muscles.

RIDE LIKE A PRO

RIDING WITH ONE STIRRUP

The great New Zealand event rider Mark Todd completed the cross-country at Badminton in 1995 minus one stirrup. The leather broke one-third of the way through his round, but this superb horseman had sufficient balance and skill to ride the huge fences without it (these days, safety rules would not allow him to continue). Sadly, the horse, Bertie Blunt, was unable to show jump on the final day but the pair won Badminton the following year. Try to watch videos of Todd riding – he is one of the best.

Mark Todd and Bertie Blunt, Badminton, 1995

THE HORSE'S BALANCE

As well as your own centre of balance, you need to consider that of the horse. The rider's position is designed to ensure that you stay in place, interfere as little as possible with the horse's balance, and help him in using his hindquarters to provide the power. You can use your weight to help him in subtle ways, such as looking into a turn or standing in the stirrups to jump, but shifting your body around too much will hinder rather than help.

Your legs are used to drive the horse forwards and your hands to assist braking and steering, but this must all be done without disturbing your core balance. As you become more advanced you will learn that much control comes from your seat, not your hands – remember that the reins are attached to the horse's mouth, which is very sensitive and easily damaged.

PRACTISING BALANCE

At some point, your lessons will probably involve riding without reins or stirrups in the controlled environment of the manège.

MOVING WITH THE HORSE

Learning to balance from your seat is the key to staying with the horse's movement, which even when walking in a straight line, is quite considerable. Different types of horse may feel different to ride – a big, solid horse, for example, might have a smoother walk than a lively pony.

FEEL THE MOVEMENT

As you walk, put one hand just above the small of your back and feel the movement within it. Now consider that the horse has four legs and a lot more bulk, so there is correspondingly more movement. Your task as the rider is to stay balanced and follow the movement of the horse without interfering with it in any way. Bear in mind that each pace involves a different sequence of footfalls, sometimes with a moment when all four hooves are off the ground. His body could be bunched up one moment and stretched out the next. If you watch a slow-motion sequence, you will also notice that the horse's body is not always parallel with the ground. In canter, for example, it tips forwards and backwards. In order to stay on and ride effectively, your body must absorb these movements through good posture and poise.

A horse is a sensitive creature, and he will feel the slightest movement of your body. The quicker he moves, the more you need to keep balanced so that you stay

GALLOPING HORSE
In gallop, you have to take your weight out of the saddle and off the horse's back to allow for the rapid sequence of movements.

with him. If you turn your body – or even just your head – or shift your weight to one side, he will feel it and move accordingly. One basic rule is to always look in the direction you want to go. If you look down to the ground in front of your left foot, for example, your weight will tip that way and it will be harder for the horse to move straight.

RIDE LIKE A PRO

HELPING THE HORSE
When professional riders jump you will see that even before they land from a fence, they focus on the approach to the next one. Watch people like William Fox-Pitt, who is a highly skilled event rider.

William Fox-Pitt

STAYING CENTRED
Looking up and ahead helps keep you centred over the horse, and helps him move freely and correctly.

“HAVING MADE SURE THAT THE HORSES ARE IN GOOD CONDITION, THE NEXT BUSINESS IS TO TRAIN THE MEN.”

Xenophon, Greek cavalryman (430–355BCE)

STAYING SUPPLE

Doing exercises while mounted will increase your suppleness, making your body more relaxed and easier for the horse to carry. It will also improve your balance and help you control the amount of tension in individual muscles and joints, giving you greater control of your body and boosting your confidence. These exercises should be done under supervision in a manège on a quiet horse.

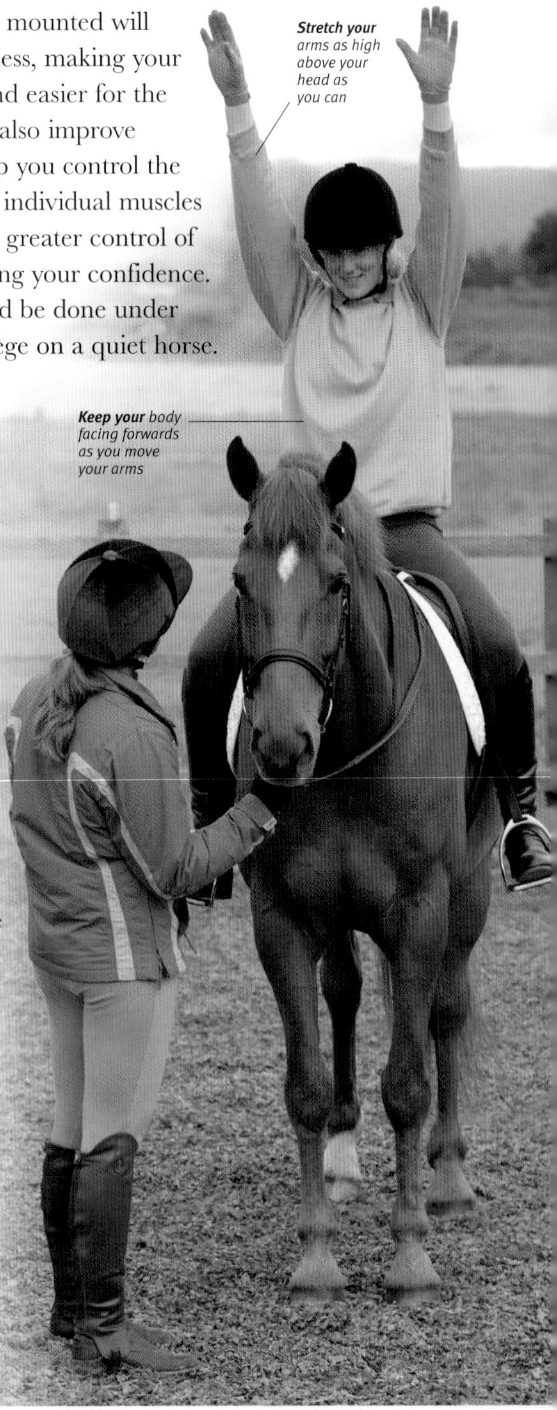

Stretch your arms as high above your head as you can

Keep your body facing forwards as you move your arms

1 SWING ARMS
Face forwards with your feet in the stirrups, or with the stirrups quit and crossed in front of the saddle. Stretch one arm in front of you and the other behind. Swing your arms down and back up in the opposite direction.

2 SWING SHOULDERS
Hang your arms by your sides. Swing them forwards and backwards slowly and rhythmically a few times before continuing the swing up above your head. Shrug your shoulders, pause, and repeat.

3 STRETCH WAIST

With your feet in the stirrups, stretch your arms out to the sides at shoulder height. Slowly turn your upper body and head from side to side. Keep the movements slow and rhythmical to avoid strain.

RIDERS' TIPS

Try these exercises at walk on a long rein, with your stirrups crossed in front of the saddle.

- **Ankles and** hips: turn your toes up, down, and out in smooth, continuous circles.
- **Knees: swing** your lower legs alternately forwards and backwards.
- **Thighs and** seat: move your upper legs away from the saddle, draw them back, return them to the saddle, and relax.

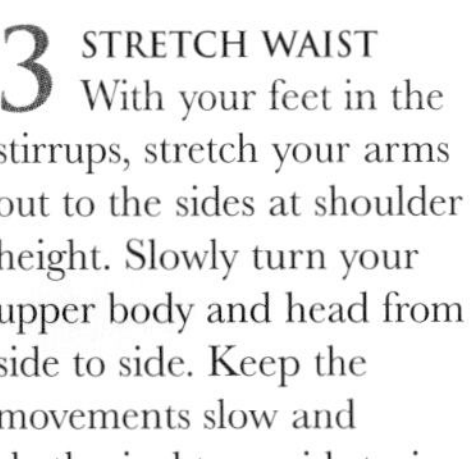

***Stretch your** arms out to the sides before starting*

***Move your** body and arms together for waist stretches*

***Sit still** with your hips facing forwards*

4 TOUCH TOES

With your feet in the stirrups, stretch up as high as you can. Bring one hand down slowly to the outside of the opposite knee and gently reach towards the foot, bending from your hips. Stretch up again, then repeat with the other hand.

KEEPING FIT

A level of aerobic and muscular fitness will make riding easier and more enjoyable. Warming up your muscles before a ride helps to loosen you up and stop you aching afterwards. For light hacking and schooling, you do not need to do specific fitness training. But for competing or trail-riding, it is worth building up your fitness as well as the horse's.

PREPARING YOUR BODY

Before you do any physical exercise, make sure your body is capable and that the exercises are suitable for your medical status. If in any doubt, consult your doctor and a qualified fitness trainer before you start. Each exercise should be repeated according to your capabilities – try five repeats to start with, then gradually increase. Always stretch your whole body gently first. Stand straight and stretch your arms above your head, and gradually stand on tiptoe so that your whole body stretches. Relax down on to your heels, then repeat several times.

FLEXING

Supple legs and ankles are helpful for making riding more comfortable. Standing upright, bring each foot in turn up behind you and catch it with the hand on the same side. Hold for a few seconds, then gently pull the ankle in towards your back and release. Repeat a few times, then gently release the leg.

SQUATS

Stand with your arms out in front of you and look straight ahead. Bend both knees and squat down slowly. Stand up, keeping your head up and back straight all the time. The bend should come from your hips, knees, and ankles. Move gently, and do not rush.

LEG AND THIGH STRETCHES
Sit with your legs stretched out in a V-shape. Folding from the hips so that you do not strain your back, slide both hands along one leg until you reach the foot. Repeat on the other leg. Do not worry if you cannot reach all the way – it is better to do the exercise correctly and partially than strain to achieve too much too soon.

RUNNING UP STEPS
Taking the stairs two steps at a time is a good way to build up strength in your legs. Make a habit of doing this whenever you can – but only in the upward direction.

DOS & DON'TS

- **Don't begin** any new physical exercise without seeing your doctor for a check-up.
- **Do always** warm up and cool down.
- **Do work** within your capabilities.
- **Do exercise** little and often, and vary your training activities so that you avoid continually putting stress on the same parts of your body.
- **Do remember** to keep working on exercises for suppleness as your muscle power increases, rather than just building up more muscle.

JOGGING
Regular jogging or cycling is a good form of aerobic training. As with any exercise, build it up gradually and learn to push yourself without exceeding your capabilities. Always wear proper running shoes if you go jogging, and remember to keep your body hydrated.

FALLING OFF

The adage that "the best riders have most falls" might not be strictly accurate, but it is true that everyone will fall off at some stage, and learning to fall correctly can help to minimize the risk of injury in some cases. Types of riding such as jumping and fast work appear to carry a higher risk, but you can just as easily fall doing flatwork or on a hack.

1 BE PROPELLED FORWARDS
Allow yourself to be propelled away from the horse in a forward arc rather than straight down. This gives you a greater chance of somersaulting instead of landing hard on one part of your body.

Rider kicks *his feet free of the stirrups*

He lets *himself fall rather than bracing his body and causing tension*

TIPS AND TECHNIQUES

PRACTISING FOR A FALL

Practise doing forward rolls on a gym mat so that you get the feel of the movement. The velocity of a fall can help propel you into a roll, especially if your stirrups are short, such as for jumping. **Step 1** Squat with your hands parallel to each other and tuck your chin into your chest. **Step 2** Put your shoulders to the ground and roll forwards, bending your legs. **Step 3** Finish in the squat position.

1 Pull in your chin

2 Roll over

3 Finish in squat position

2 DO A SOMERSAULT

As you hit the ground, go into a forward roll or at least tuck your head in and try to curl up into a ball. If you cannot roll clear, stay still and do not look up until the horse has moved out of the way. Some horses might kick out but most will try to avoid treading on you – moving will make this difficult for them.

DOS AND DON'TS

- **Don't scream** if you think you are about to fall, as this can frighten the horse.
- **Do try** to kick your feet free of the stirrup irons so that you can fall as far away from the horse as possible.
- **Don't throw** an arm out to break the fall – you are more likely to break the arm.
- **Do try** to keep hold of the reins.

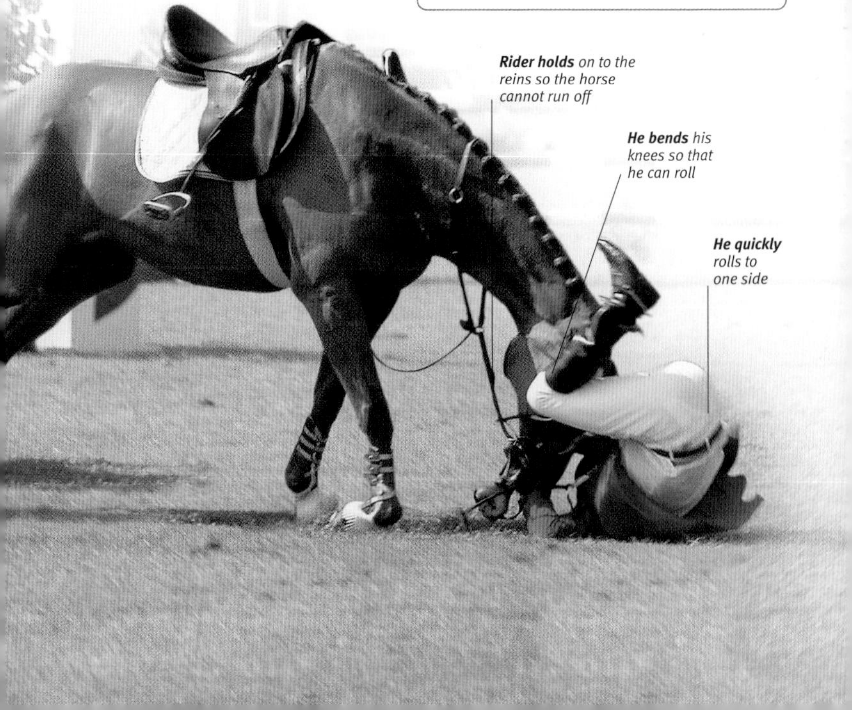

***Rider holds** on to the reins so the horse cannot run off*

***He bends** his knees so that he can roll*

***He quickly** rolls to one side*

ENGLISH RIDING

THE ENGLISH STYLE

The style known as English, or Continental, riding evolved from a merging of the old-fashioned hunting seat, cavalry riding, and dressage. Whereas the Western style of riding and saddle is best suited to flatwork, the English style can be easily adapted for both flatwork and jumping simply by altering the length of stirrups and the rider's position on a general-purpose saddle.

THE HORSE'S WELFARE

The central, uniting theme in any enlightened style of riding must always be the welfare of the horse. The best way to ensure this is through good training, using tack that is suitable for the job and fits the horse well, and by following a practical, safe routine for care and management that the horse can understand.

Ideas and equipment will always be adapted as science teaches us more about the horse – in particular the veterinary and nutritional aspects – but it is surprising how little the basics have changed over the centuries. Bits have become less harsh, and saddles are now made with sprung trees and softer padding. However, the tack used today is based on a simple, effective and centuries-old design that works as well now as ever before.

SADDLE STYLES
A dressage saddle is ideal for flatwork, but a general-purpose saddle can be used for flatwork and jumping.

TRAINING IS KEY

The English style, especially in Britain, is often seen as having a rather heavily regulated image. What it teaches, though, is a tried and

HACKING WITH FRIENDS
The English style of riding is perfect for a slow, sociable hack with friends or a fast hack that includes galloping and jumping.

trusted method designed to result in the safest, most effective and therefore most enjoyable all-round horsemanship. It is not difficult to learn the simple commands such as how to make a horse stop, go, and go faster or slower, but as you learn more about horses and their differing characters, you will discover that there is much more to riding than this. Even top riders admit that they are learning all the time.

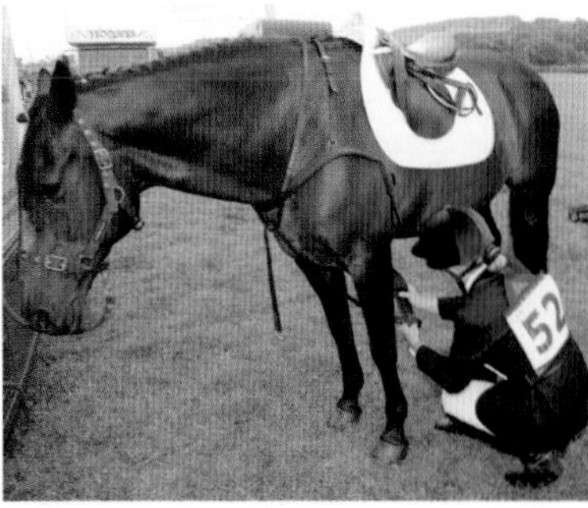

ENTERING COMPETITIONS
With a good seat and an understanding of the horse you can compete in a variety of disciplines using the English method.

VERSATILE STYLE

The training of both horse and rider in the English style prepares you for a variety of situations that you might encounter, whether at a riding school, at a competition, or on a riding holiday. You can do all this on a general-purpose saddle, which is designed both to give you the freedom to adapt your position according to what you want to do, and to ensure that the horse is always comfortable.

CROSS-COUNTRY RIDING
For cross-country riding, the rider takes their weight out of the saddle and crouches low over the horse so that he can gallop and jump freely.

FIRST LESSONS

Your earliest lessons will involve getting used to being around horses as well as riding them, so be patient and do not try to rush. You will find that there is a lot to take in, but with practice riding will become instinctive. Correct training can be done in a fun way that gives you the safest start and helps you to get the most out of riding.

MOUNTING

Using a mounting block places less strain on the horse's back than mounting from the ground, but you should be able to do both in case a block is not available – for example if you need to remount out hacking. Use a solid platform that can bear your weight without breaking or tipping, and ask someone to hold the horse if possible.

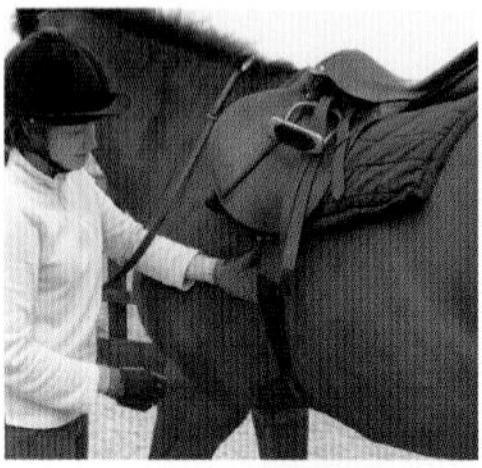

1 CHECK THE GIRTH Tighten the girth to stop the saddle from slipping round as you mount, then run down both stirrups.

2 FACE THE TAIL Gather the reins in your left hand. Place the hand in front of the horse's withers to steady you and prevent you from pulling his mouth with the reins. Face the horse's tail. Turn the stirrup clockwise towards you and place the ball of your left foot in it.

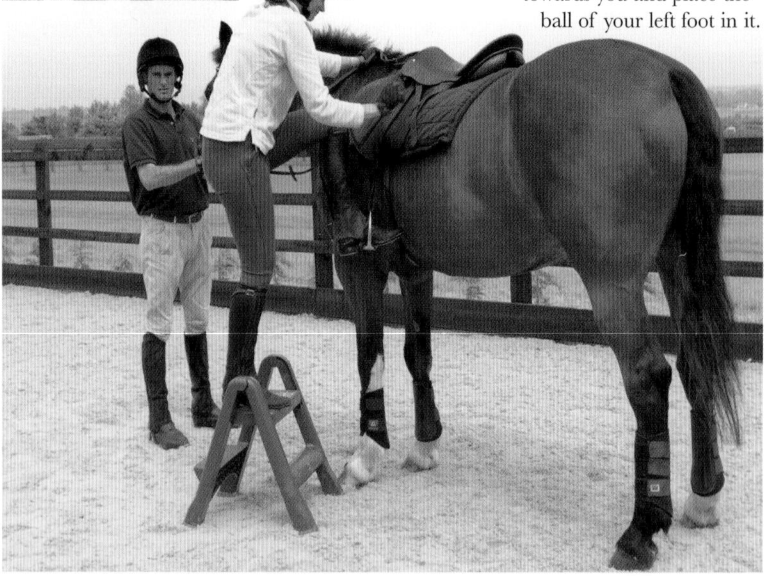

TIPS AND TECHNIQUES

MOUNTING FROM THE GROUND
Stand the horse still – if this is difficult, face him towards a wall, hedge, or fence. Tighten the girth. **Step 1** Gather the reins in your left hand, short enough to stop the horse moving. Put your hand in front of the horse's withers, place your left foot in the stirrup and your right hand on the far side of the saddle. **Step 2** Spring up, swing your leg over, and sit down gently. Take up the reins.

1 Put your foot in the stirrup

2 Swing your leg over

3 SPRING UP

Turn towards the horse with your left knee against the saddle, being careful not to prod him with your toe. Reach up with your right hand to grab the far side of the saddle and spring up, putting your weight on to the ball of your foot.

4 SWING OVER

Swing your right leg over the horse's back as you move your right hand forwards. Lower yourself gently into the saddle and place your right foot in the stirrup from the outside by turning your ankle inwards.

RIDERS' TIPS

- **To tighten** the girth when mounted, keep your feet in the stirrups. Lift one leg forwards in front of the saddle flap, lift the flap, reach down and tighten one buckle at a time.
- **To adjust** a stirrup when mounted, keep your foot in it. Grasp the end of the leather and find the buckle by feel. Put your thumb on top of the buckle, pull it out and adjust it. Then pull the inside of the leather down so that the buckle is snug against the bar.

Tightening the girth

Adjusting a stirrup

CORRECT POSITION

Sitting correctly is important both for the horse's comfort – your weight is directly over his spine and very close to his internal organs – and for effective riding. Only if you sit correctly can you be balanced enough to give the horse aids that he can understand and follow his movement without impeding him by gripping or becoming tense.

SITTING CORRECTLY

Sit in the lowest part of the saddle, balance your weight equally on each seat bone, and keep your back straight yet relaxed. Imagine that the top of your head is attached to a balloon floating above it, and gently grow tall from the waist up; this is a better way to straighten your spine than pushing out your chest or hollowing your back, both of which create tension.

To hold the reins, grasp one rein with each hand, making a light fist with your thumbs facing inwards. Bring your little fingers outside the reins, which now pass between your little and third fingers. Turn your hands upright with your thumbs on top to keep the reins in place.

SIT UP STRAIGHT

When you are in the saddle, imagine a line running from the point of your shoulder, through your hip, down to your heel.

CENTRE YOUR WEIGHT

You should sit centrally over the horse. Keep your head level; if your chin is too high it will cause tension in your neck, back, and shoulders.

ALIGN YOUR BODY

When riding straight, your head and spine should be aligned with the horse's, with your coccyx in the centre of, but not touching, the saddle.

DOS & DON'TS

- **Do keep** your body poised and relaxed.
- **Do let** your upper arms hang close to your sides.
- **Don't rock** forwards, because your whole body will tip forwards.
- **Don't sit** too far back on your seat bones, because this will make you slouch in the saddle.

Tense rider with hollow back

***Keep your** head straight so that there is no tension in your neck*

***Look ahead** in the direction that you want to go*

***Keep your** hands as still as possible; the reins are connected to the horse's mouth and fidgeting will confuse him*

ALIGN YOUR HANDS AND ELBOWS

When your hands are at the correct height, another imaginary line runs from the horse's mouth via your hands to your elbows.

***Your body** should be upright without being too stiff*

***Your weight** should be equally distributed on both seat bones*

***Your feet** should point straight forwards with the weight in the heels*

THE AIDS

You tell the horse what you want him to do via signals called the aids. The basis of the natural aids is a good seat supported by your legs, hands and, to some extent, your voice. Artificial aids such as whips and spurs can enhance the natural aids but should be used with great care. In this book, leg and hand aids are highlighted in blue and red boxes.

USING THE AIDS

Your aids must be clear and consistent so that the horse always understands what you are asking. This is only possible if you are sitting correctly and are able to use the different parts of your body independently of each other, which requires a combination of skill, subtlety, and co-ordination. Exaggerated movements are not necessary, in fact they are discouraged. Every aid should be prepared for; in other words, you put the horse in a physical position from which he is able to obey. To do this, you need to learn to synchronize your driving and restraining aids with the horse's movement.

EQUIPMENT TYPES

SPURS

The leg aids can be reinforced and given greater finesse with spurs. Spurs should be used only by experienced riders who can use their legs independently of their seat. Spurs come in various lengths, but are never more than a few centimetres and always have blunt ends. Their use should be kept to a minimum.

A spur on a rider's foot

WHIPS

There are different types of whip. For hacking and jumping, a short whip is used behind the rider's leg as an adjunct to the leg aid. To use it, you need to learn to take one hand off the reins confidently. A dressage whip is longer and can be used by more experienced riders while keeping both hands on the reins.

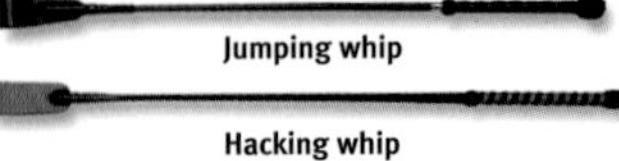

Jumping whip

Hacking whip

Dressage whip

USING NATURAL AIDS

Your seat, legs, and hands are the basis of good riding. Your voice can be helpful too, but only use it calmly and when necessary.

DEVELOPING FEEL

The horse must do as you ask, but a tactful rather than dictatorial approach is needed. You need to learn to use the aids without looking and to feel when and how the horse is responding. If a well-trained horse does not do what you ask, question whether your aids were effective. When he does as you ask, soften the aids to let him know he has done the right thing. As you become more experienced, you will learn to judge when the horse is misbehaving through real naughtiness or just a burst of high spirits.

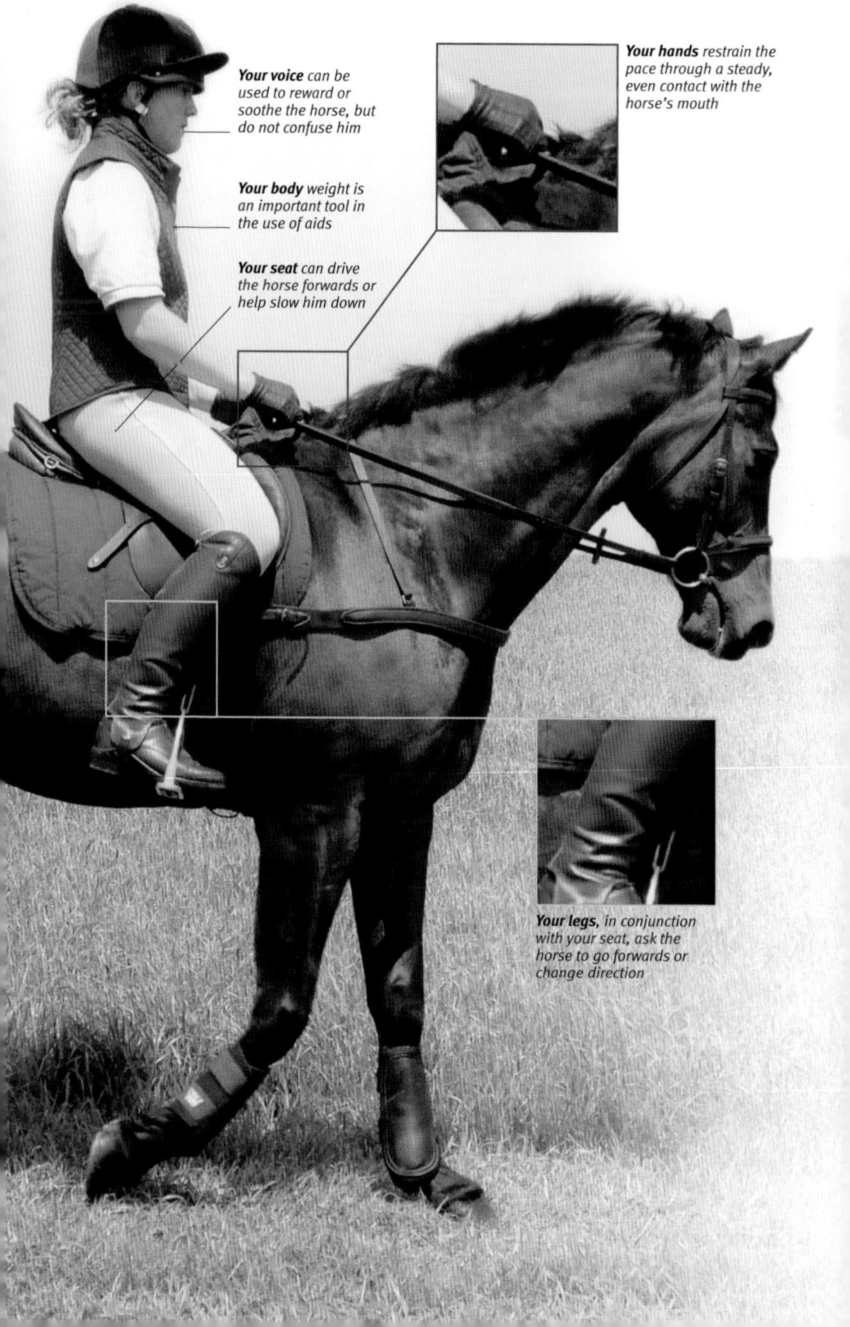

Your voice *can be used to reward or soothe the horse, but do not confuse him*

Your body *weight is an important tool in the use of aids*

Your seat *can drive the horse forwards or help slow him down*

Your hands *restrain the pace through a steady, even contact with the horse's mouth*

Your legs, *in conjunction with your seat, ask the horse to go forwards or change direction*

STARTING AND STOPPING

These are basic techniques that you need to learn before you can go faster than walk, along with balancing on the horse and holding a steady rein contact. This contact is crucial – if the reins are too long, you will have no control and will jab the horse's mouth when you pull them, and if they are too short, the horse cannot go forwards.

1 PREPARE TO WALK
Make sure you are sitting and holding the reins correctly. Take up a soft contact on the reins that allows the horse to stretch his neck forwards as he walks. Squeeze with both legs in the position known as "on the girth", which is where they hang when you are sitting correctly.

2 WALK FORWARDS
Once the horse has answered your command, allow him forwards and, while keeping the leg and rein contact, soften the aids. This tells him that he has done as you asked.

***Keep your** hands upright with the thumbs on top and maintain a soft contact*

***Keep your** feet pointing forwards so that the inside of your leg gives the aid*

HALTING

Stopping and slowing down are basic requirements that need to be mastered from all paces, but your first lesson will concentrate on halting from walk. It is not simply a matter of pulling on the reins, which would hurt the horse and possibly cause him to pull away from your hands, but is a combination of seat, leg, and rein.

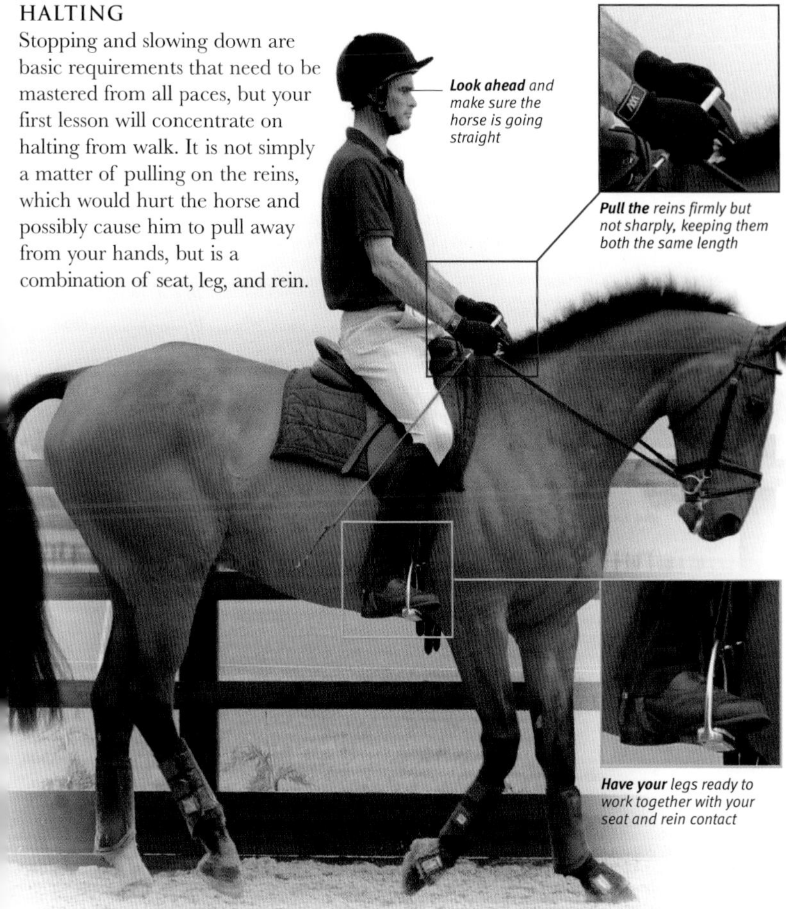

***Look ahead** and make sure the horse is going straight*

***Pull the** reins firmly but not sharply, keeping them both the same length*

***Have your** legs ready to work together with your seat and rein contact*

1 PREPARE TO HALT
Make sure you are sitting straight on the horse. Sit up tall, with your head up, sit deep in the saddle, and try to reduce the movement of your body. Keep squeezing gently with your legs on the girth.

***Sit down** deep in the saddle to help the horse bring his hindquarters under*

2 HALT
Squeeze the reins with your hands so that the horse moves forwards into the contact and is restricted from going any further, then give an even, firm pull. Relax the aids as soon as the horse has obeyed.

TURNING

When you turn left or right, you need to guide the horse with your body and legs. The reins play an important part too, but you use them to help and allow the horse to turn rather than to pull his head round. This means that the horse can make the turn with his whole body and does not lose his balance or momentum.

1 PREPARE TO TURN

Look in the direction you want to turn. With your inside hand – that is, the one on the inside of the manège and not the one nearest the fence – briefly put a light pressure on the rein then release it. This warns the horse that you are about to ask him to turn.

Move your *hand across into the turn, not back towards your body*

Keep your *inside leg on the girth and your outside leg behind the girth*

AT A GLANCE

TURNING RIGHT

The rider briefly checks the horse's forward movement then opens his inside rein. He looks right, letting his upper body follow, and uses his legs – inside leg on the girth, outside leg just behind – to keep the horse going forwards.

Keep the horse moving forwards and keep your weight centred over his body

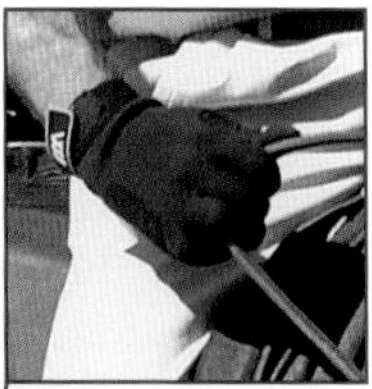

Keep allowing the turn with your inside hand until the horse is straight

Ask for the turn in good time – do not just pull the horse's head round

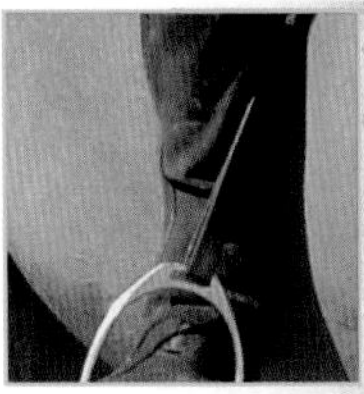

2 FLEX THE HORSE

Now move your inside hand and rein sideways in the direction of the turn. This is called "opening the rein". Keep your inside leg on the girth, move your outside leg slightly further back and squeeze with both at the same time to keep the horse moving.

Squeeze with your legs until the horse has completed the turn

3 COMPLETE THE TURN

Keep looking through the turn and squeezing with your legs so that the horse bends his whole body, not just his neck. When you have completed the turn, straighten your body, hands, and legs and ride positively forwards.

DISMOUNTING

It is technically correct to dismount from the horse's near (left) side – a practice that may have its origins in the days when men carried swords on their left side. The components of the dismount need to be put together in one fluid movement that does not startle the horse.

DOS & DON'TS

- **Don't let** go of the reins and allow the horse to wander off.
- **Do bring** the horse to a complete halt before dismounting.
- **Do hold** your whip in your left hand, lying down the horse's shoulder.
- **Do practise** dismounting from both sides.

1 LEAN FORWARDS

Take both feet out of the stirrups and put your reins in your left hand. Then put your left hand on the horse's neck for support and lean forwards to an angle of about 45 degrees. Do not collapse on to the horse's neck.

2 LIFT YOUR LEG CLEAR

Put your right hand on the front of the saddle. Take your weight on your hands and swing your right leg back, up, and over the horse's back, being careful not to touch it.

***Do not** kick the horse with your leg as you swing it over*

AT A GLANCE

DISMOUNTING

Stop the horse and keep the rein contact as you dismount. Quit your stirrups, put your left hand on the withers and your right hand on the front of the saddle. Swing your right leg over the horse's back and drop gently to the ground.

Keep hold of the reins so that they do not hang down in loops

Bend your knees and keep your back straight as you land

3 BEND YOUR KNEES

Let your body slip naturally to the ground close to the horse. Land on both feet with your knees bent to absorb the shock. Straighten up quickly, keeping hold of the reins.

TIPS AND TECHNIQUES

RUNNING UP THE STIRRUPS

After dismounting, run up the stirrups so that they do not flap. **Step 1** Loop your left arm (for left stirrup) through the reins. Run the iron up the back of the leather as far as it will go. **Step 2** Tuck the end of the leather through the iron.

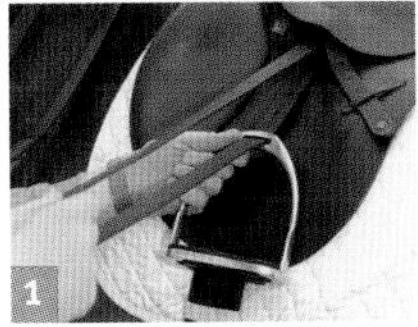

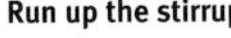

Run up the stirrup

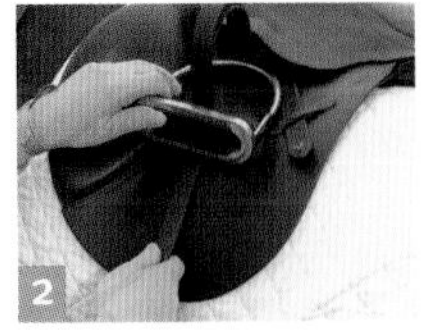

Secure the stirrup

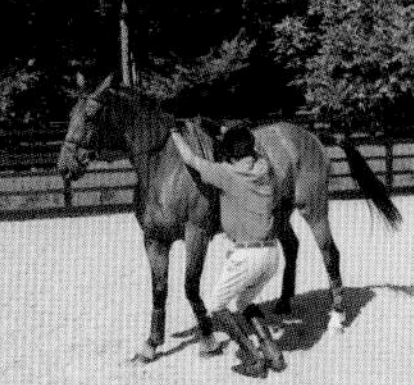

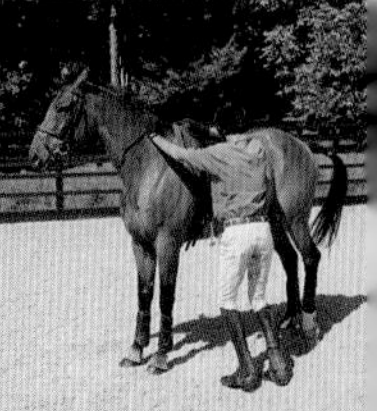

THE FOUR GAITS

Each "gait", also known as a "pace", has a distinctive feel. This is because the horse's legs move in a different sequence for each one, and because the angle of his body may change. In walk and trot his body is parallel to the ground, but in canter and gallop it tilts up as he pushes off from his hind legs and down when he stretches out his front legs.

WALKING

The walk is a four-time movement that has no moment of suspension – in other words, at least one foot is on the ground at all times. This pace tells us a lot about a horse: for example, a good, swinging walk that covers the ground and uses his muscles well means he is likely to be athletic in his other paces.

1 FOLLOW THE MOVEMENT
When walking forwards, keep both your seat bones equally balanced on the saddle. Relax your lower back so that your body naturally follows the movement of the horse. Keep an even contact on the reins, allowing the horse to move forwards.

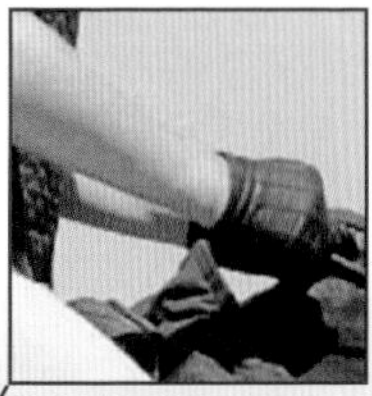

***Keep your** shoulders and neck relaxed*

***Barely change** your position from that of halt*

***Maintain a** light contact with the horse's mouth*

AT A GLANCE

WALKING
In an ordinary, workmanlike walk, the prints made by the horse's hind hooves should overlap the prints made by his front hooves. The pace should be active but unhurried, with each stride the same length.

2 KEEP IT GOING

Sit up tall and keep your legs in contact with the horse. There is no need to keep kicking or squeezing, unless the horse is unwilling. Just let the movement of his sides create a small amount of pressure against your legs. Let your hands follow the natural stretching of the horse's neck.

HORSE IN ACTION

WALKING CORRECTLY
Watch a horse walking unrestrained or on the lunge. Note how he uses his muscle, especially those over his "topline" – his back, quarters, and the top of his neck.

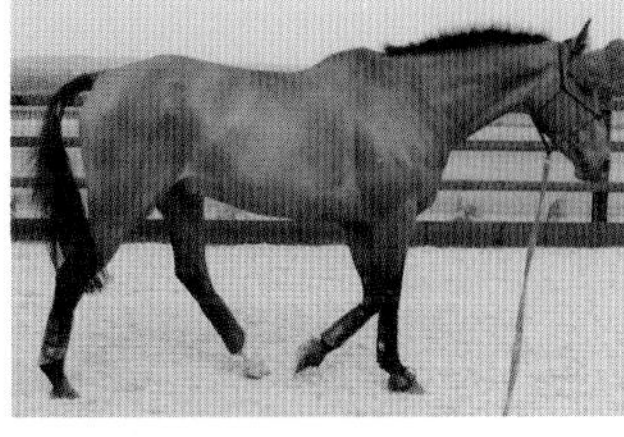

Horse walking on the lunge

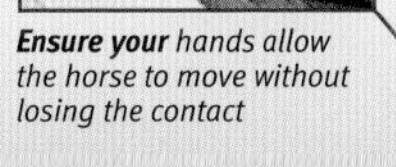

Ensure your *hands allow the horse to move without losing the contact*

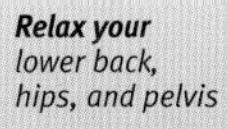

Relax your *lower back, hips, and pelvis*

Look in *the direction you are heading*

The horse *naturally nods his head while walking*

Keep your *legs in contact with the horse's sides*

WALK TO TROT

Your first attempt at trotting will feel bumpy but do not worry – walk to trot is one of the harder transitions to learn, but you will soon get the hang of it. The key is to relax and keep your posture and centre of balance correct, so that you move with the horse rather than trying to anticipate by making a forced movement or tipping forwards.

1 PREPARE TO TROT First, shorten your reins if necessary. In trot, the horse's neck does not stretch out as much as in walk and if the reins are too long, you will lose the contact when he starts to trot.

2 ASK FOR TROT Squeeze with your lower legs – just as you do when you ask him to move from halt to walk, but slightly harder. The pressure must come from both legs equally and at the same time.

RIDERS' TIPS

- **On your** first few attempts, take the reins in one hand and hold the pommel of the saddle with the other hand to help you balance. But do not let the horse's head pull your body forwards out of balance.
- **Stay in** sitting trot (*see* pp.146–147) for the first few strides. This puts you in a firmer position to establish the pace.

AT A GLANCE

WALK TO TROT

Shorten the reins and keep an even contact, then squeeze with both legs to ask the horse to go faster. Sit for a few strides, then lean your upper body slightly forwards and let the horse's movement push you up into rising trot.

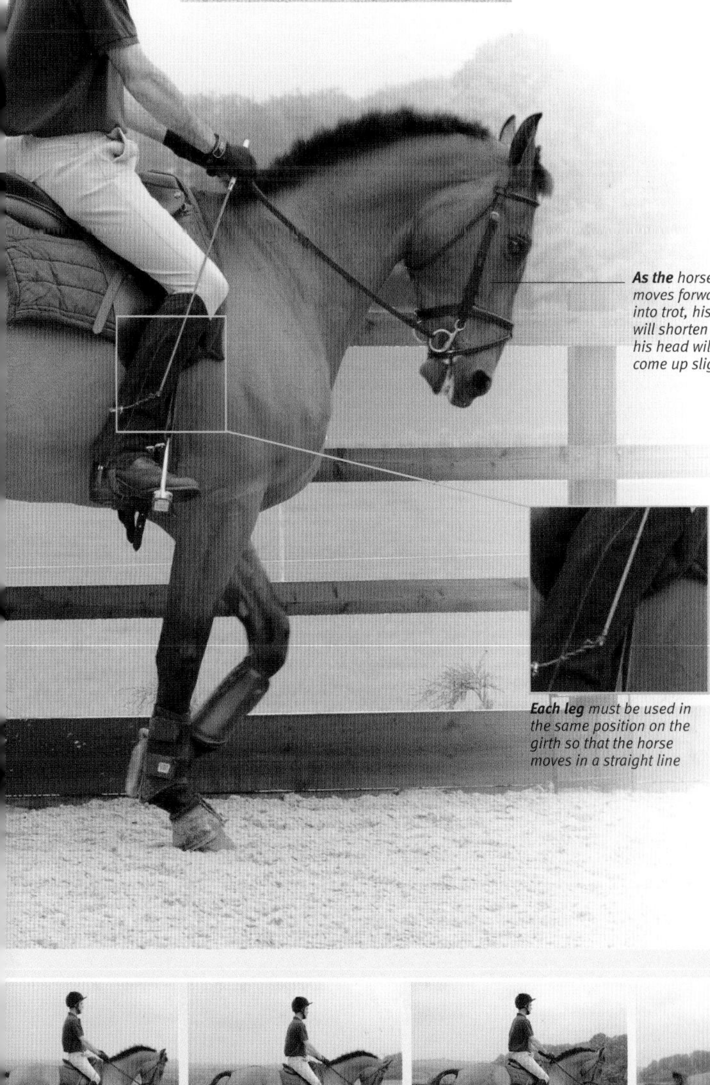

Keep looking *forwards and ahead*

3 TROTTING

When the horse starts to trot, relax your hips and back to help your body absorb the movement. It can be alarming when he first moves off, but do not pull on the reins – your legs and hands must be giving the same message.

As the *horse moves forwards into trot, his neck will shorten and his head will come up slightly*

Each leg *must be used in the same position on the girth so that the horse moves in a straight line*

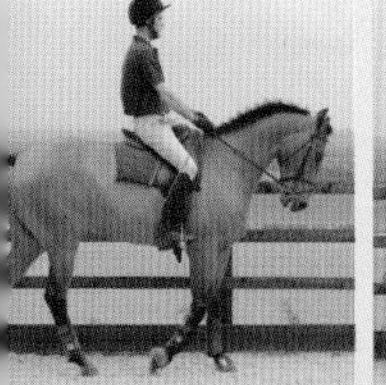

TROTTING

The trot is a two-time pace in which the horse's legs move in diagonal pairs and there is a moment of suspension. The footsteps should have an even beat. It can be ridden either by rising and sitting with each alternate stride, called rising trot, or by sitting, when your seat stays in the saddle the whole time and your back absorbs the energy.

1 STAY SITTING
Stay in sitting trot for a few steps before you start to rise. Your seat helps to ensure the horse goes forwards, and if he is reluctant or drops back into walk, it is easier to use your legs effectively while sitting.

2 RISE UP
To start rising, incline your upper body forwards slightly, push your weight down into your heels, and lift your thighs and seat up, letting your knees act as a hinge. You will find the horse's action pushes you up quite naturally.

TIPS AND TECHNIQUES

SITTING TROT

Remaining balanced in sitting trot requires an upright position and a relaxed, supple back, otherwise you will bounce, which is painful for you and the horse. Sitting trot without stirrups is a good way to improve your seat and is especially useful for schooling, but should not be over-used as it is hard work for the horse's back. You should increase its use gradually if the horse is not used to it, to allow his back muscles to develop.

Absorbing the movement through your back

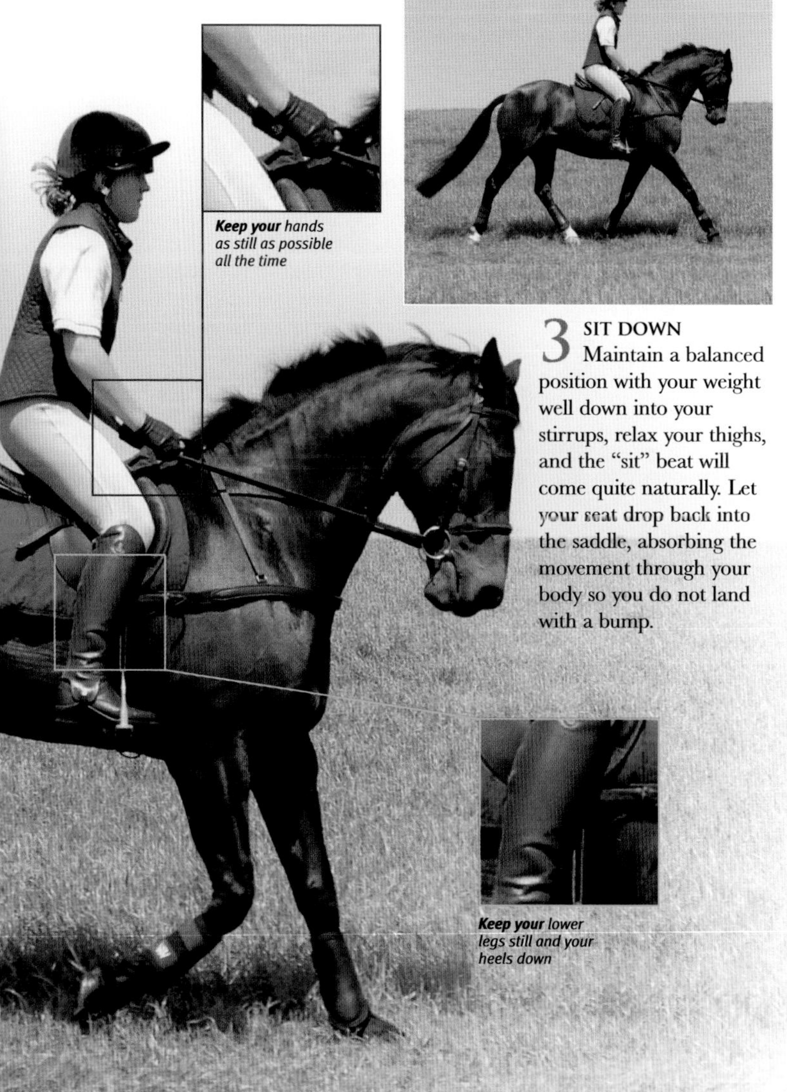

Keep your hands as still as possible all the time

3 SIT DOWN

Maintain a balanced position with your weight well down into your stirrups, relax your thighs, and the "sit" beat will come quite naturally. Let your seat drop back into the saddle, absorbing the movement through your body so you do not land with a bump.

Keep your lower legs still and your heels down

EXTRA INFORMATION

SITTING ON THE CORRECT DIAGONAL

Because the horse's legs move in diagonal pairs at trot, you can rise and sit on either diagonal. "On the left diagonal" means you sit as the left forefoot and right hind touch the ground; "on the right diagonal" means you sit as his right forefoot and left hind touch the ground. When riding a circle, the English style is to sit when the inside hind touches the ground, as this helps the horse to balance through corners and turns. Sitting on the same diagonal too often makes the horse's back muscles develop unevenly, so try to vary it even when you are hacking.

TROT TO WALK

Downward transitions need to be ridden just as positively as their upward counterparts so that the horse stays active and forward-going. Be sure to keep a steady contact, and prepare the horse for the command by moderating the pace – while maintaining the rhythm – before you ask for the transition itself.

1 PREPARE TO WALK Make sure you have an even contact on the reins. Stop rising and go into sitting trot for the last few strides before you ask for the transition. This means you can use your seat and weight to help slow the horse down.

2 MAKE THE TRANSITION Pull the reins firmly, keeping the contact and using a smooth action that does not tug the horse's mouth. Sit up tall with your pelvis deep in the saddle and keep your legs still.

***Push the** horse forwards into the reins with even pressure from your lower legs*

AT A GLANCE

TROT TO WALK

Slow the trot if necessary, but keep an even beat to the pace. Stop rising and sit up straight, relaxing your back and hips. Pull or squeeze the reins to bring the horse back to walk, then yield that pressure so he can keep moving.

3 MAINTAIN CONTACT

As the horse slows down into walk, his strides actually become longer and his neck needs to stretch forwards, so you might need to give him a slightly longer rein. To do this, loosen your fingers and let the reins slip through them a little but do not let the reins go slack – keep the contact. Keep sitting up tall because if you slump, so will the horse.

RIDERS' TIPS

- **When you** first learn this transition, do not worry about impulsion and rhythm – just go into sitting trot and give the aid for walk.
- **Once the** horse is walking, keep your position and ride positively forwards so that the horse does not slouch on to his forehand.

***Sit tall** and keep your back relaxed and poised*

***Slow the** horse down by putting slightly more weight into your seat to help slow your own movement and that of the horse*

***Keep an** even contact on the reins to avoid hurting the horse*

TROT TO CANTER

The canter is a three-time pace, which means there are three footfalls followed by a moment of suspension before the leading hind leg starts the sequence again. To strike off into canter, the horse brings one hind leg under his body and pushes off from it. To do this, the trot must be active and balanced, with plenty of impulsion.

1 PREPARE TO CANTER
Establish an active but unhurried trot with even steps. Create plenty of energy, contain the pace, then stop rising to the trot before you give the canter aids.

2 ASK FOR CANTER
To ask for canter, briefly give and take with the inside rein. Move your outside leg slightly behind the girth and give the horse's side a nudge. Keep your inside leg on the girth to maintain the impulsion.

RIDERS' TIPS

- **Think ahead** – plan every step of your transition.
- **Place slightly** more weight on your inside seat bone before you ask for the transition.
- **Sometimes it** is helpful to lighten your seat as you ask for canter so that the horse's back can move freely.
- **Remember that** when your legs ask for an upward transition, your hands must allow it to happen – do not pull the reins.
- **Yield slightly** with your hands as soon as the horse starts to canter.

AT A GLANCE

TROT TO CANTER
Make sure that the trot is energetic but controlled. Go into sitting trot for a few paces before the transition. Squeeze with both legs – outside leg slightly further back if you want a particular lead – and yield the reins.

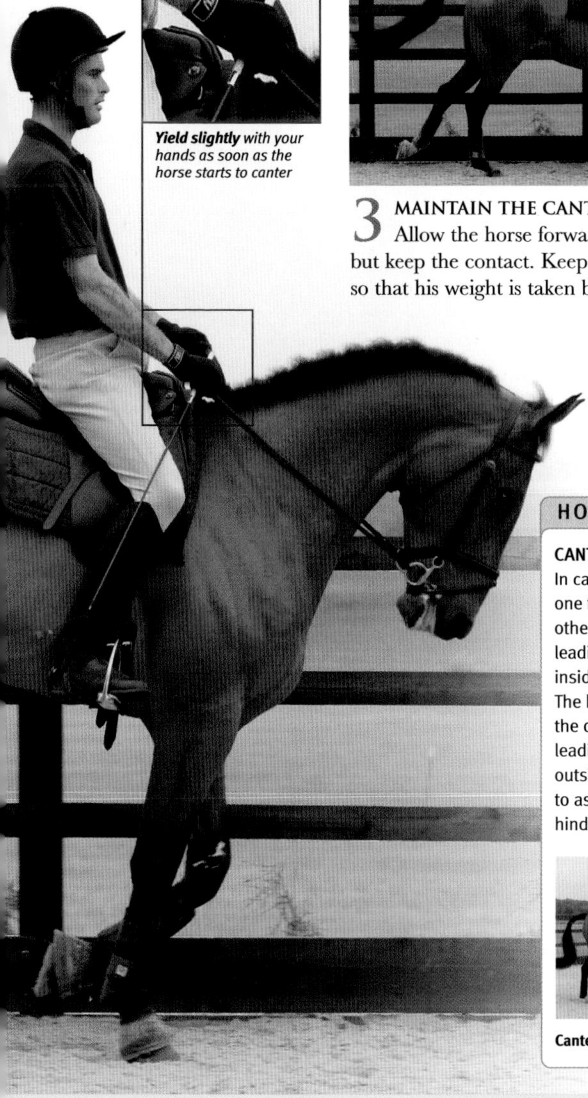

***Yield slightly** with your hands as soon as the horse starts to canter*

3 MAINTAIN THE CANTER

Allow the horse forwards with your hands but keep the contact. Keep your body balanced so that his weight is taken by his hind legs.

HORSE IN ACTION

CANTERING CORRECTLY

In canter, a horse stretches one foreleg in front of the other legs. This is called the leading leg. In an arena, the inside foreleg should lead. The horse strikes off with the opposite hind leg to the leading foreleg, so use your outside leg behind the girth to ask him to move that hind leg forwards.

Cantering on the correct leg

CANTERING

Working canter is a smooth, forward-going pace that horses find quite easy to maintain, and can be subtly varied to tackle different situations. A collected canter may be quite slow, while extended or cross-country canters can cover a great deal of ground.

1 CREATE A GOOD CANTER

A cantering horse should be balanced and forward-going, accepting the bit and controlled. Most horses are more supple and comfortable on one lead than the other, so try to use both equally, even out hacking.

DOS AND DON'TS

- **Don't let** the horse canter disunited – with his legs moving in the wrong sequence. This can happen if your transition was poor and the horse had too much weight on his forehand. It is easy to recognize because it feels completely unbalanced.
- **Do bring** him back to trot if this happens, rebalance, and begin the transition again.

AT A GLANCE

CANTERING

Working canter is an active but balanced pace. Keep a good contact for control, but allow the horse's body to move. As this sequence shows, there is a gentle rocking motion to the canter, so the rider also needs to be balanced.

***Learn to** feel which leg is leading without looking down to check*

***Sit softly** so that your body, including your hands and arms, follows the movement of the horse*

2 SIT DEEP IN THE SADDLE

For both working and collected canter, sit deep in the saddle with an upright posture. Working canter should be an energetic yet steady pace that is ideal for hacking and has sufficient control and balance for schooling. Always use working paces before asking for collection so that the horse is thinking forwards.

TIPS AND TECHNIQUES

CROSS-COUNTRY CANTER

For a more forward-going pace, you can lighten your seat (push your weight through your heels and lift your bottom) and incline your body slightly forwards. You must be correctly balanced and keep your legs still.

Cantering with a forward seat

CANTER TO TROT

When you perform a downward transition, think of the horse's hind legs continuing for one more beat than the front legs. This should help you grasp the concept of maintaining impulsion and driving the horse forwards into a restraining contact, rather than pulling him up too quickly and stopping the movement altogether.

1 PREPARE TO TROT Think ahead and take a few strides at canter to set up the transition. If necessary, use a half-halt – a brief "slow down" command that is immediately released so that the horse checks his pace but keeps moving forwards.

2 ASK FOR TROT Sit down in the saddle, keep your lower legs firmly against the horse's sides, and give a firm, even pull with both reins.

***Give and** take the reins – do not make a sharp, sudden pull*

***Your voice** can be a helpful aid in slowing down – a long, gentle "and ter-rot" with a downward inflection helps convey the message*

***Put your** weight down into the saddle and sit up tall to help slow the horse down*

3 FORWARDS TO TROT

Sit for the first few strides of trot, allowing your body to absorb the movement. Keep squeezing with your legs to keep the trot active but keep a firm hold on the reins in case the horse tries to canter again. Once the trot is established, begin to rise.

***Use your** legs to continue to ask the horse for impulsion*

DOS AND DON'TS

■ **Do ask** a horse to slow down with your hands while telling him to go forwards with your legs. This collects him into a short, round outline so that his hind legs come further under his body and the stretch of his head and neck is contained, helping him to balance and giving you greater control.

■ **Don't let** the horse's outline become long and low, as in this picture. This horse's body is also tilted on the bend. Add a rider's weight and, without some help, the horse could easily overbalance.

Unbalanced horse cantering on the lunge

GALLOPING

This is a fast, exhilarating pace, but you need plenty of space to do it. If you slowed down a sound recording of a galloping horse you would hear four even beats followed by a pause, which is the moment of suspension. You should attempt to gallop only if you are a competent rider and know you can pull up your horse safely.

1 ASK FOR GALLOP Shorten your reins and establish a powerful, forward canter. Then nudge with your legs until the horse speeds up. Take up a forward position with your seat out of the saddle so that as your body leans forwards, your centre of balance remains the same.

2 GIVE HIM SPACE Let the horse stretch out his neck and lengthen his outline, otherwise he cannot gallop. The forward position allows you to do this with your hands while keeping the reins short enough for control.

RIDE LIKE A PRO

FLAT-RACING

To see horses gallop spectacularly fast, watch a flat-race – stand near the start and see them leap out of the boxes. Note how the jockeys crouch over the horses' backs.

Racehorses on the flat at Kentucky, USA

AT A GLANCE

GALLOPING

The horse's outline becomes long and low as he stretches out. With his right foreleg leading, the sequence of his legs is: left hind, right hind, left fore, right fore, then a moment when all four feet are off the ground.

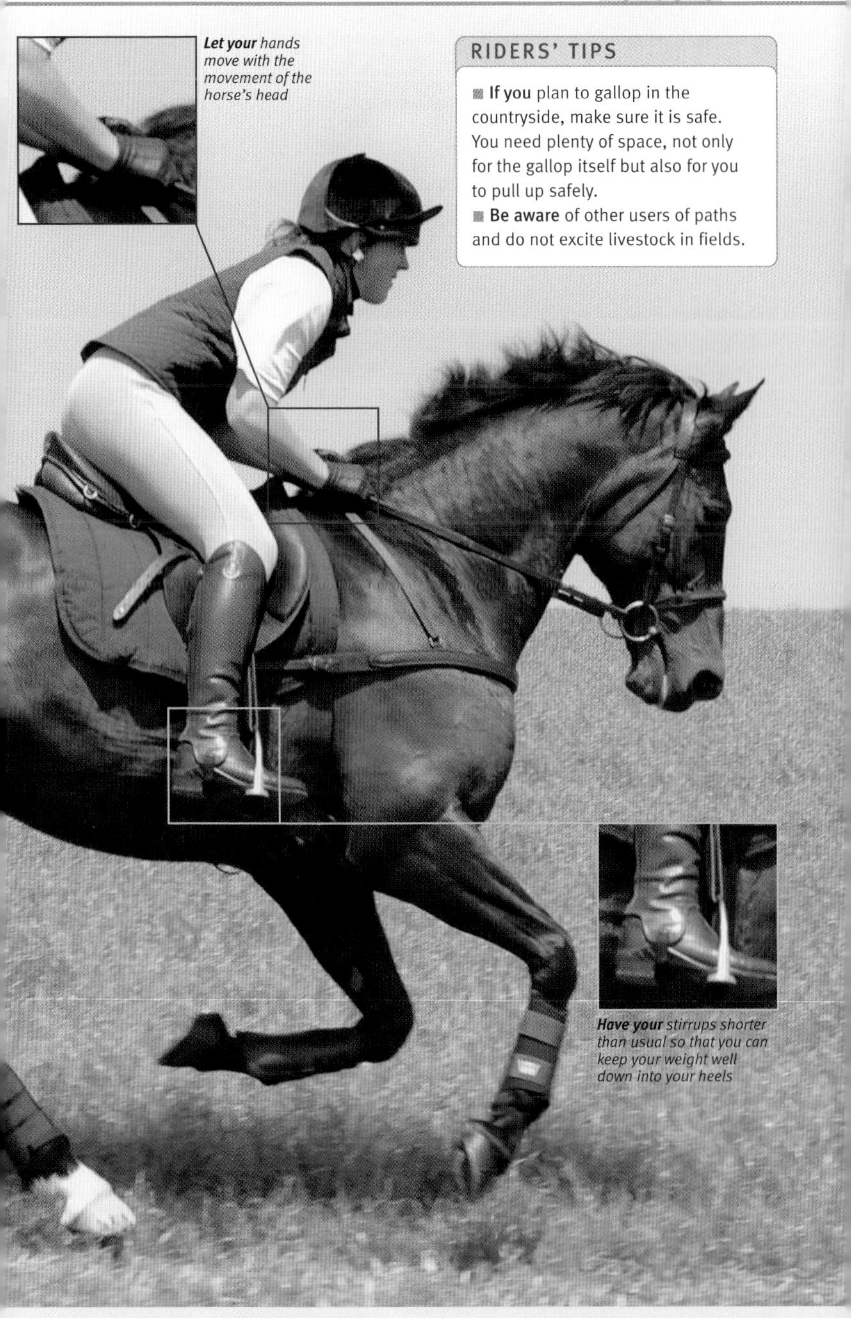

***Let your** hands move with the movement of the horse's head*

RIDERS' TIPS

- **If you** plan to gallop in the countryside, make sure it is safe. You need plenty of space, not only for the gallop itself but also for you to pull up safely.
- **Be aware** of other users of paths and do not excite livestock in fields.

***Have your** stirrups shorter than usual so that you can keep your weight well down into your heels*

ADVANCED PACES

The ordinary, or working, version of every pace can be slowed to a collected version or have its strides lengthened into medium or extended paces. In collection, the horse takes shorter, higher steps and his outline is compact. Medium and extended paces cover more ground, with the horse in a longer outline but no change in the rhythm of his footfalls.

WALKING

When training a young horse, less emphasis is placed on the walk than the trot and canter because it is easy to ruin a naturally good walk with over-training.

One important tool you will need for schooling is the half-halt, used to rebalance the horse. Give the aids to go forwards into halt but, as the horse begins to pause, immediately allow him forwards again.

MEDIUM WALK

As you gain experience, you can gradually "compress" the walk, asking for more activity from the hindquarters but less speed until you achieve medium walk. The horse should accept the bridle with his nose in front of the vertical.

COLLECTED WALK

The walk is the most difficult pace to collect. It is easy to hurry the horse in your effort to add impulsion, thus pushing him out of his natural rhythm. Wait until you and the horse are relaxed in the other paces before trying collected walk.

FREE WALK

To reward the horse for hard work in schooling, you should allow him regular intervals at free walk. It is an essential pace for relaxing the horse. Keep a light contact, but allow him lots of rein so he can stretch his neck.

RIDE LIKE A PRO

EXTENDED TROT

With tremendous power coming from the hindquarters, the front feet should stretch right out as if the horse is pointing his toes. His whole outline lengthens even more than in medium trot.

Mary Hanna from Australia riding in extended trot

TROTTING

The trot is used more than any other pace when teaching both horse and rider because it has the most natural impulsion and is therefore the easiest in which to work. Some horses have a good natural rhythm, others have to be taught to relax and not to hurry, but the horse cannot relax his back if the rider's back is tense. Rising trot places less strain on the horse, while sitting trot without stirrups is a great tool for developing poise in the rider.

MEDIUM TROT
The horse should cover quite a lot of ground in medium trot, but do not let him run away with you or fall on to his forehand. To help you learn medium trot, use the corners and short sides of a manège to rebalance before sending the horse up the long, straight side in medium trot.

COLLECTED TROT
Working forwards is essential in developing collection – too much emphasis on slowing down will mean a loss of momentum. Work on medium trot first, and when you have achieved it, learn to contain it into the collected version. As always, balance, rhythm, and suppleness are the keys.

CANTERING

It is important to establish an easy, forward-going canter before you start trying to make adjustments within the pace, but do not let the horse run away with you. The angle of the horse's body will change slightly according to where he is in the sequence of footfalls. The moment of suspension, which you will learn to feel, is the moment to ask for changes. Your back and hips must be relaxed so that the horse can move freely.

MEDIUM CANTER
Once you can achieve a balanced working canter, you can ask for longer strides. These must come from impulsion created by the hind legs, not from the horse stretching out in front. The prints from the hind feet should be on top of or in front of those made by the front feet.

COLLECTED CANTER
In collected canter the steps are shorter, the hind legs come well under the horse, and his outline is much rounder than in medium work. Establish a good forward canter first, then use half-halts to rebalance and slow the pace while keeping the impulsion.

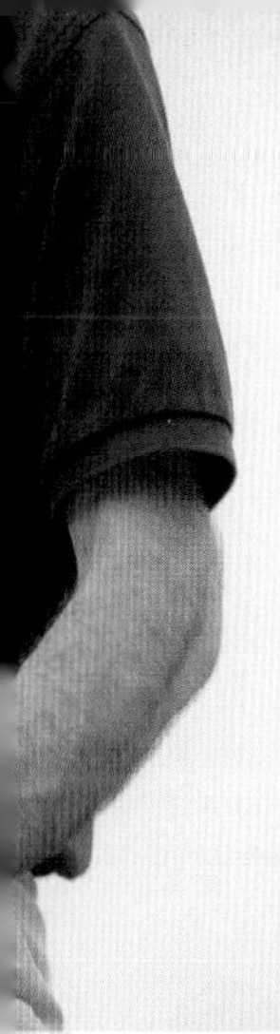

IN THE SCHOOL

The flat area of grass or sand designed specifically for riding has become known as a manège – derived from *manage*, the French for horsemanship. Often they are simply called sand-schools, or just schools. If you do not have access to a purpose-built one, you can easily set up markers in a field if the ground is reasonably level.

RIDING IN A MANÈGE

The sand-school, or manège, is used for all kinds of riding, from lessons to advanced schooling. It should be at least 40 x 20 m, but any size will do provided there is space to ride properly. It is helpful to mark at least the points A, C, B, and E to give you some structure. A track will form around the outside, but try to ride your own course.

THE SURFACE

A manège can have a variety of surfaces consisting of single or mixed components, from grass and sand to silica and rubber. Note how the surface feels underfoot – pure sand, for example, can be quite hard, while a mix of sand and small pieces of rubber may be more springy – and watch out for any areas that do not drain properly as they can become slippy. Care of the manège is important; you should remove droppings after your ride and the surface should be harrowed or raked regularly.

MARKERS IN A MANÈGE

The letter markers are helpful in many ways. Your instructor will use them in lessons, for example, "change the rein from M to K". It is also helpful to have a specific point to aim for when you are carrying out a movement. You will find that all dressage tests are written with the markers in mind. A full-size

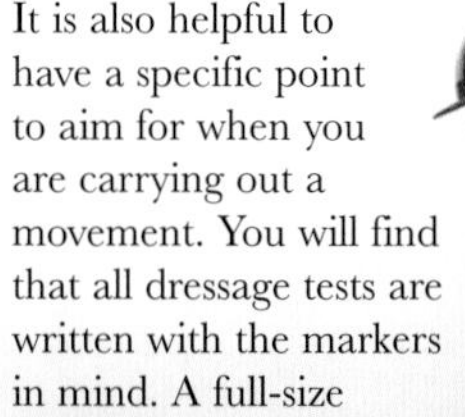

TROTTING POLES
Using trotting poles in the manège is a useful exercise that can be tackled by most riders and horses.

dressage arena (*see* p.274) has more markers than the more common 40 x 20 m size, but they are always in the same place. You also need to get to know the points where physical markers cannot be placed, such as X, which is in the centre of the arena.

SHARING WITH OTHERS

Having a sand-school to yourself is a luxury – you are more likely to be sharing with other horses, and working independently of them requires awareness and sense. As a rule, keep at least one horse's length between each horse and do not cut in front of another rider or interrupt their work. When passing in opposite directions, pass left shoulder to left shoulder. For example, if you are working on the right rein, take the inside track. Always show courtesy to others – if you are setting up jumps or trotting poles, place them on an inside track so that other riders can avoid them if they wish.

GOOD USE OF THE MANÈGE
Make good use of the whole schooling area. Learn to use the corners fully and to ride accurate circles and turns rather than simply riding from one marker to the next.

EXTRA INFORMATION

THE MARKERS IN A MANÈGE
The accepted size for a manège is 40 x 20 m or 60 x 20 m. The smaller size is perfectly adequate for riding and teaching, with space for several horses and for jumping. The standard markers are always the same, but if you do not have room for the whole set, at least mark A, C, B, and E.

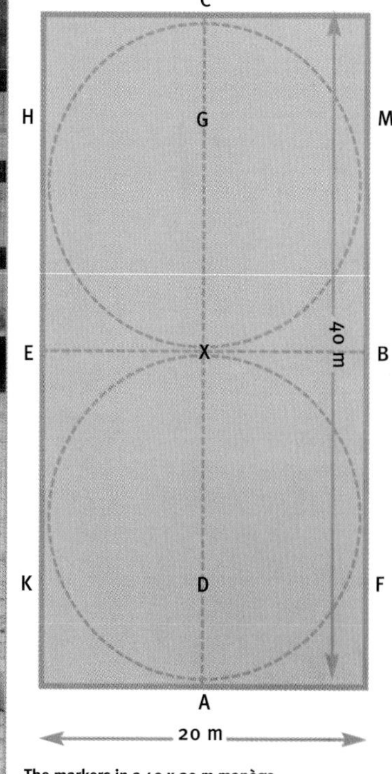

The markers in a 40 x 20 m manège

HAVING LESSONS

Lessons are not only essential, they can also be great fun. And they need not be just for beginners – even top professionals work with their own trainers to fine-tune their skills and help them with specific problems. There are advantages to both working on your own and as a group, so this section looks at both.

TYPES OF LESSON

Some riding schools prefer you to have your first lessons individually until you have basic control of the horse, but others will teach groups from the start. After that it is a matter of choice. Individual lessons are more intensive and expensive; group lessons are cheaper, but the instructor's attention will be divided between the group. You might be offered a lunge lesson, in which the instructor will control the horse by way of a long rein from the centre of a circle, leaving you free to ride without using reins or stirrups. This is an excellent way to help you to develop an independent seat and good balance. Lunging can only be done on a one-to-one basis with a suitable horse.

TAKING GROUP LESSONS
A good instructor will make the experience of riding with others useful, and will tailor their teaching to each rider's needs.

KEEP YOUR DISTANCE
In a group lesson, keep about 1.5 m (5 ft) away from the horse in front – this is about the same as the length of one horse.

***Work on** your own riding when the instructor is busy with someone else – do not just follow the horse in front*

RIDING OUT

Some instructors put beginners on a lead-rein for hacking, others wait until you can control the horse on your own. Riding along a road or in an open space feels quite different from being in a manège, so be patient and trust their judgement.

GOOD INSTRUCTORS

A good instructor should be enthusiastic, confident, and knowledgeable, and able to inspire the same qualities in their pupils. They should be observant and able to get along with people as well as horses. Health and safety regulations mean that instructors have to be very careful in the exercises they set, but that does not mean every lesson should consist of going round and round the manège – there are still plenty of ways to make a lesson fun.

PASSING LEFT TO LEFT
When you need to pass someone who is going the other way, pass left to left with about 1.5 m (5 ft) between you.

You should *be able to see the heels of the horse in front of you through your own horse's ears*

TERMS

GO LARGE
When you have been working on any movement that uses only part of the school, your instructor will use the command "go large" to ask you now to use the whole school.

RIGHT AND LEFT REIN
Being "on the right rein" means you are going round to the right, or clockwise. Being "on the left rein" means you are going to the left, or anticlockwise.

OUTSIDE TRACK
This runs around the perimeter of the school. It may be clearly defined by hoofprints if the school has not been raked recently.

INSIDE TRACK
An imaginary track about 1.5 m (5 ft) further in than the outside track, used to pass other horses or to start movements.

CHANGE THE REIN
Changing direction – often done diagonally across the school, e.g. from K to M, or straight across between E and B.

DIAGONAL
This refers to rising and sitting on the correct pair of legs in trot (*see* p.147). Being on the correct diagonal helps the horse to balance.

WHOLE RIDE
The command used in a group lesson to ask everyone to do the same thing, e.g. "whole ride trot".

LEADING FILE
When a command is given to the "lead file", it is directed at the rider in front.

CORRECT WAY OF GOING

Think of the horse's hindquarters as a "rear engine" that pushes him along with the balance and momentum he needs to use his muscles correctly and carry a rider. If he pulls himself along with his shoulders, all his weight goes downwards into his front legs, or "forehand". This can cause problems, from foreleg strain to stumbling and tipping the rider off.

FORWARD MOVEMENT

The key to the correct way of going is forward movement. When you use your hands to restrain the horse, always yield the pressure once it has achieved the desired effect. By slowing his speed with your seat and hands, while still squeezing with your legs to make him go forwards, you can channel some of the forward energy into upward movement. The horse then picks up his feet higher, rather than faster, and can push himself along from his hindquarters – this is called impulsion. Ridden in this way, with a steady rhythm to his steps, he can come naturally and correctly on to the bit.

DOS AND DON'TS

Some horses try to evade the bit because it seems easier – rather like doing a gym exercise wrongly. In particular, they do this in two ways.

■ **Don't let** the horse tuck in his nose too far, known as "overbent". It may look impressive to an untrained eye, but usually means he is tense and not working properly.

Overbent horse

■ **Don't let** the horse hold his nose too high in the air, or "above the bit". His back will hollow, causing discomfort, and you will lose control.

Horse above the bit

ON THE BIT

When a horse is on the bit, he should be stepping through from his hindquarters. His neck and poll should be relaxed with his head just in front of the vertical.

***Sit with** the correct posture to help you to ride effectively*

***You should** feel in harmony with the horse*

***The horse** has an active stride without great speed*

***A horse** going correctly should look happy, attentive, and comfortable*

IMPULSION VERSUS SPEED

Impulsion and speed can be compared to the gears in a car. In fifth gear, a car coasts along at higher speeds but lacks the power and wheel control that a lower gear gives you. A horse that is above the bridle and pulling himself along from his shoulders might travel fast, but would probably skid on a corner. Whereas, if the power is coming from his hind legs and is channelled into upward as well as forward movement (called impulsion), he will be far more controlled and comfortable.

HORSE IN ACTION

WHAT IT FEELS LIKE

The correct way of going gives you an unmistakable feeling of harmony. You find yourself directing a smooth-running unit of power and energy, yet with a very light rein contact. You are relaxed but poised; the horse moves forwards with unhurried but active, even steps and is responsive to your aids; and you can feel his back swing as you sit.

CIRCLES AND LOOPS

Variations on the circle are among the most basic and most useful suppling exercises. Just as people are right- or left-handed, most horses are stiffer through one side than the other. As well as helping to improve the balance of both horse and rider, bending teaches the horse to go straighter by suppling his muscles and learning to accept both reins.

RIDING A CIRCLE

The aids for a circle are basically the same as for turns, but are applied continuously. Prepare the horse by making sure that his hind legs are working so that his whole body will bend together, not just his neck. Allow the horse to flex in the direction of the bend – you should just be able to see his eye.

USING YOUR WEIGHT

In theory, you can ride a circle using your legs and upper body with very little guidance from the reins. By looking in the direction you want to go, and turning your shoulders accordingly, the distribution of your weight tells the horse what you want him to do.

***Look in** the direction you want to go*

***Turn your** body to indicate the direction you wish to turn*

***Support the** outside shoulder by keeping your outside hand close to the horse*

***Flex the** horse's poll in the required direction*

SUPPORTING THE SHOULDER

Your inside hand gives slightly so that the horse can flex. Your outside hand supports the other shoulder, giving just enough to allow him to make the bend and prevent him from evading the turn through the opposite shoulder.

KEEPING THE BEND

Pressure from your legs keeps the impulsion and helps to indicate direction. Your inside leg, used on the girth, keeps the forward momentum. Your outside leg stops the horse swinging his quarters out and losing the shape of the circle.

SCHOOL MOVEMENTS

RIDING CIRCLES

The most commonly ridden circle is 20 m in diameter. It allows variety and suppling work without placing strain on the horse's muscles. Smaller circles are used as the horse becomes more athletic. Each helps him to improve his way of going.

C

H M

E X B

20 m

15 m

10 m

K F

A

Different sized circles

RIDING FIGURES OF EIGHT

Two circles can be joined together into a figure of eight. Until you are more experienced, each circle should be 20 m in diameter. Whatever the size of circle, aim for a few strides on a straight line before you change direction.

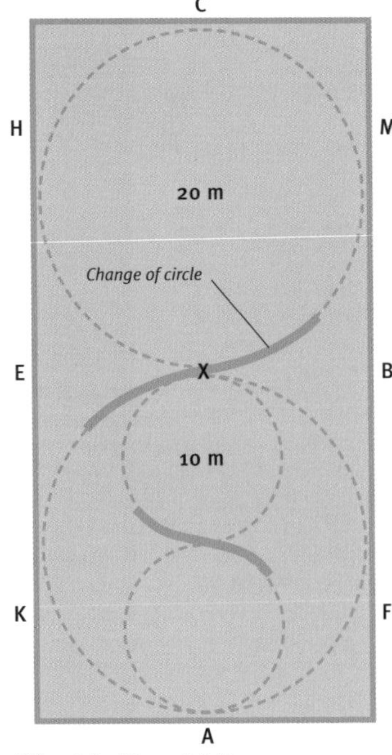

Different sized figure of eights

USING SERPENTINE EXERCISES

Your aim is to ride an accurate, evenly shaped serpentine with the horse balanced and working in an even rhythm so that you can correctly change the bend with each turn. Introducing transitions is a more advanced variation on this exercise to improve balance and collection. For example, you could ride the straight sections in working trot and curves in collected trot, or the straight sections in trot and the curves in collected canter.

From C, *make sure you have enough impulsion, and use a half-halt to rebalance the trot*

Ride in *a straight line for a few strides across the centre of the manège*

Keep your *hips and hands parallel on the straight line*

Start applying *the turn-aids before the corner*

Do not *let the horse drift on to his forehand*

RIDING A SERPENTINE

First establish a good, active pace with impulsion and rhythm, with the horse listening to your aids, because too much speed or uneven steps will compromise his ability to perform the turns. Make sure the horse is warmed up and be aware that he might find it difficult at first.

SCHOOL MOVEMENTS

THREE-LOOP SERPENTINE

Starting from A on the left rein, ride a half circle of about 15 m, turning before B. Ride straight across the arena then make another half circle over E. Ride straight again then circle back to C and go large.

FOUR-LOOP SERPENTINE

Starting from A on the right rein, ride half a 10 m circle, cross the school into another half-10m circle before B; cross straight to E, ride half a 10 m circle, cross again and half-circle back to C. Go large. Small loops are more difficult for the horse.

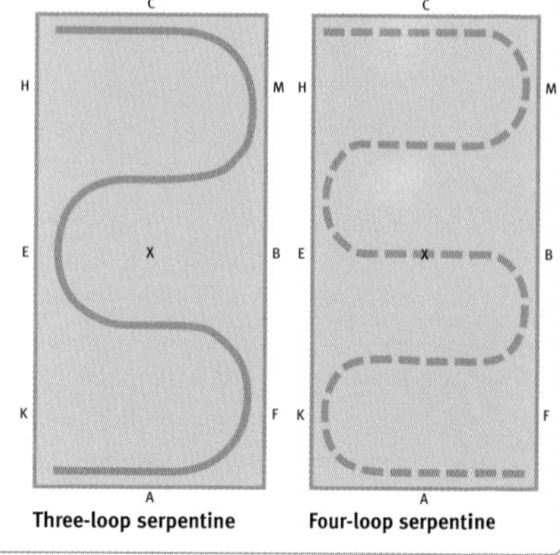

Three-loop serpentine **Four-loop serpentine**

Use your *hands to indicate direction and to support the outside shoulder*

Keep looking *in the direction you want to go*

Before you *reach the track, apply the aids for circling right*

Make the *loops of your serpentine smooth and seamless*

RIDING A LOOP

Loops are usually ridden 5 m, 10 m, or 15 m in from the outside track. Rebalance the horse with a half-halt and ride the preceding corner with the correct bend so that you make a flowing shape. Aim for a soft curve, using the aids for circling in each direction.

PLENTY OF SPACE
Use the long side of the sand-school for riding loops.

SCHOOL MOVEMENTS

5 M LOOP
The angles in this loop are very gradual. The movement starts at A or C and takes the form of three gentle part-circles.

10 M LOOP
Your first and third part-circles are smaller than the middle one, which should be a gradual curve taking you through X.

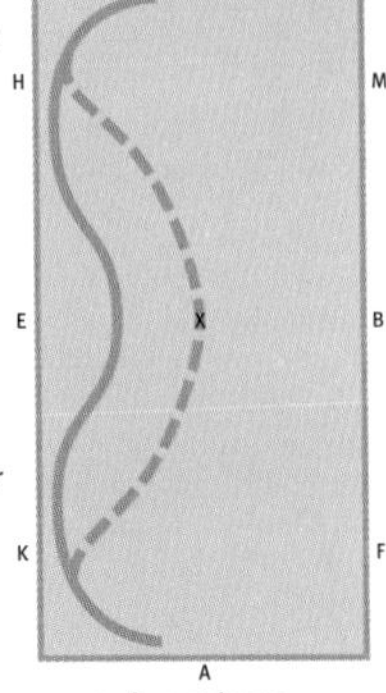

5 m and 10 m loops

REIN-BACK

In the rein-back, the horse should step backwards moving his legs in diagonal pairs rather than in the normal four-time walk sequence, with the steps having a definite lift and not dragging. He needs to develop strong back muscles and a good halt, with his feet forming a square, before you try it, and one or two steps is enough to start with.

AT A GLANCE

REIN-BACK

The rider balances the horse, asks for halt, lightens his seat, and begins to ask for rein-back. As the horse obeys, the rider lightens his hands to avoid resistance. After a few steps they walk forwards.

1 ASK FOR REIN-BACK
Once you can achieve a balanced halt without losing momentum (*see* p.135) you can try rein-back. Keep your seat light and squeeze with your legs, but at the same time use firm yet soft rein pressure to stop the horse going forwards.

The horse's *back is slightly raised in this movement*

2 REIN BACK

Keep your body upright and your hips and back supple so that the horse can round his back sufficiently to perform the movement. Keep the rein aid light and yield slightly with each step – never pull him back with your hands as this will only teach him to resist.

3 WALK FORWARDS

Once you have achieved two or three strides, ask the horse to walk forwards again. It is important to focus him more on moving forwards than going backwards, as this can cause behavioural problems.

***Sit up** straight with your weight in your stirrups to lighten your seat*

***Resist forward** movement so that the horse understands what is required, then yield with each backward step*

***Maintain impulsion** and straightness with your legs*

***The horse's** legs should move rhythmically in diagonal pairs*

DOS & DON'TS

- **Don't ask** the horse to continue with the movement if he raises his head, because he cannot do it with a hollow back. Go forwards, collect the pace, and ask for halt again.
- **Do send** the horse forwards immediately if he tries to go back too fast. Begin the exercise again with more emphasis on your legs.

BASIC LATERAL WORK

Lateral work, in which the horse moves at an angle on two or more tracks, is the equivalent of gymnastics for horses. When performed correctly it develops the horse's muscles and balance, encouraging him to become supple, but if performed incorrectly it can be damaging, so a few good strides is better than lots of poor ones.

LEG-YIELD AND SHOULDER-FORE

Most instructors teach leg-yield before other, more difficult lateral movements. You ask the horse to move forwards and sideways on two tracks with his head flexed slightly away from the direction of movement and with his body straight. Another exercise called "shoulder-fore" can help you to learn to apply the aids while maintaining your direction. To do this, walk or trot along the outside track, position the horse's shoulder on a slightly inside track, and keep moving in the same direction.

RIDE LIKE A PRO

PERFORMING A HALF-PASS

Half-pass and leg-yield can be easily confused by the amateur onlooker, but half-pass is the more difficult movement and therefore the one you will see advanced dressage riders performing. In half-pass, the horse's body should be bent in the direction in which he is going. His shoulders should be slightly in the lead and his outside legs should cross in front of the inside legs.

German rider Martin Schaudt performs a half-pass

***Flex the** horse's neck to the outside with your outside hand*

***Apply pressure** behind the girth with your outside leg to push the horse across*

***The horse's** outside leg should cross over in front of the inside leg*

RIDING LEG-YIELD

When leg-yield is done correctly, the outside legs, especially the hind, cross over in front of the inside legs as they step forwards and underneath the horse. This can only happen if his body is straight and he has enough impulsion.

RIDERS' TIPS

- **Keep the** impulsion and rhythm going, otherwise the horse will drift sideways or slow to a halt.
- **Too much** bend in the horse's neck will make him put his weight in the leading shoulder or bend his body too much.
- **Control of** the quarters is important – allowing them to swing either way will put the horse in the wrong position for leg-yield.
- **A few** correct steps of a lateral exercise is more useful than doing too many steps badly, which can be detrimental.

Control the *horse's shoulders with your leading hand*

Use your *seat to push the horse forwards*

Keep your *inside leg on the girth to keep the forward momentum*

FLEXION & SHOULDER-IN

Flexion and shoulder-in are lateral exercises that help the horse to develop balance, strength, and suppleness, encouraging him to move smartly off the aids and work from his quarters with a good natural outline. This, in turn, helps to teach the rider to avoid the common pitfall of trying to put him on the bit by over-use of the hands.

RIDING FLEXION

Mastering school movements depends on the rider's ability to control every nuance of how the horse moves at a given moment. One of the most basic but important exercises that helps to develop this type of control is flexion, in which you ask the horse to flex his neck while keeping his body straight. His neck should only bend from just behind the poll, and should be relaxed through its whole length. The rider should just be able to see the horse's eye and nostril. Learning to be soft through his poll in this way helps the horse learn to work on the bit.

RIDING SHOULDER-IN

Shoulder-in is a three-track movement. While moving ahead, for example along the outside track, the horse's body is bent just enough to bring his shoulders off the track to an angle of about 30 degrees. This puts the outside foreleg and the inside hind on the same track, while the outside hind

ASKING FOR FLEXION
Keep your weight evenly on both seat bones and squeeze the inside rein with your hand, yielding slightly with the outside hand.

ASKING FOR SHOULDER-IN
Position the horse as if riding a small circle to take you naturally into this movement.

***Use your** inside leg to establish the bend and create impulsion*

and inside fore each make a separate track. The inside hind must come well under the horse's body as he steps forwards, thus encouraging collection. As well as suppling the horse, this exercise helps to straighten and balance him – the more supple the horse is, and the better his response to sideways and bending aids, the more able he will be to go straight when asked.

FURTHER LATERAL EXERCISES

To the untrained eye, travers, shoulder-fore (*see* p.174), and renvers might look similar to shoulder-in or leg-yield, but there are key differences. In shoulder-fore, the horse's shoulders are brought off the track at a similar angle to shoulder-in, but his body is straight, not bent round the rider's leg. Travers and renvers are more difficult movements in which the horse's body is bent in the direction of travel. In travers, the quarters are brought off the track, in renvers, his shoulders are off the track.

Forward impulsion and the position of the horse's body are equally important in all lateral exercises. Many riders, especially while learning, fall into the trap of positioning the horse at too great an angle because it seems easier to push him straight across than both forwards and across.

Look straight *between the horse's ears*

Soften the *inside rein to allow the required bend and flexion of the horse's neck*

Use the *outside rein to guide the horse's outside shoulder and control his forward movement*

Lateral exercises *such as this help to engage the hind legs and create power*

Use your *outside leg slightly further back to control the angle of the quarters*

Inside fore *is on first track*

Outside fore *and inside hind are on second track*

Outside hind *is on third track*

TURN ON THE FOREHAND AND QUARTERS

Turning the horse about his forehand helps him learn to understand the sideways leg-aid and teaches novice riders to stay in balance during such a movement. The turn on the quarters, which is used to engage the hind legs, should not be used until the horse is more experienced and the rider has learnt not to be dependent on the reins.

TURN ON THE FOREHAND

Turning on the forehand is one of the first stages in the progression towards true lateral work. It is performed from the halt and involves pushing the horse's quarters round while his forelegs turn on the spot. Stepping sideways is not a natural movement for horses, so this helps them develop the right muscles and learn to balance their weight and the rider's. It is not necessary to turn 360 degrees, especially to start with; quarter turns and half turns are sufficient.

1 KEEP THE RHYTHM Make a brief halt after a good, active walk so as not to lose rhythm. To move the quarters away from your right leg, first flex the horse's neck to the right (*see* p.176).

2 APPLY YOUR LEGS Use your right leg behind the girth to push the horse's quarters across. Keep your left leg on the girth to maintain impulsion. The front feet should mark time, not shuffle.

TURN ON THE QUARTERS

In turn on the quarters, the forehand is pushed round while the hind legs turn on the spot. The horse should be bent slightly in the direction of the turn and must not step forwards or back. The hind feet should make a small half-circle and the outside foreleg should step across in front of the inside leg. This movement helps the horse learn to use his hindquarters properly and achieve more collected paces. Be careful not to pull his mouth too hard.

1 FLEX THE HORSE To move the forehand round to the left, ask for a half-halt, flex the horse to the left, and while sitting upright, put more weight on your left seat bone.

2 CONTROL THE BEND Use your left leg on the girth and control the quarters with your right leg. Your left rein asks for the bend while your right rein controls it.

3 RESTRAIN FORWARD MOVEMENT

Use gentle rein pressure to stop the horse from walking forwards. Continue to apply your right leg to ask the horse to step across with his hind legs.

4 FINISH THE TURN

When you have completed the turn, ask the horse to move positively forwards in trot or even canter for a few strides before starting any other lateral movement.

3 ASK FOR MOVEMENT

Keep using your legs to ask for movement and rhythm. Use your outside rein to stop the horse from leaning on that shoulder.

4 FINISH THE TURN

Check the movement with your hands but do not pull back hard on the reins. Walk forwards as soon as you have completed the movement.

COUNTER CANTER

In counter canter, you ask the horse to lead with his outside foreleg instead of the inside one. This is a fairly advanced exercise that is used to develop the horse's balance and work towards flying changes, and the canter needs to be active but controlled. The simplest way is to canter throughout a shallow loop but you can use a small half-circle, as here.

1 SET UP THE CANTER

When starting on the right rein establish right-lead canter, then at the end of a long side, ride a small half-circle – or *demi-volte* – to change the rein.

Look up *and ahead and keep your body as stil as possible*

Keep your *weight correctly balanced for the lead you require*

2 MAINTAIN THE RIGHT LEAD

Keep your weight on your right seat bone and maintain a slight flexion towards the leading leg to help the horse stay in balance.

The horse *is on right-lead canter on the left rein*

For counter *canter, use your inside leg further back than normal*

RIDE LIKE A PRO

A FLYING CHANGE

During a flying change, the horse jumps from one canter lead to the other during the moment of suspension. To do flying changes the rider must be able to give precise aids at exactly the right moment and the horse must be perfectly balanced, which is why counter canter is an essential part of the build-up in training. This is the Dutch rider Anky van Grunsven, one of the world's leading dressage exponents.

Anky van Grunsven performing a flying change

AT A GLANCE

COUNTER CANTER

Establish a controlled canter and ride a *demi-volte*. As you change direction, maintain the same flexion, distribution of your weight, and position of your legs so that the horse does not change lead.

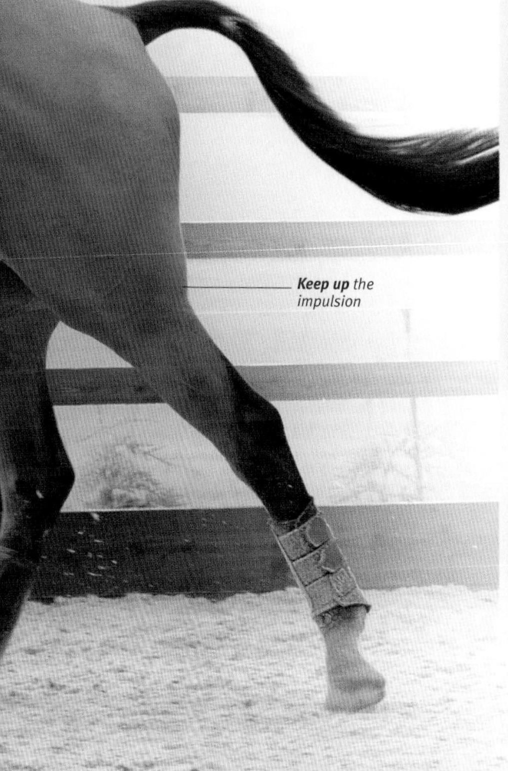

A SCHOOLING SESSION

Schooling involves working to make the horse as supple and relaxed as possible, so that he can work effectively. It can be part of a fitness regime, a warm-up for a lesson or competition, or just a routine ride, but the horse's muscles and mind – as well as your own – need to be relaxed and focused.

WORKING IN THE SCHOOL

Regular schooling has great benefits in terms of fitness and obedience, but be careful not to overdo it. Horses can become bored as easily as people, and will show their boredom by rebelling or misbehaving, which is both counter-productive and potentially dangerous. Thirty to forty minutes is often enough.

Riding simply but correctly will do more for your horse in the long run than being too ambitious and performing movements incorrectly. A good instructor will know just how far to push you in order to teach you or the horse something new, but on your own it is best to stick to what you already know. Start by working on the outside track and 20 m circles. Spend a few minutes in walk on a loose rein, then take up more contact and ask the horse to trot and canter on each rein. Once he is warmed up and going forwards, take up a firmer contact and start the real work.

Work can be quite simple and involve nothing more than walk, trot, and canter using the whole arena and large circles, transitions, turns, and halts. Your aim is to put your horse "in front of the leg", which means that he responds instantly when you ask without a moment of hesitation.

Basic lateral movements, such as leg-yield and flexion, and small circles, loops, and serpentines can be introduced as you gain experience and the horse becomes sufficiently fit and supple.

WORKING CORRECTLY
Concentrate on rhythm, balance, and impulsion. Too much emphasis on getting the horse on the bit can stop him going forwards properly.

WORK BOTH SIDES

Change the rein regularly so that the horse's muscles are worked evenly on both sides.

RIDERS' TIPS

- **Vary the** work but keep it simple. Do not confuse the horse with too many different exercises but do change the rein and use transitions to make it interesting.
- **Out hacking,** use a quiet, level track to practise exercises such as flexion and shoulder-in. Riding turns and transitions correctly wherever you are is also helpful.
- **Watch the** professionals. Go to demonstrations, watch instructional videos, or simply watch them compete.

***Make sure** you and the horse are warmed up properly to avoid straining muscles*

***The horse** should be forward-going and alert to your commands*

***Help the** horse to achieve impulsion with suppling exercises and transitions*

JUMPING

As well as being a great gymnastic exercise for both horse and rider, jumping can also be a tough competitive discipline. Most horses will happily hop over a small jump in lessons or on a hack, but not all are cut out for larger fences – it is a case of knowing your horse and your limitations. Jumping needs to be learnt under supervision on an experienced horse so that you develop confidence and technique. You do not have to jump high to be a good rider.

HOW A HORSE JUMPS

Jumping comes naturally to most horses but their technique, as well as the rider's, needs to be honed in order to become safe and comfortable. The training of both horse and rider is crucial in developing not only the practical skills but also the right mindset so that you are both ready to have fun tackling fences with control and confidence.

THE JUMPING ACTION

The horse's back should make a round arc known as a "bascule" as he jumps. It enables him to clear the obstacle in a smooth movement with his legs tucked up carefully. This places minimum strain on his muscles and limbs and is also comfortable for the rider. But it is a technique that most horses have to learn. Training on the flat and over carefully distanced grids (*see* pp.190–191) enhances the bascule. Remember that the horse can only make this shape if you are in the correct jumping position.

***Look up** and ride positively into the next fence, turn, or task*

PHASES OF THE JUMP

There are five distinct phases to every jump – the approach, the take-off, the airborne moment, the landing, and the getaway.

DOS AND DON'TS

- **Do set** up the approach and prepare correctly.
- **Don't expect** the horse to approach fences "on the bit" – he needs to be able to see and assess the task.
- **Don't look** directly at a jump once you are approaching it – look up and over it because that is where you want to go.
- **Do keep** your weight off the horse's shoulders so he can take off unhindered.
- **Do fold** from your hips as the horse takes off, but learn to make it a natural movement – do not throw your weight forwards.
- **Don't practise** over big fences all the time – this is boring for the horse and places more strain on his limbs than is necessary.

RIDERS' TIPS

- **If you** or your horse suffers a set-back, do not be afraid to go back a few steps to rebuild your confidence.
- **The control** achieved through flatwork will help your jumping technique.
- **Watch the** professionals in action – be inspired by their jumping technique but also notice how well-schooled their horses are on the flat around and between fences.

Gradually sit *up so that your weight does not fall on to the horse's front end as he lands*

Make sure *your hands allow the horse's neck to stretch out as he becomes airborne*

Allow the *horse the freedom to lift himself*

Let the *horse see the fence ahead as you approach*

LEARNING TO JUMP

The early stages of learning to jump involve practising the forward jumping position, learning to keep your balance, and then jumping small fences. You might be keen to attempt something more ambitious, but you will soon discover that with the approach, take-off, landing, and "getaway" to be considered, there is more to jumping than the fence.

THE JUMPING POSITION

The horse needs space and freedom to arch his back, stretch out, and keep his balance on landing, so your aim is to give him all that while keeping your own balance and not interfering with his. A comfortable, safe jumping position enables your body to fold forwards and follow the horse's movement without compromising your centre of balance or causing your legs to swing back – and it ensures your seat is well clear of the horse's back.

Your stirrups should be shorter than for flatwork, but not so short that you cannot effectively use your legs. The idea is to raise your seat out of the saddle by closing the angle of your hips, knees, and ankles and pushing your weight into your heels. Your seat is pushed back and you can then fold forwards correctly.

***Fix your** eyes on a point beyond the jump, such as the top of a tree – do not look down*

FOLDING FORWARDS

With shorter stirrups, your hips, knees, and ankles take on a more acute angle, enabling your body to fold forwards without tipping.

***Make sure** your feet are firmly in the stirrups so you can push your weight down into your heels*

STARTING TO JUMP

Practise the jumping position first at halt and then at walk, trot, and canter. At first, the shorter stirrups will feel strange and keeping your seat out of the saddle can make you feel vulnerable. This is a good test of your balance. Learn to fold your body rather than pushing yourself up from the stirrups. Practise maintaining a good contact without holding on too tight, as well as slipping and re-taking the reins.

DOS AND DON'TS

- **Don't bury** the horse in front of the jump – look up.
- **Do be** determined. If you let the horse know you do not want to jump the fence, neither will he.
- **Do use** your legs to keep the impulsion and to help you keep your balance.
- **Don't throw** yourself forwards suddenly – stay with the movement.

1 APPROACH IN BALANCE When you start learning, approach the fence in the jumping position. A line of trotting poles before the fence will help you learn to maintain this position.

2 GO WITH THE HORSE Do not worry if you cannot anticipate where the horse is going to take off – this will come with practice. Be ready to go with him whenever he takes off.

3 SIT UP ON LANDING As the horse lands, return to an upright position, absorbing the impact through your knees and ankles. Allow this to happen rather than forcing it, so you do not sit down hard on the horse's back.

DEVELOPING THE JUMP

Once you have mastered the take-off, jump, and landing, you will start to learn about the approach and how to tackle different types of fence. Different heights and shapes can make fences more tricky – but when you first learn, you will probably jump a crossbar, which has a shape that is easy for both horse and rider to judge. Changing the profile of the fence, for example by adding a pole in front of or behind the original one, encourages the horse to use his back more and perhaps take off from further out.

TIPS AND TECHNIQUES

SEEING A STRIDE

The term "seeing a stride" means judging where the horse might take off – but do not focus on it too much. Learn to get a feel for it from several strides out, let the horse work it out for himself, and be ready to go with him.

1 FOCUS WELL IN ADVANCE
Preparation is important. Focus the horse's attention, and your efforts, well before the jump. Steer the horse and keep up the power, without pushing or rushing him. Once you are within a few strides of the fence you should interfere with the horse's mouth as little as possible.

GRIDWORK

Doing gridwork is a great way to work on your balance and the horse's agility – which is why it is also known as gymnastic jumping. It helps you learn to create the impulsion well before a fence and maintain it throughout the line. The grid can consist of a variety of ground poles and fences, which can be several strides apart or just a bounce. You need to have the horse in front of your leg before you enter the grid, and either stay in jumping position throughout or fold and sit up again as each fence demands.

1 LOOK AHEAD
Be sure to look up at a point on the horizon as you go through the grid – looking down at the fences will make you lose momentum.

Keep your *back flat and your centre of balance in line with that of the horse*

Allow your *hands to follow the movement while keeping contact*

Look ahead *and prepare for the next task*

Lower your *seat gently back into the saddle as you land*

Keep both *your lower legs still*

Do not *let the horse fall on to his forehand*

2 FOLD FORWARDS
Keep your weight in your heels and your legs still against the horse's sides to maintain steering and power. As he takes off, fold forwards and let his head take your hands forwards. Bringing your seat off the saddle is important as it allows the horse to bascule and clear the fence.

3 KEEP THE FORWARD MOMENTUM
As the horse's hind legs touch the ground and he takes the first getaway stride, it is important to keep the forward momentum and the rein contact to help him balance. Aim for a point several metres beyond the jump, such as a marker at which you intend to pull up.

2 STAY FOCUSED
If there is a stride or more between the fences, you have time to sit down and use your seat to push the horse forwards and maintain the power.

3 KEEP YOUR POSITION
With a bounce distance, when the horse takes off immediately after landing, stay in jumping position throughout and use your legs firmly.

"THERE'S SOMETHING ABOUT JUMPING A HORSE OVER A FENCE THAT MAKES YOU FEEL GOOD."

William Faulkner, author (1897–1962)

CROSS-COUNTRY

The term "cross-country" has become the accepted one for jumping solid, natural-style fences in open countryside, or more often, parkland. Good cross-country riding is both an art and a skill and, when done correctly, can be great fun for both horse and rider.

RIDING ACROSS COUNTRY

Cross-country obstacles, such as the log shown below, are inviting for the horse to jump, but they are solid and fixed in place, so you do not have the same margin for error that show jumps give. You need some natural instinct and courage to enjoy this type of riding, but you must recognize the risks and learn good technique so that you ride as safely as possible. You should wear a body protector, which must conform to the latest safety standards and be correctly fitted, and be sure to check that your tack is in good repair.

STIRRUP LENGTH

Your stirrups should be slightly shorter than for normal jumping. This will make it easier to ride at the greater speed and cope with the unpredictable nature of the terrain.

***Look up,** keep your legs on and keep the contact so the horse moves smartly away from the fence*

***Let your** body come upright without hitting the horse's back*

TIPS AND TECHNIQUES

RIDING IN OPEN SPACES

Before you try cross-country jumping, get used to fast hacking in open spaces. Learn to maintain the lighter forward seat in canter for longer periods of time and, if possible, practise jumping somewhere other than in a manège. Even in the relatively controlled setting of a schooling course, this type of riding feels quite different to being in an enclosed area, and you need an extra element of control and steering. Some horses become excited and stronger than usual.

Excited horse on a schooling course

Look ahead *so your weight does not tip on to the horse's forehand*

Go with *the horse and do not interfere with his movement*

Sit up *and make sure the horse focuses well before the fence*

Keep your *contact but slip the reins if necessary*

HONING YOUR APPROACH

In cross-country jumping, the approach to the fence is especially important. It is likely to be longer and faster than in show jumping, and the fixed fences give little margin for error. By five or six strides out, the horse must be focused and ready to jump. You should sit still, wrap your legs round to keep the horse's "engine" going, and interfere as little as possible – leave the actual jump to the horse. Folding forwards too soon could interfere with his balance.

SOLID FENCES

Cross-country fences can look more daunting than show jumps because you cannot see through them, but the shapes are often quite kind – a roll-top or round, log fence mirrors the shape the horse makes as he jumps.

TIPS AND TECHNIQUES

USING STUDS

For jumping on muddy or slippery ground, it is advisable to put studs in the horse's shoes for extra grip. These are available from tack shops, and you need to ask the farrier to fit special shoes with stud holes, into which you screw the studs.

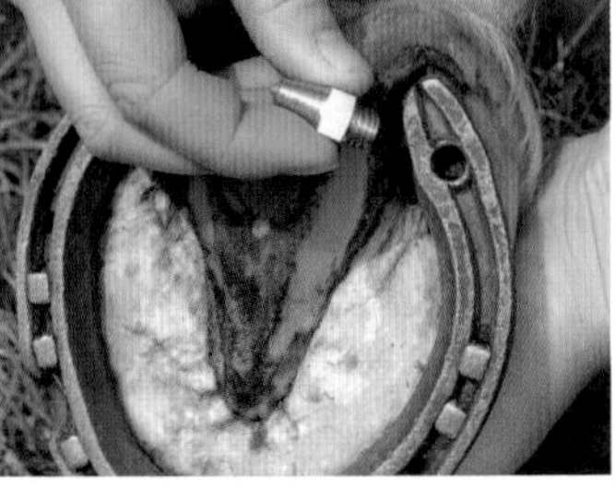

Fitting a stud

Look ahead *and stay with the movement, keeping your contact but slipping the reins if necessary*

The horse *will soon learn to respect solid fences and lift his feet properly*

JUMPING STEPS
Riding up and down steps requires the same techniques as riding up and down slopes – lean forwards to go up and sit upright to go down.

PUT IN THE PRACTICE

Once you are competent at jumping in an enclosed space, have a go somewhere more open. This may be an enclosed field with natural obstacles such as logs set up around the edge, or logs and small streams out hacking. Some horses are harder to control in open spaces – to start with, try jumps that are set in a hedge or fence so that you jump from one open area to another but the horse cannot run past. Progress to fences that have one end against a hedge so that there is only one direction in which the horse could run out. Then try a fence with open space on both sides; the horse might be distracted and it is your job to steer him over it.

The beauty of a schooling round is that you can miss out any fences that look too difficult, and you do not have to do the whole course at once. You can practise specific types of fence that you have problems with or that you do not usually have access to, such as drops, steps, and water. Some typical cross-country fences, such as corners and "skinnies", can be replicated at home with show jumps.

If you do not have a chance to walk the fences before you jump them, walk the horse around them and have a look – check for features such as a drop on the landing side. If you are not on a course that is designed to specific standards and regulations, check the depth of any water by riding slowly through it. In official courses there is a maximum depth for water and the ground should be good underneath it, but other courses might not be built to the same high standards.

RIDING THROUGH WATER
Practise by walking through shallow water, then trotting and cantering. Next, add a small fence just after the exit. Do not try to jump into water.

JUMPING CORNER FENCES
Before you attempt to jump corner fences, both you and the horse need to be skilled and confident because they are tricky to judge.

COMMON PROBLEMS

When horses do not respond to the aids we give them, there are often several possible reasons and solutions which may depend on the horse, the rider, or the circumstances. Here are some common problems and possible solutions but, in practice, there may be other factors to take into account, including physical problems in the horse.

RIDING PROBLEMS

FLATWORK

PROBLEM	POSSIBLE CAUSE	SUGGESTED SOLUTION
The horse slows down, or will not go forwards when asked.	Rider is pulling too much on one or both reins, preventing the horse from going forwards; ineffective use of legs.	Yield with your hands to allow the horse forwards; squeeze with both legs. Also ensure your back and seat are relaxed so that they do not restrict the movement.
The horse will not go in a straight line.	Rider is looking or leaning to one side; leg aids are not clear.	Position your body straight and look ahead – aim for a marker in the distance if you wish. Give clear forward aids, ensuring both your legs are on the girth and your hands are held evenly.
When asked to turn, the horse turns his head but not his body and throws weight on to his outside shoulder.	Unclear aids; poor preparation; rider not looking through the turn; lack of impulsion.	**Starting to turn** Set up the turn in good time, look the way you want to go and give the correct aids (*see* pp.136–137). Maintain impulsion. In trot and canter, use a half-halt to rebalance the horse before asking for the turn.
On circles, the horse bends his neck more than his body and circles become increasingly large.	Inside rein is too strong; rider is using hands to position the horse's head instead of using legs and body to direct.	Give and take the inside rein to encourage the horse to soften through that side. Use the outside rein to limit the bend in his neck. Keep your inside leg on the girth and your outside leg further back to control the quarters. Look where you want to go.
Bending and circles are more difficult on one rein than the other.	Most horses are stiffer on one side, as are most people; problem could lie with either of you. Horse may not have been sufficiently warmed up.	Warm up before schooling; work the horse forwards, aiming to make him use his hind legs evenly – exercises such as leg-yield and loops can be helpful. Learn to recognize difficulty and encourage and praise the horse. Check your own muscles and posture for stiffness and unevenness; do warm-up exercises before riding.

RIDING PROBLEMS

PROBLEM	POSSIBLE CAUSE	SUGGESTED SOLUTION
The horse hollows his back or throws his head up when asked to slow down. **Head thrown up**	Rider is using too much rein pressure.	Use a controlling seat in conjunction with leg aids to send the horse forwards into a restraining hand. Alternate strong rein contact with yield so that the horse can use his back and neck.
The horse pulls his head forwards causing the rider to tip and lose balance.	Rider is relying to much on reins for balance; seat is not independent.	Learn to balance without the reins. Take lessons in a controlled environment where your instructor can safely devise exercises without reins and/or stirrups.
The horse slows down or goes too far sideways in leg-yield.	Lack of forward impulsion; aids unclear or sideways aid too strong.	Yield the inside rein; ride forwards then re-apply the leg-yield aids.
The rider becomes impatient and creates an argument with the horse.	Horse is confused by unclear aids; rider started out stressed.	Take some deep breaths and clear your mind of everyday stress before you get on – horses are sensitive to moods and to any tension in your body. Apply the aids clearly so that the horse can understand. Encourage and reward him for good efforts.

JUMPING

PROBLEM	POSSIBLE CAUSE	SUGGESTED SOLUTION
The horse rushes at fences and jumps too big or knocks down the top rail.	Poor approach; horse is over-excited or scared, perhaps because of a previous bad experience.	Work on a balanced, confident approach; concentrate on rhythm and impulsion, not speed. Jump from trot or even walk.
The horse slows down several strides before the jump, and stops or runs out.	Lack of impulsion; rider looking down or not using legs; horse or rider nervous.	Lower the fence if necessary to regain confidence. Work on the approach and impulsion. Keep your hands steady to direct the horse straight forwards. Look beyond the jump to a point on the horizon.
The rider lets the reins become long over jumps and has difficulty regaining control on landing.	Rider is behind the movement; hands are too rigid and not following the horse's neck as it stretches.	Your arms must follow the movement of the horse's neck, maintaining rein contact as he stretches over the fence. Gridwork can be helpful in developing your balance (*see* pp.190–191). **Going over a jump**
The rider loses balance on landing.	Rider has leant too far forwards; weak lower leg position; gripping with the knees.	Shorten your stirrups and practise riding in jumping position on the flat. Push your weight down into your heel so that your lower leg does not tip back. Go with the movement on take-off rather than throwing your upper body forwards.

RIDING OUT

Riding out in the countryside must surely be one of the most relaxing pastimes. You can cover so much more ground in a shorter time than on foot and enjoy the views from the vantage point of the horse's back. If you are quiet, you might also see plenty of wildlife, as shy creatures are less likely to run away from horses than from humans or dogs.

GOING FOR A HACK

Enjoying the countryside is one of the great attractions of riding. All the control and schooling techniques that you learnt in the manège will come into play, helping you to cope with everything you meet and to make the most of this delightful experience. Remember, though, to behave courteously towards other people who are using the tracks.

HOW THE HORSE MIGHT BEHAVE

There is an exciting world out there involving a range of joys and hazards, from litter in the hedge to wide open spaces and other horses. Horses enjoy hacking and they can be quite exuberant. A responsible riding school will not send you out on a hack until you are ready and they will choose a suitable horse for you. Remember to concentrate on the riding while you admire the countryside!

TIPS AND TECHNIQUES

RIDING UP AND DOWN HILL

A steep uphill slope is hard work for the horse and he might want to trot or even jump up. Lighten your seat and adjust your weight forwards and keep your legs firmly against his sides to help him keep his balance and momentum. Take steep downhill slopes at walk. Sit upright, or, if very steep, lean back slightly to keep your weight off the horse's shoulders. Push your weight into your heels and do not let your lower legs slide back.

Lean forwards to ride uphill

Lean back slightly to ride down steep slopes

RIDE SAFELY
Relax and enjoy, but ride properly and stay in control.

KEEPING CALM

If the horse takes hold and does not want to stop, keep calm and use the collection skills you learnt in the manège. A firm hold on the reins is important but some horses respond to increased pressure on the bit by pulling harder, so be prepared to "give and take" one or both reins. Put your weight down into your seat, keep your legs firm, and do not lean forwards, as this will encourage him to go faster. If space allows, turn a circle. Use your voice to help calm your horse and regain his attention, especially if he has bolted through panic or fear.

SPOOKY HORSE

If you approach a hazard, such as roadworks, flapping litter, or someone gardening behind a hedge, do not focus on it. Keep your legs against the horse's sides, look ahead, and ride forwards.

DOS & DON'TS

- **Do bend** low over the horse's neck to go under overhanging branches. Keep your legs on and your contact on the reins. Look ahead. If you cannot go round or safely underneath while mounted, dismount and lead the horse.
- **Do use** collection and steering to avoid catching your legs on trees in narrow, tree-lined paths.
- **Do dismount** to cross narrow, slippery, or high bridges. On bridges specifically designed for horses, ride or lead your horse across according to the conditions.
- **Don't let** your horse roll in water. Keep in balance and ride carefully but positively forwards, especially if he tries to stop and splash the water with a front foot.

A horse splashing in water

OPENING AND CLOSING A GATE

Most riders will have to open and close gates while mounted at some time, whether on a hack or going into the manège. A horse that responds to sideways aids and can turn on his forehand and quarters is a great advantage, while gates are a good way to practise these moves away from the school environment.

1 STAND PARALLEL TO THE GATE
Approach the gate in walk and bring the horse parallel to it, facing the catch end. Take your reins in the hand furthest from the gate then lean down and release the catch with the nearest hand.

2 PULL THE GATE OPEN WIDE
Push the horse sideways with the appropriate leg as you gradually open the gate, keeping hold of the catch. Make sure that he moves clear of it and it does not touch him.

3 START TO GO THROUGH
When the gate is open wide enough to pass through safely, do so – there should be enough space that your tack and legs will not catch on anything. If in doubt, dismount and lead the horse through.

4 KEEP HOLD OF THE GATE
If the gate is heavy or is likely to swing shut, it can be easier to keep hold of the catch as you go through, provided there is enough space and your horse is sufficiently manoeuvrable.

5 TURN ROUND
Now turn round, remembering to use your legs as well as your hands, and place the horse parallel to the gate again. Grab the gate and pull it towards you.

6 MOVE SIDEWAYS
Push the horse sideways as you shut the gate, taking care not to catch his legs with it. At all stages, make sure your reins or martingale are not caught up.

7 SHUT THE GATE
Fasten the catch, making sure you have done so properly, turn round carefully and walk away – do not let the horse get into the habit of moving away faster.

***Make sure** the gate is shut properly*

***Keep your** feet in the stirrups and make sure the irons do not catch on anything*

RIDERS' TIPS

- **Practise this** routine before hacking out to make sure both you and the horse are familiar with it.
- **Be sure** you can dismount and remount on a hack in case you need to lead the horse through a gate.
- **If you** have to open a gate always close it again.
- **If a** gate is open, decide sensibly if this was careless or intentional. As a general rule, close it if in doubt.

"NO HOUR OF LIFE IS WASTED THAT IS SPENT IN THE SADDLE."

Winston Churchill,
statesman and author (1874–1965)

SAFETY AND ETIQUETTE

Riding out is fun but it is also a responsibility that should not be taken too lightly. Horses can become excited and distracted away from home and it is important to be in control. There are sensible precautions you can take before and during a ride to minimize risk and to help promote goodwill towards horse riders among other users of the roads and countryside.

RIDERS' TIPS

- **Make sure** the horse you plan to ride is used to being hacked out and is suitable for your skill level.
- **Check that** all your tack is in good condition.
- **Tell someone** where you are going and for how long.
- **Take a** mobile phone with the numbers of your yard and vet.
- **Ride with** someone else if possible, and always if you are a beginner.

RIDING ON THE ROAD

Sadly, most of us have to ride on roads in order to reach bridlepaths, and even the quietest country lane is a potential risk for horses. Many drivers do not realize that even if a horse is not frightened of vehicles, it could be alarmed by other factors such as the sound of a

***Wear a** correctly fitting, properly fastened riding hat. In some countries it is illegal to ride on the road without one*

***Make your** signals clearly and in good time*

TURNING LEFT OR RIGHT

Use the standard arm signals for turning left and right. Give drivers plenty of warning and make eye contact if possible.

THANK YOU

Thank drivers who show you courtesy with the universal "thank you" hand signal or, if it is not safe to take your hand off the reins, a smile and a nod.

lawnmower behind a hedge. A rider therefore has to be not only fully in control of the horse, but also aware of and alert to everything going on around them. Be aware of conditions underfoot, such as ice and slippery road surfaces. Corners and worn tyre tracks are often slippery and you should approach these with caution, preferably in walk.

As a rule, you should ride in single file on the road and keep as close to the horse in front as is safely possible. Large rides should split into smaller groups to let traffic pass.

Do not cross the white line at junctions until it is safe to do so. You should be able to keep the horse standing still and have him move forwards promptly when you ask – all that schooling will stand you in good stead here.

MEETING OTHER PEOPLE

Other people are entitled to use bridlepaths. Walk past them, giving them as much space as possible. Thank people who move out of your way or hold dogs for you to pass. Treat other riders with respect, too. Call out if you come up behind another horse, and if you need to overtake, check the rider is happy for you to do so, and put a reasonable distance between you before going any faster.

STAYING VISIBLE IN POOR LIGHT
A wide range of reflective clothing is available, from coats and hat covers for riders, to leg bands, breastplates, and tail guards for horses.

DIFFICULT TERRAIN
Ride slowly over rough, cluttered, or muddy ground and try to avoid obvious hazards such as tree roots. Deep mud can hide potholes and roots. Let the horse look where he is going.

STAYING VISIBLE IN ANY LIGHT
It is advisable to wear a high-visibility garment such as a plain, fluorescent yellow tabard. This can give a driver several extra seconds to brake.

CHECK LIST

RIDING IN THE COUNTRYSIDE

- **Keep to** bridlepaths; if you are allowed on the edges of fields, keep to the edge (or headland) and never trample crops.
- **Be aware** that there may be birds breeding in the hedgerows which are vulnerable at certain times of the year.
- **Walk past** livestock.
- **Close gates** behind you.
- **Respect people's** privacy – try not to conduct a loud conversation when riding past houses and gardens.

DEALING WITH PROBLEMS

We all hope that nothing too eventful will happen while we are out riding. Most problems that occur are small and entail nothing more than getting back on or leading the horse home, but what sort of things can go wrong and what should you do about them? A little knowledge and a lot of common sense will be a great asset at these times.

LOOSE OR LOST SHOE

A shoe that becomes loose during a ride should cause little problem. Ride gently and report it to the yard when you return. If a shoe comes off cleanly and the foot is undamaged, the horse will probably be able to walk home without much problem. However, lost, or "cast" shoes often take a chunk of hoof off with them, which can make the horse's foot quite sore.

SUDDEN LAMENESS

If the horse suddenly starts to limp and there are stones underfoot, dismount, cross your stirrups over the saddle and check his front feet for stones. You might not be able to reach his hind feet safely unless there is someone else there to hold him – never let go of the reins – so your only option may be to lead him home.

It is all too easy for a horse's foot to be punctured by a nail or other sharp object on the ground. This will make him lame and can be very serious, but the cause may not be immediately obvious, especially if the ground or hoof is muddy. If walking is causing the horse pain, you have no choice but to phone for help. Be clear about your location so that you can be found easily.

TACK TROUBLE

If a stirrup leather breaks, there is a fair chance you will be able to ride quietly home without it. A breakage in any other part of the tack, however, is more of a problem. A broken girth strap means you will certainly have to lead the horse home, holding the saddle on his back. Run up the stirrups and secure the girth so that it does not flap.

Broken reins can be knotted if the break is near the buckle and you can hold both reins, but a break in any other place again means you will have to dismount and lead the horse. If any part of the bridle other than the noseband breaks, you have no way to control the horse. A piece of baler twine carried in your pocket can provide a superficial mend that might see you home but on no account try to ride if your bridle is broken. If you are too far away to walk home or there is a busy road to negotiate, phone for help.

LEADING A HORSE FROM ANOTHER
This should be done by a skilled rider. Bring the reins over the horse's head and hold the buckle firmly in the nearest hand.

WALKING HOME
If it is not safe for the horse in trouble to be led home on his own, someone should ride quietly alongside him.

FALLING OFF

Try your utmost to keep hold of the reins when you fall: there are any number of reasons why a horse could run away – through naughtiness or fear – and a serious accident could be the result.

With luck, you will be able to dust yourself off and get back in the saddle, even if you then have to turn for home rather than continuing the planned ride. If a fallen rider is unconscious, they might need to be put in the recovery position. It is possible that they could have a back injury, but your priority is to save their life, so first-aid training is invaluable. Make the situation as safe as possible and phone for help. If a rider has hit their head do not remove the hat, especially if they are unconscious, as doing so could make the injury worse.

Air Ride

WESTERN RIDING

THE WESTERN STYLE

Western riding evolved on the cattle ranches of the American West, influenced by the style of riding brought to the New World by the Spanish conquistadores. Swinging into a Western saddle certainly can make you feel like a cowboy, but today's Western riding discipline is not just a comfortable way to ride the range – it is a competitive sport with many different divisions, and is practised all over the world.

EFFICIENT AND SECURE

Riding a well-trained, or "finished", Western horse, can be compared to driving a brand-new fast car. It is responsive, predictable, quiet, and powerful. The resulting partnership between horse and rider makes for a comfortable and relaxed ride.

Every aspect of Western riding arose from the need to be efficient and secure while working in the saddle. A cow herder needed to be able to have a hand free for roping, so the technique of "neck reining" developed, where a horse is guided by one hand using rein pressure against the neck. This enabled the cow herder not only to rope cattle, but to open gates, crack a whip, and carry out other tasks on the ranch.

NECK REINING
In this technique, the rider moves her hand to right or left to ask the horse to turn.

WESTERN EQUITATION

The most obvious difference between English and Western riding is the tack, but there are other distinctions. Most English horses are ridden with steady, consistent contact on the bit, but in Western riding, the horse is ridden with minimal contact. The horse is highly attuned to the bit's balance and position within his mouth, and that, combined with the rider's natural aids – the seat, legs, and hands – keeps the horse on the bit and quick to respond. A horse is trained to be ridden Western style – an English-trained horse cannot suddenly be ridden Western style, and vice versa, as he would not understand.

A Western rider's equitation is similar to, but not the same as, that of an English rider. The rider remains naturally erect at the walk, jog, and lope, but the leg position is longer, resulting in a deeper seat position. Generally, when the horse is ridden in a curb bit (*see* pp.76–77), the reins are held in one hand, and the other hand rests naturally on the leg or at the rider's side.

Many riders make the mistake of thinking that the horse is controlled by the mouth, but in reality the rider strives to control the shoulders and the hindquarters. Being able to move over the horse's front end or elevate it makes the horse more responsive and gives the rider maximum influence. If the rider has the horse moving from his haunches, he is able to ride with energy, and collect and extend any gait.

WORLDWIDE APPEAL

What was once a purely American tradition is now making its way across the globe. It has been refined and adapted from its utilitarian origins, but it still remains a practical, useful way to ride a horse.

Just as with English riding, Western riding has its own set of competitions and events. There are classes in which the rider's equitation is judged; others that evaluate the horse's manners. In some classes, the horse's agility and obedience are tested, while in others the horse and rider race against the clock in gymkhana events.

These competitions are held not just in North America. Riders from all over Europe are increasingly taking up Western riding and competing not just in local shows, but also qualifying for international competitions held all over the world. Southern hemisphere countries such as Brazil, South Africa, and Australia are also turning out world-class Western riders.

And as a practical way to "hit the trails", people are riding Western style in more and more places around the globe. International riding tour organizers often offer Western riding as an option on trail-riding holidays, due to the appeal of the comfortable style to novice riders.

ON THE RANCH
Western riding was borne out of the need to rope cattle from the saddle.

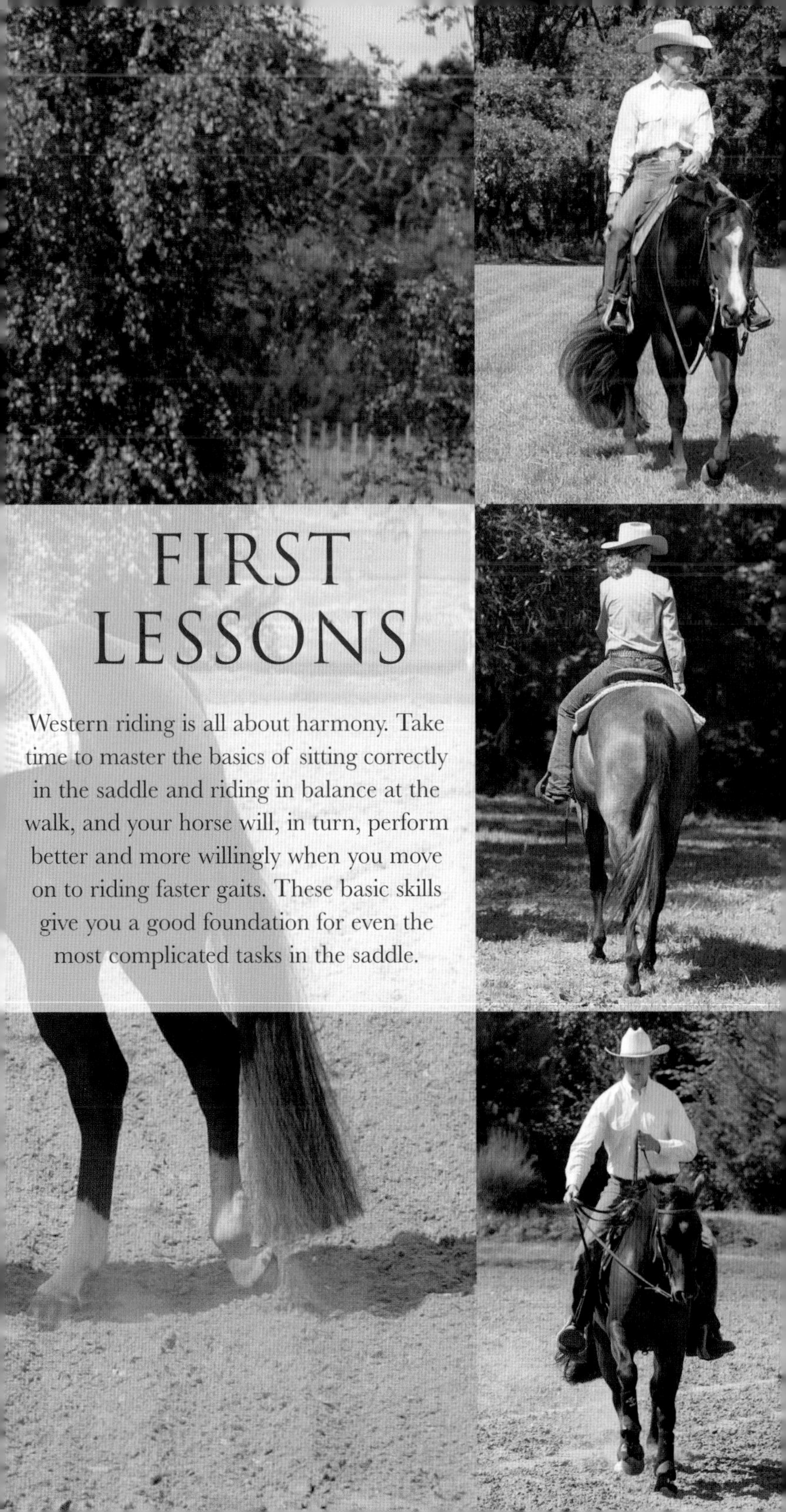

FIRST LESSONS

Western riding is all about harmony. Take time to master the basics of sitting correctly in the saddle and riding in balance at the walk, and your horse will, in turn, perform better and more willingly when you move on to riding faster gaits. These basic skills give you a good foundation for even the most complicated tasks in the saddle.

MOUNTING

Most horse breeds that are ridden in the Western style, such as the American Quarter Horse, are not as tall as their English counterparts, which makes it easier for a novice rider to mount. However, it is important not to alarm the horse while mounting, so you need to learn how to mount gently and quietly.

1 FACE THE REAR Always mount the horse from the near (left) side. Face the rear of the horse, hold the reins in your left hand and rest it on the front of the saddle. Turn the stirrup towards you and place the ball of your left foot in it.

TECHNIQUES

ALTERNATIVE MOUNTING
Some Western riders mount by holding the reins and withers with the left hand, grasping the horn with the right hand, and facing the horse's front end. However, this method is not liked by some riders, so discover which is best for you.

2 TRANSFER YOUR WEIGHT Put your right hand on the cantle and, with a small hop, push off the ground from your right foot while transferring your weight into your left stirrup. Push yourself up with your left leg.

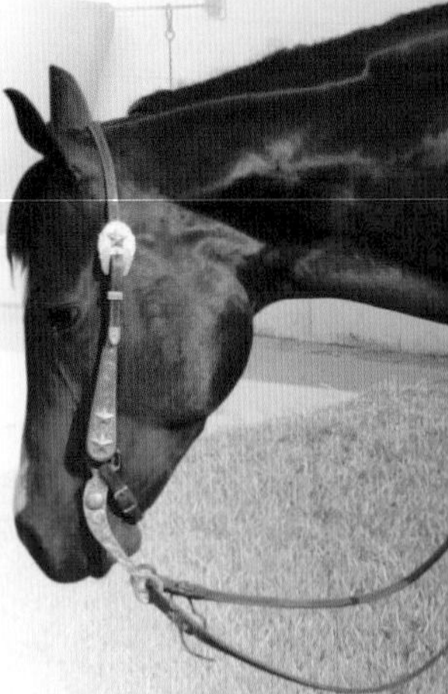

3 SWING YOUR LEG Lean over slightly as you push yourself up into a position where your left leg is straight and you are leaning over the top of the horse. Gently swing your right leg over the horse's back as you let go of the cantle. Avoid kicking him.

4 SETTLE IN THE SADDLE Allow yourself to settle slowly into the saddle. Do not thump your weight down suddenly. Turn the right toe upwards to find your right stirrup, and adjust it so that it falls under the ball of your foot.

***Aim to** mount the horse in one smooth, continuous movement*

***Lift your** leg well over the horse's back*

HOLDING THE REINS

There are different options for holding the reins, depending upon the type of bit in which a horse is being ridden, or the level of his training. A horse wearing a snaffle bit will always be ridden with two hands, while a horse in a curb bit is generally ridden with one hand, but occasionally with two hands for schooling purposes.

SNAFFLE BRIDLE

The reins on a snaffle bridle, that is, a bridle with a snaffle bit, are split reins. You can hold them in two different ways – crossed or bridged, whichever you prefer – with your hands about 10 cm (4 in) apart. By having both hands on the reins, it makes it easy to adjust the rein length if necessary. A horse ridden in a snaffle bit reacts to direct pressure on his mouth, so the rider must be able to use both hands independently.

CROSSED REINS
When riding a horse in a snaffle bridle, you can cross the reins over his neck. Cross them so that the left end hangs on the right side of the horse and the right end hangs on the left.

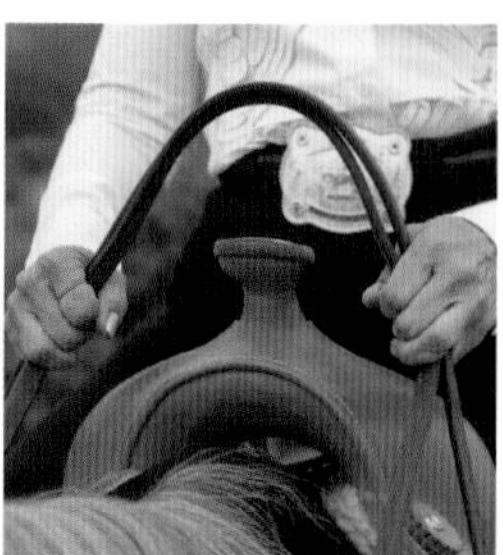

BRIDGED REINS
You can bridge snaffle reins over the neck in a shallow loop. Place your thumbs underneath the reins at each side of the neck and wrap your fingers loosely around them.

ROMAL REINS

The ends of romal-style reins are braided together to form a long, whip-like extension called a "romal", or "quirt". This style of reins originated with the vaqueros of California. The rider holds the reins with the left hand just below the romal knot and the right hand on the quirt in a relaxed spot at mid-thigh level.

THE QUIRT
Never let go of the quirt and let it hang loose while riding. It is usually about 1m (3.25 ft) long and could get caught in the horse's legs.

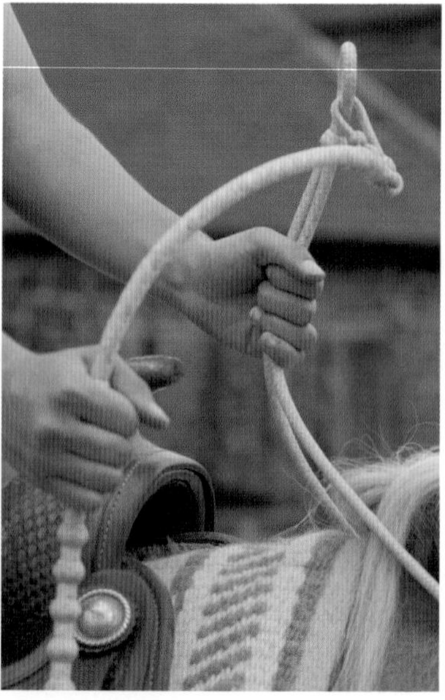

HOLDING ROMAL REINS
Close your hands around romal reins with your thumbs on top and about 40 cm (16 in) apart. Lower your right hand to hang relaxed.

CURB SPLIT REINS

A bridle with a curb bit has split reins. In the wrong hands, a curb bit can hurt the horse, so a rider must use it carefully, using just enough pressure on the reins for the horse to respond. The bit can have more or less of an effect according to the rider's hand position and the length of reins, so it is important to hold the reins correctly.

LENGTH OF REINS
The reins should loop from your hand to the horse's mouth. Hold them as softly as you can.

***Hold your** rein hand relaxed and naturally, close to the horn of the saddle*

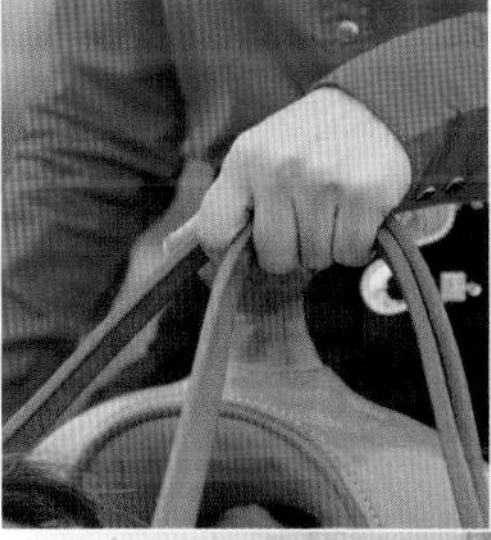

INDEX FINGER BETWEEN
Hold both reins in your left hand with your index finger between them and your knuckles angled slightly inwards.

LOOSE FIST
Split reins can also be held in a loose fist. Keep your thumb on top as this stops the reins from slipping through your fingers.

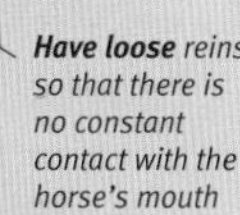

***Have loose** reins so that there is no constant contact with the horse's mouth*

DOS & DON'TS

- **Do hold** your rein hand slightly above and in front of the saddle horn when holding the reins in one hand.
- **Don't thrust** your hand too far ahead of the saddle horn and withers – this is uncomfortable and unnatural.
- **Don't hold** your hand too far back because if you cannot move it back any further, it will reduce the effectiveness of your communication with the horse.

Hand too far forward

Hand too far back

POSITION IN THE SADDLE

Western aids are very similar to English aids. As with all types of riding, a good position in the saddle is essential, since a poor position will result in imbalance and mediocre performance. You should always appear to be natural and in balance, no matter what gait the horse is in or what manoeuvre he is performing.

SITTING CORRECTLY

When you are sitting correctly, an imaginary line would run from your ear through your shoulder and hip to the back of your heel. Your back should be flat, not arched or slouched, and you should sit up tall for an elegant posture in the saddle. Your arms should always be relaxed and hang from the body naturally, with the upper arm held close to your body. In non-competitive riding, you can hold your free hand and arm in any comfortable position, from resting on the thigh to hanging straight down.

TIPS AND TECHNIQUES

STIRRUP LENGTH

Your stirrup length will have an effect on how you sit in the saddle. If you feel as though you are constantly trying to reach for your stirrups, or if you are sitting in a chair position because your stirrups are too short, adjust them. Work with your natural balance and centre of gravity, and do not force yourself into a position just because it looks right.

POSTURE AND AIDS

The seat is just as important in Western riding as it is in English riding. You should sit even deeper, opening up the pelvic bone to rest on your two seat bones. You will use weight shifts, balance, and a version of half-halts, the same way English riders do. If your posture is bad, you will find it almost impossible to make these aids effective.

DOS AND DON'TS

- **Do sit** in a comfortable, natural way.
- **Don't arch** your back. If you do, you will be stiff and unable to tell the horse what you want. It will be nearly impossible to give any seat aids.
- **Don't lean** back. Your centre of gravity will be behind the horse and your lower leg and inner thigh will not have good contact with the horse's sides, so your aids will be ineffective.

Arched back

Leaning backwards

__Hold up__ your head without jutting out your chin

__Look ahead__ in the direction you are going

__Keep your__ shoulders square, rolled back, and down

__Hold your__ rein hand above or slightly in front of the horn of the saddle

__Bend your__ left arm at the elbow

__Point your__ feet forwards and slightly out, with the stirrups on the balls of the feet for stability

RIDERS' TIP

LEG POSITION

To have effective leg aids, press your knees against the saddle so that your thighs and knees are close against the saddle. Your calves should be in light contact with the horse.

Effective leg position

WALKING

Even though the walk is the slowest gait, the horse still needs to perform it with energy. This does not mean hurried, however. A horse with energy is controllable and manoeuvrable at any speed. Always think of impulsion creating energy from within the horse whenever you ride.

1 MOVE FORWARDS

Nudge the horse with your lower calf – and your heel, if he needs a little more defined aid. The horse should move off promptly, picking up each of his feet individually.

***Sit up** straight, keeping your back flat*

***Let your** seat move with the horse as he walks*

***Allow your** rein hand to move with the motion of the horse's head*

***Bump the** horse with your heel if he is moving too slowly*

RIDERS' TIP

Imagine putting your car into neutral at 10 km/h (6 mph) and then trying to turn a corner. Since the car has no momentum or power, it makes it very difficult for you to steer it properly. The same applies to a horse. The horse's inner energy, starting with his hindquarters, gives him a push at any gait to do what you ask him to.

2 WALK ON Discourage the horse from shuffling with another nudge of your leg. Do not keep squeezing the horse constantly, however, as this will desensitize him, or make him "dead-sided".

***The horse's** ears should be about level with his withers*

***The profile** of the horse's head should be just in front of the vertical, so that he is accepting the bit and ready to respond to any rein aid*

FAULTS AND FIXES

FAULT	FIX
Jigging – a nervous half-trot, half-walk	Raise your hands high with rein contact and release them low on the horse's neck the moment he takes a walk step. Sitting deep in the saddle instead of inclining forwards (which tells a horse to go faster by your balance) also reinforces the walk.
Behind the bit – nose behind the vertical	Carry your hand above the saddle horn and use subtle bumps of each heel, in rhythm with the horse's walk, to encourage him to walk with energy.
On the forehand – too much weight on the front end	Lift the horse's shoulder by putting him on a circle and, with your inside leg at the cinch and your outside leg 8 cm (3 in) behind the cinch, apply contact to both reins. This will make the horse flex at the poll, engage his hindquarters so that he steps well underneath himself, and carry his weight on his hindquarters, lightening his front end.

WALK TO HALT

The quality of the halt is important because it shows the level of training the horse has and how responsive he is to the aids. Pulling back on the reins may make a Western horse stop, but it will look horrible. The horse should stay relaxed when he halts.

1 PREPARE TO HALT As you prepare to halt, sink your weight down into your stirrups through both legs and your seat. Concentrate on sitting very deeply into the horse's back.

***Sit deeply** into the saddle*

***Push your** weight down into the stirrups*

RIDERS' TIP

■ **If the** horse resists and does not stop, say "whoa" and use the arena fence as a boundary. If he still resists, use one rein to pull his head around to your leg. This will put him on a tight circle and he will eventually want to stop.

AT A GLANCE

WALK TO HALT
The rider allows his weight to sink into his seat and stirrups, stops the natural movement of his upper body, and takes a slight pull against the reins. Then he relaxes the reins forwards when the horse is standing quietly.

2 PERFORM THE HALT

Keep your body still by stopping the natural movement of your seat and torso. Sit up tall and take up a slight contact on the reins. The horse will respond with an even halt and should stand squarely on all four legs.

Keep your *upper body erect and still*

Move your *hands towards the horse's head to release the rein contact*

Relax your *seat softly into the saddle*

3 RELEASE THE CONTACT

Once the horse stops, immediately release your rein contact by relaxing the reins forwards. This is the signal to the horse that he has halted correctly.

TURNING

The Western horse is trained to respond to very light aids on a loose rein, so keep this in mind when you are guiding the horse. It can be a difficult feeling to get used to, because the first thing most riders want to do when they feel insecure is grab hold of the reins and pull back, or yank the horse's head around.

1 START TO TURN Holding your rein hand slightly above and in front of the saddle horn, move your hand sideways and in the direction you would like to go, without picking up slack in the reins. If you are turning right, you should move your hand 5 to 8 cm (2 to 3 in) towards the right.

Move your *hand to the right to make the left rein come into contact with the horse's neck, telling him to turn right*

Keep your *inside leg passive*

RIDERS' TIPS

- **If your** horse twists his neck away from the direction of the turn, use your hand to guide him more and remember to keep your outside leg against his body.
- **If your** horse steadily pulls against your hands, take a little slack out of the reins and give a slight pull to help him focus.

AT A GLANCE

TURNING

The rider moves her hand over so the outside rein lies against the horse's neck, telling him to turn. Her outside leg aids the turn with pressure; her inside leg supports the bend. She turns her head to look in the direction of the turn.

2 SUPPORT THE TURN

Your outside rein will lie against the horse's neck, and the horse will move away from the slight pressure. Support the turn by pressing with your outside calf. If the horse needs a stronger aid, nudge him with your outside heel.

Use your *hand lightly to guide the horse through the turn*

Look in *the direction you are going*

Keep your *shoulders in line with the horse's body*

Think of *the horse bending around your inside leg*

Use your *outside leg to ask the horse to bend his body through the turn*

TECHNIQUES

USING A SNAFFLE BIT

A horse in a snaffle bit is ridden two-handed (*see* p.220) and guided with a direct rein. Pressure on the right rein tells the horse to turn right, and pressure on the left rein tells him to turn left. Your hands should not be further apart than 10 cm (4 in), and you should never pull the horse round with the rein. You can give subtle signals by moving the reins with the little fingers.

DISMOUNTING

Once you have finished your ride, it is time to dismount, untack, groom your horse, and put him away for the day. Dismounting is not a difficult task, but it can be a little awkward at first. Keep the reins in your left hand all the time so that your horse does not walk off.

1 FREE YOUR FOOT
Shift your weight into your left stirrup and take your right foot out of the stirrup. Grasp the saddle horn in your left hand.

2 RAISE YOUR RIGHT LEG
Lean forwards so that you do not fall, and your shift in weight does not move the saddle. Raise your right leg up and back.

3 SWING YOUR LEG OVER
Lift your right leg over the back of the horse, making sure you clear the hindquarters and the saddle's cantle.

4 STEP DOWN
Put your right foot to the ground. Land at a good distance from the horse's side so that your left leg is not too twisted.

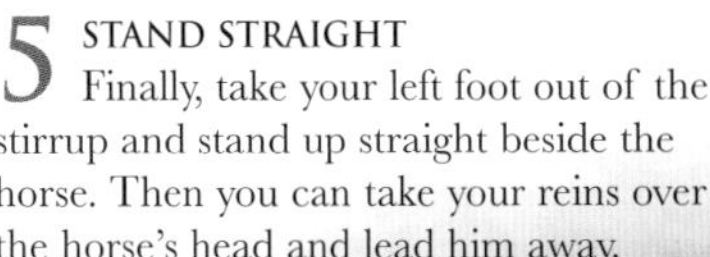

5 STAND STRAIGHT

Finally, take your left foot out of the stirrup and stand up straight beside the horse. Then you can take your reins over the horse's head and lead him away.

DOS & DON'TS

- **Do take** your left foot out of the stirrup promptly. If the horse was to spook and move off with your foot still in the stirrup you could get dragged along the ground.
- **Don't let** your left foot turn into the horse's body when you remove it from the stirrup, because you must avoid kicking the horse with your toe.

RIDERS' TIP

- **If you** prefer, you can land on the ground with both feet together when you dismount. Swing your right leg over until it is next to the left, as if you are in a standing position. Place your right hand on the cantle, take your left foot out of the stirrup, and slide down to the ground, reins in your left hand.

MOVING ON

The Western horse should always move with an easy, smooth rhythm. The gaits may seem slow, but there is a reason for this – the objective is to make the horse a pleasure to ride with as few aids as possible. A Western horse is expected to move at a measured, relaxed pace, but he should still have plenty of impulsion in all his gaits.

JOGGING

The English trot and the Western jog are essentially the same gait, in which the horse's legs move in diagonal pairs, but the jog is more collected, covering less ground with the same rhythm. The jog originated because the trot is too quick for a leisurely trail ride or for moving cattle.

1 SQUEEZE WITH YOUR LEGS

Ask the horse to jog with a light squeeze and release of your lower legs and heels. Support this with a squeeze of your upper thighs and seat. Place your rein hand forward and in front of the saddle horn.

***Hold your** rein hand in front of the saddle horn*

***The horse** travels slowly, but with impulsion*

***Use your** legs and heels to remind the horse to move with energy*

2 KEEP IT MOVING

Press your heels into the horse's ribcage slightly and pull your feet upwards to help him round his back and keep moving at a steady jog. Sit up straight with your seat aligned under your torso. Use your legs to ask the horse to move his entire body straight, not crookedly with haunches trailing or shoulders leading.

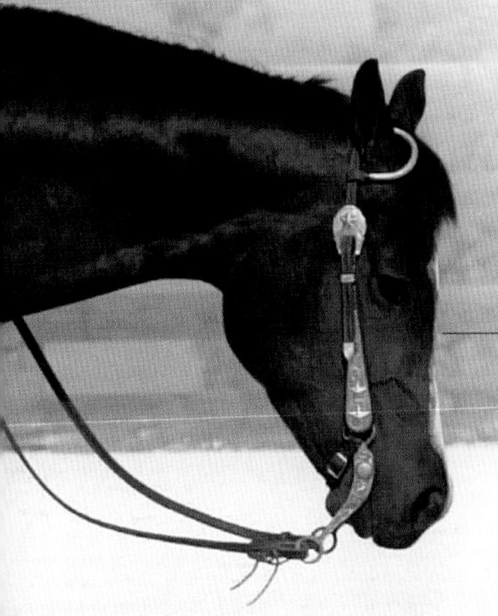

***The horse's** head is perpendicular to the ground*

AT A GLANCE

JOGGING

In competition, excessive speed is penalized so the horse is trained to travel slowly, with impulsion coming from the hindquarters. He should exhibit a smooth, flowing two-beat gait with little knee action.

DOS & DON'TS

■ **Don't let** a horse lose impulsion from his hindquarters, as he will end up pulling himself along by his front end.

■ **Do improve** a shuffling gait by allowing the horse to extend his jog to a trot and rising to the trot to regulate the rhythm. Loosen the reins so that he can travel forwards in a long, low frame. Continue to drive the horse forwards but raise your reins to lift his head up. Finally, return your hands to the normal position and collect the horse back to a jog, and this time he should have more impulsion.

Rising to the trot

LOPING

The lope should be a pleasure to sit to, with its easy rhythm and relaxed, smooth stride. It is like the English canter, with three distinct beats, but it is more collected. You should help the horse create his lope with energy from the hind end, and not slow him down with the reins to the point where his movement becomes disjointed.

1 ASK FOR LOPE Pick up a slight contact on the reins, with your inside leg providing support and your outside leg asking for the correct lead. Turn the horse's head slightly towards the inside of the arena so that you can see his inside eyelashes.

RIDERS' TIP

■ **If your** horse begins to four-beat lope, it may be because you are asking him to lope too slowly. Bring his head up and in, and allow him to rebalance himself by extending his stride a little. Keep your leg on, that is, gently squeeze his sides, and encourage him to lift his front end.

Sit upright *with a slightly deep seat to push the horse into lope*

The horse *begins to lope with his inside hind leg first*

Drive your *weight down into the stirrups*

Let your *seat move with a rocking motion*

Keep a *relaxed leg and thigh against the horse*

Hold your *hand in a position where you can take up a contact or guide the horse*

2 ABSORB THE MOVEMENT

The lope has a natural rocking movement, not unlike that of a rocking horse. Absorb the movement as you would on a rocking horse, relaxing your thigh and seat muscles.

There are *three distinct beats to the lope*

3 KEEP THE IMPULSION

Use your seat to keep the impulsion coming from behind so that the horse can shift his weight to his hindquarters and off his shoulders. This will result in a natural lope. Then ask for a little collection by maintaining a light contact on the bit.

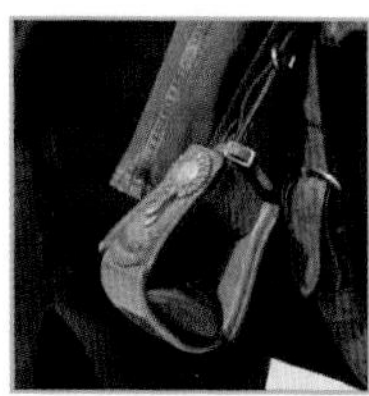

Support the *horse with your legs so that his body does not get strung out*

GALLOPING

A gallop is exhilarating. Whether it is a controlled run in a reining pattern, or a fast gallop in the open, you will never forget the feeling of freedom and speed. Before you gallop, you must be secure in the saddle at the walk, jog, and lope. Once you feel confident about your balance and your aids, you can ask for this fast gait.

RIDERS' TIP

■ **If you** believe your horse is running away with you, sit upright and ask him to come back with short pulls on the reins. Do not cling to him or go into the "foetal position". If you tighten up he will think you are telling him to keep going.

1 DRIVE WITH YOUR SEAT

To obtain the gallop, first ask your horse to lope, then use a driving seat by tightening your abdominal muscles and squeezing with your buttocks and upper thighs. Shift your weight forwards without leaning too far forwards.

2 GO FORWARDS

Encourage the horse to go forwards by holding your rein hand halfway up the horse's neck. Give a slight thrust with your pelvis at every stride and increase your leg pressure with a squeeze at every stride.

AT A GLANCE

GALLOPING

To get a transition to gallop, the rider first asks for more speed at the lope. He then follows the horse's neck movement forwards with his rein hand, and inclines his upper body forwards keeping his seat in the saddle.

***Encourage the** horse to go forwards by moving your rein hand forwards and therefore allowing him more rein*

***Keep your** upper body a little ahead of the vertical*

***The horse** must be allowed to stretch his neck as he gallops*

***Nudge the** horse with your heel to ask for more speed*

LEG-YIELD

In the leg-yield, the horse travels sideways and forwards. It is called a two-track movement because the horse adds an additional track of footprints as he travels diagonally. During the leg-yield, the horse is slightly bent away from the direction of travel and one pair of legs moves towards the other pair as the horse travels.

***Keep your** body upright and centred over the horse*

1 BEGIN TO BEND THE HORSE

Use a deep, active seat to maintain the forward motion. Begin to bend the horse around the leg you want him to move away from, in this case the right leg. Slowly take your left leg off the horse's side while increasing the pressure with your right leg.

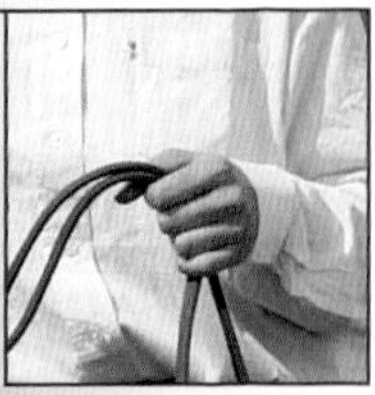

***Use the** reins to reinforce your leg aids by asking for a slight bend in the horse's neck and head*

***Take your** left leg off the horse's side when leg-yielding to the left*

RIDERS' TIPS

- **If the** horse does not start to move sideways, move your right leg further behind the cinch and ask with squeezes for him to move his haunches over.
- **If he** turns his head but will not cross his legs, better support with the right leg and more energy in his walk will help solve the problem.

2 STAY OVER THE HORSE'S RIBCAGE

Shift your hips slightly to the left to stay over the horse's ribcage as he moves forwards and sideways. Keep the right leg completely against the horse's side at the cinch and nudge him with your right heel if he needs encouragement to move.

Keep your *body tall but move your hips over slightly towards the direction of travel*

Keep your *hands high and wide when you are learning, if you like, so that your signals to the horse are clearer*

AT A GLANCE

LEG-YIELD

The horse is bent around the leg the rider wants to move away from. The rider's inside leg is at the cinch; her outside leg is behind it to keep the hind-quarters moving across.

SIDE-PASS

In the side-pass, the horse steps sideways, keeping his shoulders and haunches straight. It is an advanced lateral movement that will help improve your riding and your horse's balance and athleticism. It is also used as part of competitive events, such as trail classes, when you have to side-pass over a log or open and close a gate.

1 ASK THE HORSE TO MOVE OVER
Start a side-pass from a halt in the middle of the arena. Keep an even pressure on both sides of the horse's mouth. For a side-pass to the left, place your right leg several centimetres behind the cinch and press with your entire leg to ask the horse to move over.

2 CONTINUE TO ASK
Keep asking for the side-pass with your right leg, and when the horse moves away from the leg, reward him by releasing the leg pressure. Try to keep his body bent away from the direction of travel, and keep enough pressure on his mouth to prevent him from moving forwards.

RIDERS' TIP

■ **Because lateral** work is difficult for a horse that is not supple in his body, he may try to evade your aids. If this happens, do not force the issue. Instead, stop attempting the movement, walk in a circle and in a straight line, then try giving the aids again. Once the horse understands the aids, he will be more willing to perform the movement.

3 SIT UP STRAIGHT

Keep your body tall and centred in the saddle. It is important to use your seat as well as your legs and hands through all advanced movements. Increase your weight in the outside stirrup and seat to aid the horse.

The horse *performs a "crab-walk" in the manoeuvre*

Relax your *hands when the horse has responded to all your aids and completed the manoeuvre*

Use your *leg to push the horse's ribcage over*

The horse's *outside leg crosses over the inside leg*

Nudge with *your outside heel if you need to ask the horse to align his haunches better with his shoulder*

REINING

Now an internationally recognized riding discipline, reining has sometimes been referred to as "the dressage of Western riding". The horse is required to perform complex manoeuvres at lightning speed, and he must show control in all his movements. The best horse and rider pairs make the sport look effortless, but it is very demanding and only advanced riders with trained horses should try it.

WHAT IS REINING?

Reining, like other working cowhorse events (*see* pp.304–305), originated on the ranches of the American West. The cowboy's horse needed to be agile, anticipate the movement of cattle and react accordingly. The rider had to be able to guide his horse with the lightest of aids, so that he could focus his attention on his work.

THE ORIGINS OF REINING

The sport of reining has been honed and adapted from the traditional working methods used by cow herders. In competition, the horse and rider pair completes a designated pattern of various manoeuvres that are inspired by real ranch work – the horse will be asked to lope and run (a controlled gallop) a series of circles, flying lead changes, roll-backs, spins, and stops.

TRAINING THE RIDER
Work with a professional on a well-trained horse to build up your skills as a reiner.

THE REINING HORSE

Whether chasing down an errant calf, moving a herd, or holding a heifer at the end of a taut rope, an obedient horse was crucial to the rancher's success. Reflecting this, a reining horse exhibits complete control in all its movements. The rider's aids need to be only subtle, as the horse responds instantaneously and willingly.

Prospective reining horses are sometimes started as early as two years of age, but most training occurs when the horses are three and four years old, due in part to the strength and flexibility they need to perform the difficult manoeuvres.

When horses are going to perform movements such as the stop and the spin, an arena with a special surface, comprising a hard clay base underneath a combination of light sand and silt, is required. And even when a reining horse is only practising, it should work in an arena where the surface has been freshly harrowed.

REINING LOPE
A reining horse should show more animation in his gaits than a show-horse, although the horse needs to show clear changes in speed.

INTERNATIONAL SPORT

In 1966, The National Reining Horse Association was formed in America to promote the sport and organize its first official bylaws and competitions. From there, the American Quarter Horse Association, the world's largest breed register, also began to organize reining competitions for different levels.

In the past decade, reining has seen tremendous growth around the world and it is the fastest-growing equestrian sport. It became the first Western riding discipline of the United States Equestrian Team as well as of the Fédération Equestre Internationale (International Federation of Equestrian Sports) (FEI). The sport of reining made its debut as a medal discipline at the World Equestrian Games in 2002, in Jerez, Spain, where there were teams representing nine countries: USA, Canada, Italy, Great Britain, Germany, Brazil, Austria, Japan, and Switzerland. There were also individual riders from the Netherlands and France. Medals went to the USA, Canada, and Italy.

TRAINING THE HORSE

It takes patient training before a horse is ready to perform the complex manoeuvres necessary in reining, such as flying lead changes, stops, and spins.

The horse *should always appear relaxed and confident*

All reining *work is done on a loose rein*

FLYING CHANGE

In a reining pattern (*see* pp.296–297), the horse may be required to execute a flying change on a circle, in which he changes his leading leg at the lope without stopping and starts a circle in the opposite direction. He should not change his gait or speed, and must perform the lead change at the location specified in the pattern. He should not leap exuberantly into the next lead or anticipate the lead change before the rider has asked for it.

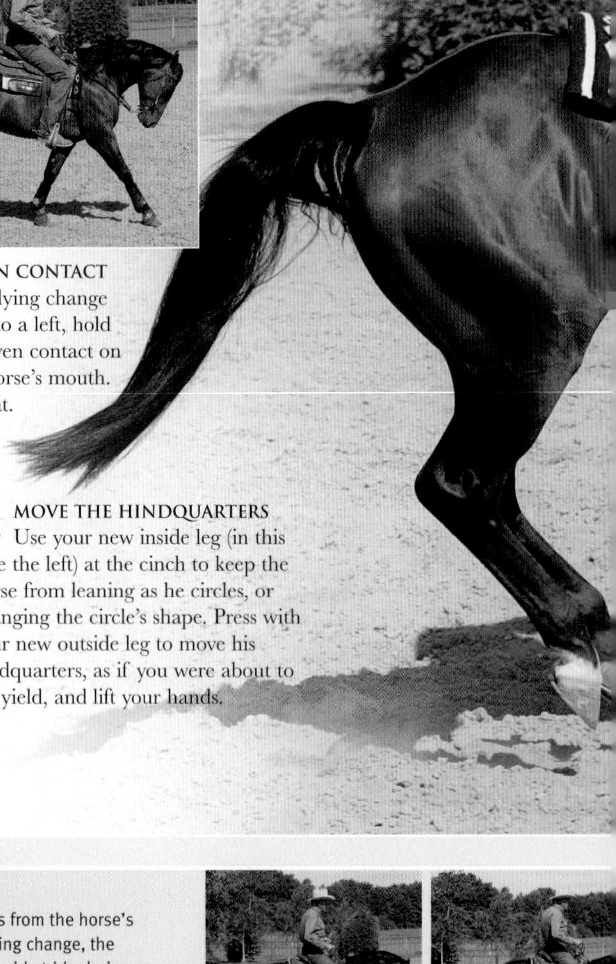

1 HAVE AN EVEN CONTACT To execute a flying change from a right circle to a left, hold the reins with an even contact on both sides of the horse's mouth. Drive with your seat.

2 MOVE THE HINDQUARTERS Use your new inside leg (in this case the left) at the cinch to keep the horse from leaning as he circles, or changing the circle's shape. Press with your new outside leg to move his hindquarters, as if you were about to leg yield, and lift your hands.

AT A GLANCE

FLYING CHANGE

The lead change starts from the horse's hind end. During a flying change, the horse swaps his lead mid-stride during the moment of suspension, when he moves his hips laterally towards the new lead.

Sit centred *and upright and keep your seat in the saddle to drive the horse forwards*

Keep your *hands steady and low, just above the saddle horn*

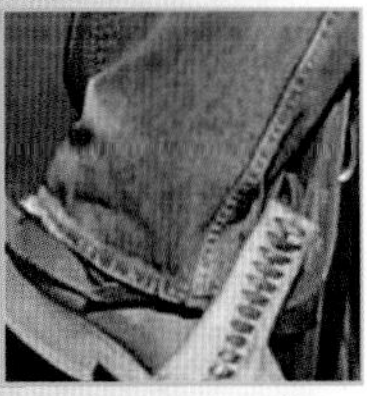

The horse *changes the direction in which his body bends as he starts to lope on the new circle*

Push the *horse laterally with your inside leg to disengage his hindquarters*

The horse *changes his lead leg during the moment of suspension*

3 START THE NEW CIRCLE

On the new leading leg, begin to circle in the opposite direction. The horse should not interrupt his stride or change his tempo as he continues on his new lead around a circle.

SLIDING STOP

The sliding stop is the distinctive feature of reining. It is a difficult manoeuvre that should only be attempted by experienced riders. The horse travels in a straight line, changing from lope to gallop. He gains speed with each stride until he is travelling fast. Then he slides to a dramatic halt.

1 INCREASE SPEED
To perform a sliding stop, a horse needs momentum to lift his front end and sit back, so you must first ask the horse to increase speed. Then ask him to slow down and start to slide by stopping all driving motion and relaxing immediately into the stirrups.

2 PUSH YOUR WEIGHT DOWN
Sit in balance at all times and just subtly push your body weight straight down through your hips. Keep your back straight so that you do not affect the horse's balance. Pulling back is not necessary and will not earn any points in competition.

AT A GLANCE

SLIDING STOP
The horse curls his hindquarters, drops his haunches, rounds his back, and braces his hind legs, sitting back deeply over his hocks. He slides 3–6 m (10–20 ft) to a stop, then stands motionless and relaxed.

EQUIPMENT TYPES

SHOES FOR SLIDING STOP

A reining horse wears wide, flat shoes called sliding plates. These allow him to slide over the arena more easily. The top layer of the arena must be sandy and fluffy so that the horse's feet do not go in too deep where he cannot slide properly.

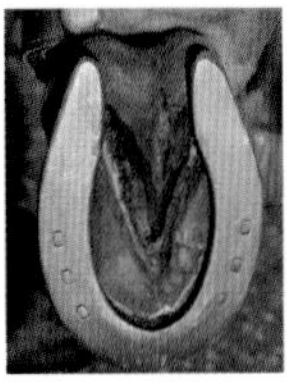

Sliding plate

You can *sometimes use the word "whoa" to make the horse respond*

Keep a *straight back so you do not throw the horse off balance*

The horse's *front end is elevated as he slides*

Keep the *reins loose and do not pull them during the slide*

Push your *weight into the stirrups and push your heels down*

The horse *is still in motion, "crawling" with his front legs in the same rhythm as his lope*

ROLL-BACK

A roll-back is a pivot turn of 180 degrees, done in one continuous movement without hesitation. It is usually performed after a stop. The horse runs down a straight line to a sliding stop then turns his shoulders round to face the opposite direction, arcs his body, pushes off with his inside hind leg, and leaps into a lope in the new direction.

Place the *outside rein against the horse's neck, but with plenty of slack*

1 SAY "WHOA"
One stride before reaching the stopping point, ask the horse to perform a roll-back by saying "whoa" to encourage him to rock his weight on to his hindquarters.

The horse *shifts his weight over his hindquarters during the turn*

2 OPEN THE REIN
Before stopping, initiate the turn by moving your rein hand out in the direction you want to turn, with a steady, firm contact. Use your outside leg to encourage the horse's body to follow his nose through the turn.

AT A GLANCE

ROLL-BACK

A roll-back is an advanced movement. The inside hind leg pushes deep and holds steady as the horse reaches round with his shoulders. The front legs cross over each other without hitting each other, or "interfering".

3 RELEASE THE REINS

Once the horse has passed the half-way point in the turn, release all contact on his mouth, allowing him to complete the turn on his own. Too much contact past that point in the turn is restrictive and slows down the horse's departure in the opposite direction.

***Keep the** outside rein low and loose throughout the turn*

SPIN

Spinning is one of the most exciting reining manoeuvres, but it is difficult to master so should only be tried by experienced horses and riders. In a spin, the horse plants his inside hind leg firmly into the ground and performs a rapid series of 360-degree turns. He then "nails the shut off", or stops, at an exact point in the turn after a certain number of spins.

***Keep your** weight slightly back in the saddle*

***The horse's** poll and chin are relaxed, not rigid*

***Tell the** horse to keep turning by pressing the outside rein against his neck*

1 INITIATE THE SPIN Sit with your weight shifted slightly back. Keep your outside leg close to the horse's side. To initiate the spin and keep it going, keep your outside leg close to the horse's side. Take your inside leg away from the horse's side.

***The horse's** inside front leg takes the first step of the spin*

***The horse's** inside hind leg acts as a pivot*

AT A GLANCE

SPIN

The horse pushes himself around, keeping his back level. He builds speed for the spin with his outside hind leg and front legs. He should perform his spin series all in one spot, with his hindquarters as the anchor.

2 KEEP SPINNING

Once the horse starts to spin, put your outside leg and rein on him only if you need to remind him to keep going. To stop the spin, return your legs, hands, and body to a central position and say "Whoa". The horse should then stand motionless.

TIPS AND TECHNIQUES

TEACHING THE HORSE

A rider teaches a horse to spin by first putting him on a series of small circles at the walk with his nose tipped towards the inside. His rein hand is low so that the horse puts his head down. This teaches the horse how to position his body so that his front legs do not interfere. From there, the rider moves his hand to wither level, in the direction of the spin, with outside leg reinforcement. He stays centred over the horse to aid his balance. Riders will often cluck to a horse to tell him to keep spinning, and say "whoa" to tell him to stop.

BACK-UP

A horse shows his responsiveness and obedience when he performs a back-up. In most patterns, the horse has to back up in a straight line for a distance of at least three metres (ten feet). The proper form is for the horse to transfer all his weight to his hindquarters, rounding his back and lowering his croup as he takes quick steps backwards.

1 APPLY LOWER LEG PRESSURE

To back up the horse, take up a little slack in the reins and squeeze your lower legs against the horse's sides, with the same amount of pressure on each side. Your legs create energy while your hand restricts the horse's forward motion, so that he steps backwards.

Keep your contact on the mouth steady but not severe

Take up the slack in the reins smoothly

The horse willingly keeps his head down as he moves backwards

Keep your seat square in the saddle

The horse quickly performs the back-up without shuffling his legs

2 MAINTAIN MOVEMENT

Once the horse has begun to travel backwards, you can release some of the rein pressure, but you must keep your legs firmly active at the horse's side. When you cease your leg pressure, it is the signal for the horse to stop his backward movement.

AT A GLANCE

BACK-UP
To perform a back-up, the horse first elevates his front end. He then shifts his weight to his hindquarters and begins stepping back with his hind legs. He then follows with his front legs. He should take several steps backwards in a straight line without dragging his feet or drifting off the track.

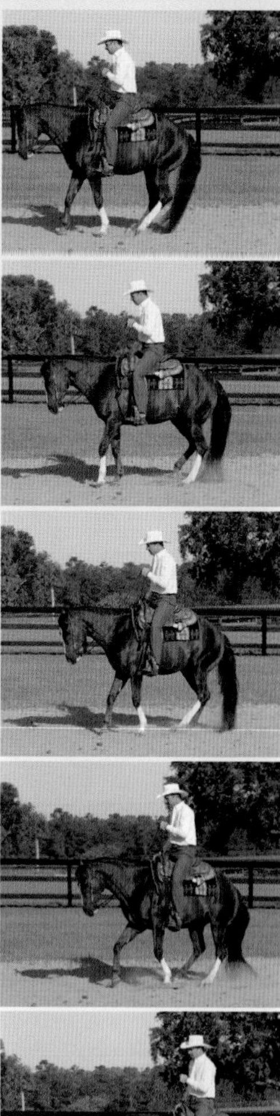

RIDERS' TIPS

- **If the** horse does not back up, release your aids and then try again, this time with more leg.
- **If the** horse begins to drift off the straight line while he is backing up, use the leg on the side to which he is drifting to push him back on to your intended path.
- **Do not** pull the reins or "see-saw" them against the horse's mouth – he will only raise his head and resist the pressure.
- **Give the** lightest cues possible to get the horse to back up. Harsh hands often intimidate a horse, and he may overreact and scurry backwards, which is incorrect and will lose points in a competition.
- **To stop,** release both rein and leg contact and allow the horse to stand quietly.

PIKE
Roeckl

COMPETING

STARTING TO COMPETE

Competing can be taken seriously or treated as fun, but in the long run you will succeed only if both you and the horse enjoy it. Even at Olympic level, equestrian sports have retained a degree of old-fashioned sportsmanship that many others have lost, perhaps because all competitors share the common goal of horse welfare.

THE RIGHT START

The most popular disciplines include dressage, showjumping, eventing, hunter trials, showing, polo, and Western reining. Fixture lists for these, and the myriad others available, can be found through the organizing bodies or in national and local equestrian press. Some are gentle and suitable for all riders, others require more skill or bravery.

Choose a competition that is suitable for both you and the horse. Most well-schooled horses can have a go at a local show, but it is important that neither of you is over-faced. You will both have to contend with an unfamiliar place and lots of other horses milling around. With so much going on, it can be an exciting occasion for the horse and make him more difficult than usual to ride, so you need to be confident that you can cope. If possible, make your first few attempts on a horse that is used to competing and go with someone more experienced.

HUNTER TRIAL
A novice or height-restricted class at a local hunter trial is a good first cross-country competition to try.

LOCAL SHOWS

The easiest place to start is at a small venue with just one arena, usually an ordinary manège or field. Many competitions are held at local equestrian centres or riding clubs and welcome all comers. Having a go at a basic dressage test, clear-round jumping (in which you just try to jump a clear round and are not competing against anyone), or a showing class – ridden or in-hand – is a fun way to test your skills or just do something different.

JOINING A RIDING CLUB

If you compete regularly, joining a local riding club is a good idea. This gives you access to different training facilities and club shows, which should offer good standards in terms of both organization and course quality, reduced entry fees at open shows that they organize, and the chance to compete in teams. They often ask you to help out at shows too, which is not only a good way to support their efforts

WESTERN TRAIL CLASS
Competitions for Western riders include the trail class, which tests your horse's obedience and skill at manoeuvring on the trail.

RIDERS' TIPS

- **The busy** roads that invariably have to be negotiated make hacking to shows a fairly limited opportunity these days. When you can, though, it is a nice way to start the warm-up and relax at the end of the day.
- **Horses will** get used to travelling in trailers and lorries but they need practice and reassurance to start with.
- **Rather than** going out and buying your own lorry or trailer straight away, take a lift to your first few shows with someone who knows the ropes. It is always best to travel with someone else so that you can help each other out and share fuel costs.

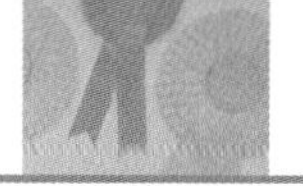

but also a chance to see how competitions are run, watch other people compete, and make new, like-minded friends.

AFFILIATING

Those who compete seriously beyond club level will eventually need to affiliate to the national governing body of the discipline they have chosen. Affiliated competitions are only open to members, offer consistent standards, and allow you to progress to the highest international level. Each country's governing bodies for eventing, showjumping, dressage, driving, endurance, reining, vaulting, and paraquestrian are in turn affiliated to the Fédération Équestre Internationale, based in Switzerland (*see* p.337).

A SMART APPEARANCE
Good turnout is an important element of competitions. It is part of the respect you owe your horse and the volunteers who run shows.

PREPARING FOR COMPETITIONS

However well you have learnt the course or test, you need to have put in enough ridden and mental preparation beforehand to make it all come together on the day. Winning is not important – as long as you know you have tried your best, then the experience will be more enjoyable and leave you feeling positive.

BEING PREPARED

How you perform is the culmination of all the work and training you have put in up to that day – but you need the right gear too, so do not leave any preparation until the last minute.

Be sure of what you have to do. Learn your dressage test thoroughly or make sure you know the jumping course: at starter level, with just a few small, straightforward fences, knowing the route is usually enough, but you will be given a chance to "walk the course" before riding it.

It is also important to learn about the competition, its rules, what the judges are looking for, how to gain points – and how not to throw them away – and how other people have succeeded.

Do as much as you can in advance. Prepare all your clothing and equipment the day before the show. This way, on the morning of the show you are free to concentrate on the horse, which will need to be groomed and perhaps plaited.

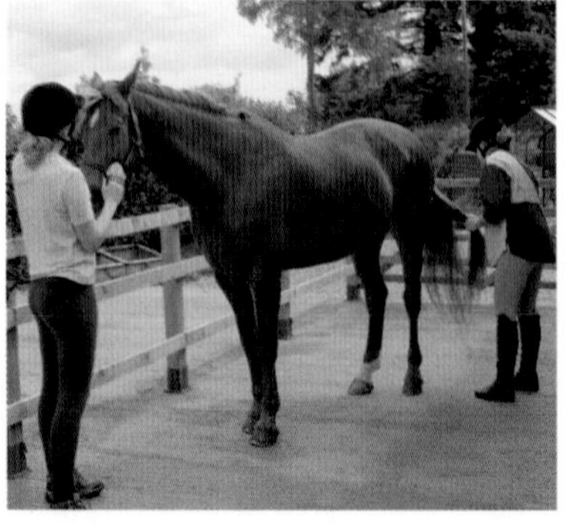

GETTING READY
Before you set out for the show, allow plenty of time to groom the horse and check him over thoroughly. Remember to also check his shoes.

LEARNING THE ROPES
For your first few shows, borrow a horse that knows the ropes and do not expect great results – just go for the experience.

Allow plenty of time to get to the venue and enough time on arrival to collect your number from the secretary, find out which ring you should be in if there is more than one, and walk the course if necessary. You will also need riding-in time, especially if you travelled in a horse box. Late preparation will leave you flustered and

RIDERS' TIPS

- **Take a** book or crossword to while away spare time. At Badminton 2005, Pippa Funnell confessed that as she waited for her turn to show jump, she took her mind off her overnight lead by doing Sudoku.
- **Before your** class, imagine riding the test or course in your mind the way you would ideally like to do it – then take this positive mental image in with you.
- **Identify the** start and finish. In jumping competitions you can be eliminated for either failing to cross them or crossing them more than once.
- **Take a** cooler or sweat-rug to put on the horse when he is standing around. In cold weather a blanket or exercise sheet is useful.

worried and the horse will pick up on that mood. Being calm and organized and knowing the task ahead means that you can go into the competition in a clear, positive frame of mind.

THE RIGHT MINDSET

Top-level success requires skill and determination in huge amounts. To succeed with horses at any level, you need a measure of toughness, but also the sense and training to recognise your limitations, as well as the horse's. As long as what you are attempting is within your capabilities, a positive, calm attitude will help you on the day. Event riders, in particular, have been helped by sports psychologists in this way.

ARRIVING AT THE SHOW

When you arrive at a show, see to the horse's comfort first, then take a few minutes to yourself.

CHECK LIST

THE DAY BEFORE

- **Clean your** tack and check it is all in good repair.
- **Make sure** your own clothes are clean and ironed.
- **Check when** your class starts, or your individual start time if you have been allocated one (you may be asked to phone a day or two beforehand).

ON THE DAY

- **Groom the** horse thoroughly and plait him if necessary. Remember to wipe his eyes and nose.
- **If you** are doing more than one class, make a schedule for warming up before each one.
- **Pack any** food, water, and equipment you and the horse will need. The horse will need separate buckets for drinking and being washed down.

WASHING A HORSE

The best way to keep a horse clean and tidy is by thorough, regular grooming. An occasional bath before clipping or going to a show is fine provided you keep the horse warm and dry him quickly, but it should not be done too often. Horses that live out, in particular, need the natural grease in their skin to protect them from the elements.

1 SOAP THE MANE AND NECK

Start with the neck, wetting the coat thoroughly with a large sponge. Either apply the shampoo directly to the coat or dilute it in a bucket of water. Wash the mane at the same time as the neck, keeping the soap clear of the ears and eyes.

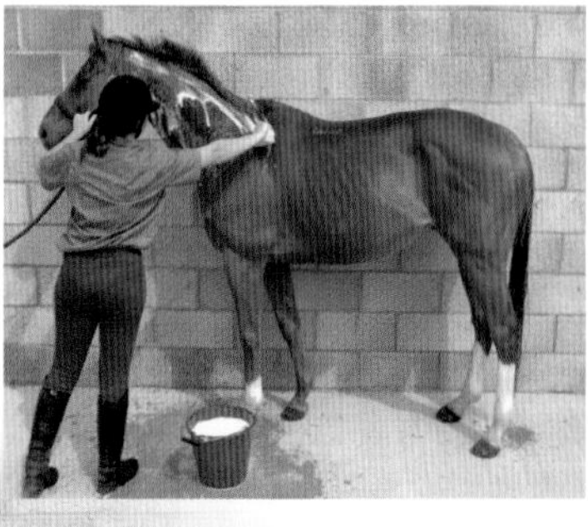

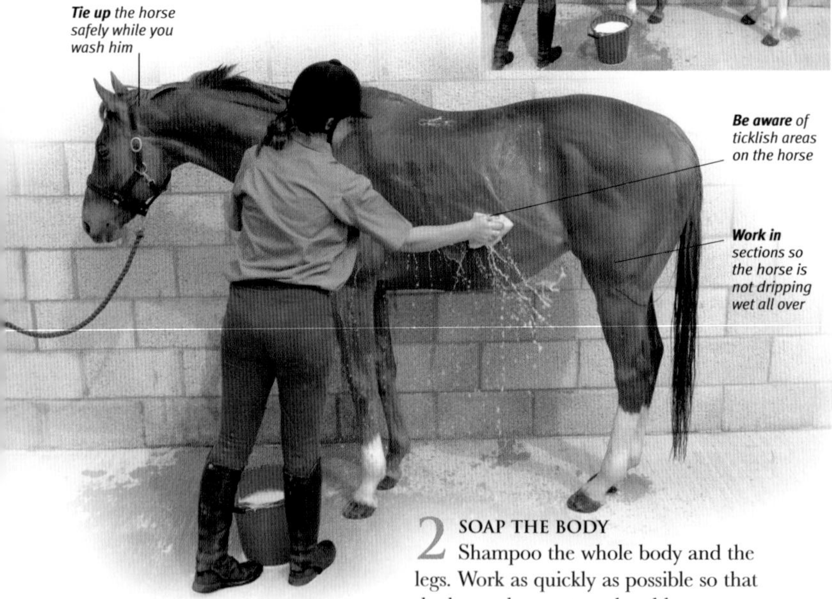

***Tie up** the horse safely while you wash him*

***Be aware** of ticklish areas on the horse*

***Work in** sections so the horse is not dripping wet all over*

2 SOAP THE BODY

Shampoo the whole body and the legs. Work as quickly as possible so that the horse does not catch cold.

TIPS AND TECHNIQUES

WASHING THE TAIL

Step 1 Wet the tail thoroughly and shampoo. A quiet horse might allow you to immerse most of his tail in a bucket but you will need to use a sponge at the top. **Step 2** Rinse the tail well in clean water then squeeze out the water with your hands. **Step 3** Hold the bottom of the dock bone and swing the lower part of the tail to help dry it.

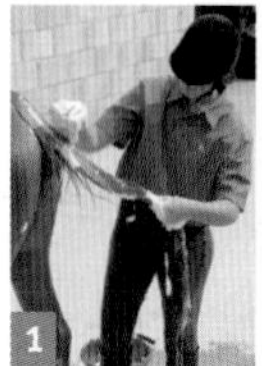

Soap the tail

Rinse in water

Swing to dry

3 WASH THE FACE

Sponge the face with plain water only to avoid getting soap in the eyes, nostrils, and ears. Take care because some horses dislike water dripping down their faces.

Rinse thoroughly *because soap can irritate the skin*

Keep sensitive *areas such as the loins and kidneys warm*

Keep the *bucket at a sensible distance from the horse's legs*

4 RINSE WELL

Using clean water and a sponge, rinse the horse thoroughly, paying attention to fiddly areas such as under the belly.

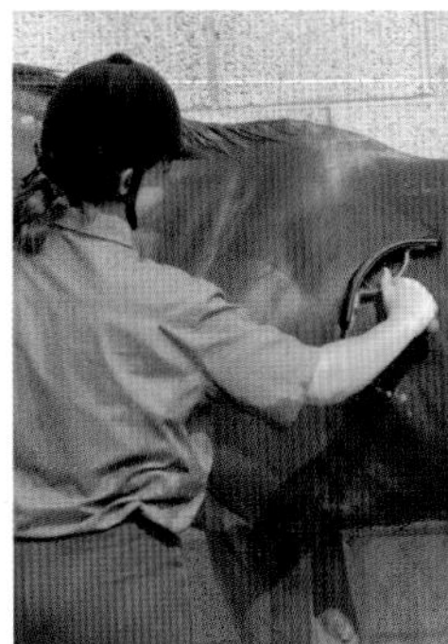

5 USE SWEAT SCRAPER

Remove excess water from the neck and body with a sweat scraper. Then put a wicking cooler or fleece rug on the horse.

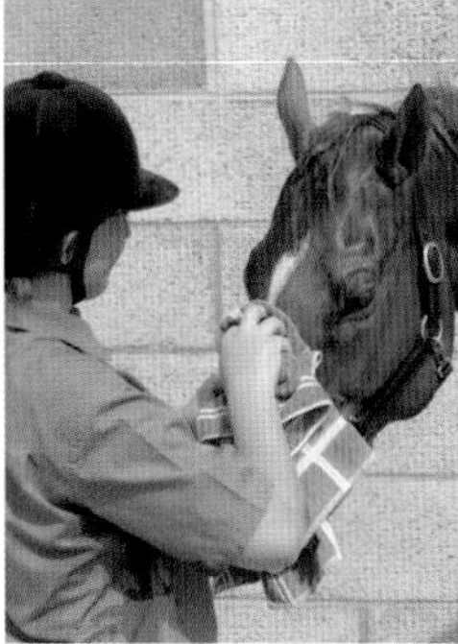

6 TOWEL-DRY FACE

Dry the face gently with a towel in the direction of the hair. Towel-dry the mane. Do not brush a wet mane.

7 TOWEL-DRY HEELS

Dry the heels carefully with a towel to prevent any aggravation of skin conditions such as cracked heels or mud fever.

PLAITING

A neatly plaited mane and tail put the finishing touch to a good turnout for competing. Plaiting at least the mane is considered polite for dressage, and may be the norm in some showing classes, but it is not always correct to plait. Mountain and moorland pony breeds, for example, should be shown with their manes and tails loose.

PLAITED MANE
Cotton looks best but rubber bands are useful if you need to remove plaits quickly.

PLAITING A MANE

The main reasons for plaiting are to improve turnout and to help train the mane to fall on one side of the horse's neck. There is no set number of plaits, but you should have an odd number along the crest plus one for the forelock. The mane should be evenly "pulled" to a reasonable length. Damp the mane before plaiting but do not wash it, as this will make it slippery to handle.

1 DIVIDE INTO THREE Divide the mane into the desired number of equal-sized sections. Starting behind the ears, split each section of mane into three strands.

2 PLAIT THE SECTION Plait the section of mane. The plait should be neat and tight enough to stay in place, but not so tight that the hairs are pulled at the roots.

PLAITING A TAIL

Thicker tails look superb when plaited, but it only works if the hairs at each side of the dock are long enough. Many people who compete regularly prefer to keep their horses' tails neatly pulled instead of plaiting them each time. This is useful for horses whose tails tend to be thin and do not hold a plait, but some horses hate having their tails pulled, so it is not always advisable. It is also difficult to do well, so it is worth asking an expert to tidy up your first few attempts.

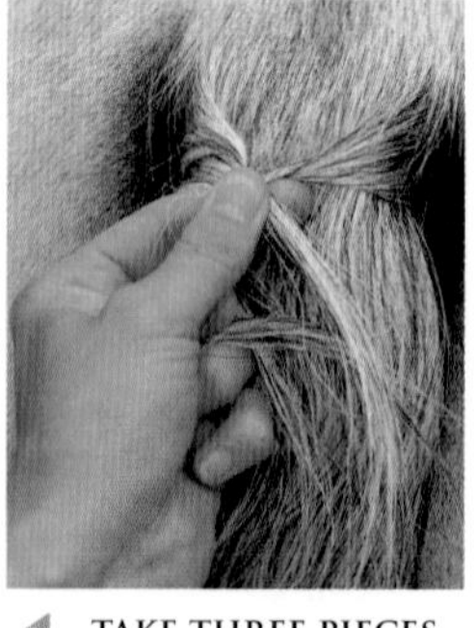

1 TAKE THREE PIECES Damp the top half of the tail with a water brush or sponge. Take three small bunches of hair from as near to the top as possible, one from one side and two from the other.

2 START PLAITING Start plaiting, taking in successive small bunches of hair from the sides. Keep each side as even as possible and make the plait tight enough to stay in without pulling the hairs.

TIPS AND TECHNIQUES

MAKING QUARTER MARKS

These add a glamorous finishing touch, especially for showing classes, and can enhance the horse's shape. The simplest design is a chevron or square design that can be done with a dampened brush, working alternately against and with the direction of hair. Some riders and grooms have a bit of fun with them – for example, Scottish event rider Ian Stark has often presented his horses with thistle-pattern quarter marks.

Square-design quarter marks

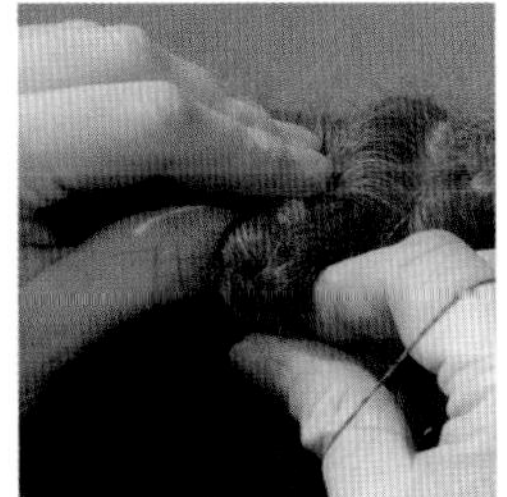

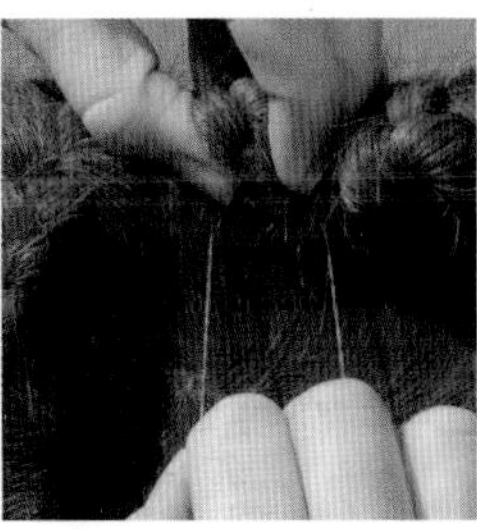

3 SECURE THE PLAIT Secure the end of the plait tightly with a rubber band. (If using a needle and cotton, include the cotton in the plait and wrap it round the end.)

4 ROLL THE PLAIT When you have plaited each section, roll up each plait. Double the plait under itself, and then again, until it is rolled close to the crest.

5 FINISH THE PLAIT To secure the plait, wind the band around it several times. (If using cotton, push the needle through from underneath and stitch through.)

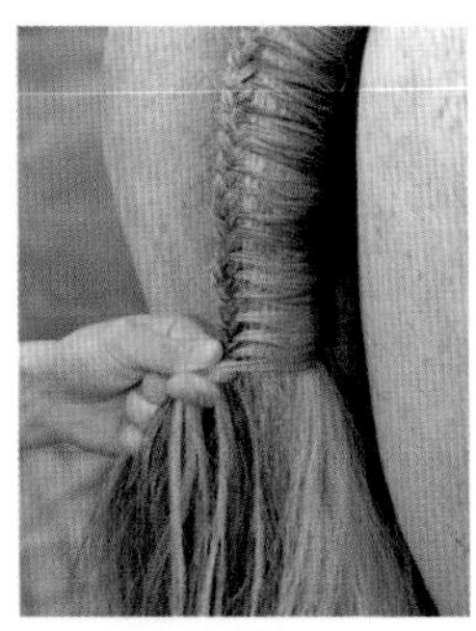

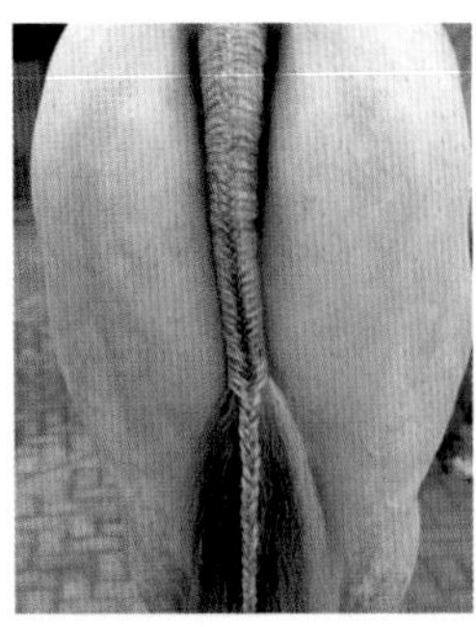

3 PLAIT DOWN Work to about three-quarters of the way down the dock bone, taking in more hairs as you go. Then finish plaiting any hairs left in your hands, without bringing in new ones.

4 FIX A LOOP Secure the end with thread or an elastic band that matches the colour of the tail. Loop the plait under itself and secure it firmly with cotton or a rubber band.

5 FINISHED PLAIT Always take plaits out at the end of the day. They can become uncomfortable for the horse, who will probably scratch his mane or tail and cause a lot of hair to fall out.

WESTERN GROOMING

The Western horse's appearance reflects his rider's level of horsemanship, and grooming chores are taken very seriously. For the competitor, a well-presented horse shows not only a commitment to the sport, but also tells the judge that he or she wants to win. Riders ensure their horses stand out by making their coats incredibly shiny and paying attention to minute detail.

WESTERN MANES

When competing in Western pleasure, trail, horsemanship, and other rail classes (*see* p.292) a horse has his mane kept short and he can wear it on either the left or the right side. The mane is usually pulled to about 10 cm (4 in) in length and banded. For the working divisions, such as reining, working cow horse, and speed events, horses are shown with unpulled manes, with some horses sporting flowing manes up to 60 cm (24 in) in length.

BURNISHED COATS

The coat of the Western show horse should always carry a flawless sheen. To achieve this, horses are heavily rugged up during the winter to prevent them from growing winter coats, and many Western show barns regulate indoor lighting for the same reason. Other show horses are clipped early in the season so that their coats grow out without becoming dull, and are sprayed with sheen products to bring out highlights.

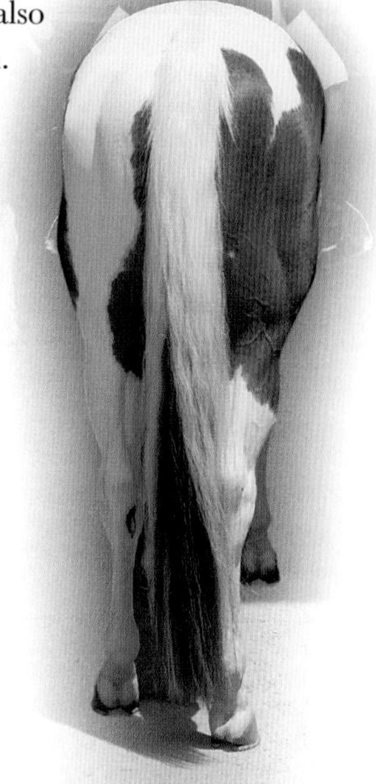

GROOMING WESTERN TAILS
Western horses' tails are blunt-cut at the bottom and end at the fetlocks. Many owners use tube-shaped tail bags – the tail is washed, conditioned, dried, then braided and put in the bag to keep it neat and smooth.

BANDING THE MANE

During shows, the mane can be banded with small elastic bands to give the horse a more refined profile. The mane needs to be clean, and you will need banding mousse, a comb, hair clips to keep non-working parts of the mane out of the way, and bands to match the horse's colouring. You should pull the mane before you band it, so that it is of even length all the way along.

1 DIVIDE THE MANE Use a mane comb to section off a lock of hair about 2.5 cm (1 in) thick. Comb the hair through.

2 SPRAY THE MANE Dampen the section of mane with water and apply banding mousse to make it easy to manipulate.

CLIPPING AND TRIMMING

The coat of a Western show horse is always removed, or clipped, to some extent. Clipping defines the horse's outline, and can accentuate his good points and disguise any flaws. The ears are often shaved with an electric clipper so that there is no hair visible inside, and whiskers and chin hairs tend to be completely removed. The throat and muzzle are also clipped close to the skin. Coronet bands, white socks, and fetlocks are trimmed with precision. It is essential that show horses are clipped without leaving behind any marks, razor burns, bald spots, or jagged patches.

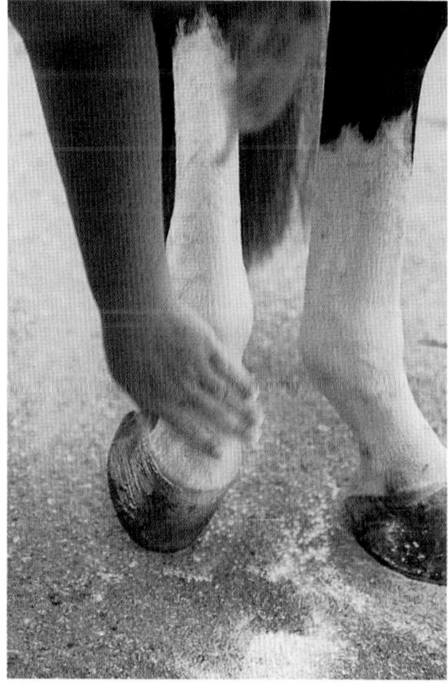

MAKING THE MOST OF COLOUR
Chalk powder can be dusted on the horse's socks just before a show to give a dazzling white appearance. Many riders also bathe their horses using colour-enhancing shampoos, and some apply baby oil to the face to enhance dark muzzles.

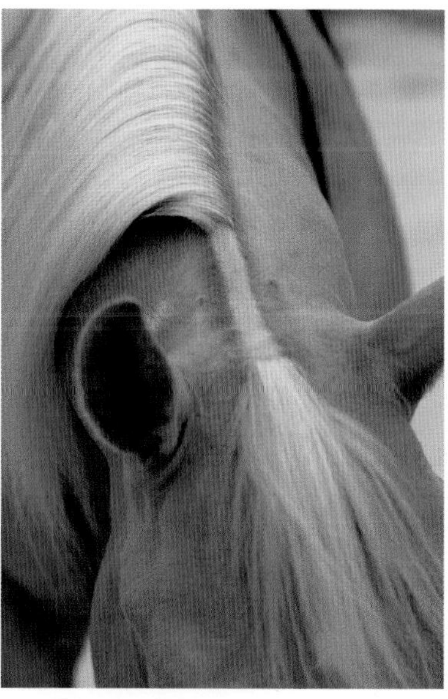

CREATING A BRIDLE PATH
A bridle path is created by shaving a section of mane, just behind the ears, down to the scalp. It should be clipped so that the shaved area is no longer than the horse's ear-length. This provides a polished look against finely clipped ears and face, and allows the bridle to lie flat.

3 START TO BAND
Begin winding the elastic band around the lock of hair. Pull the hair down as you twist the band.

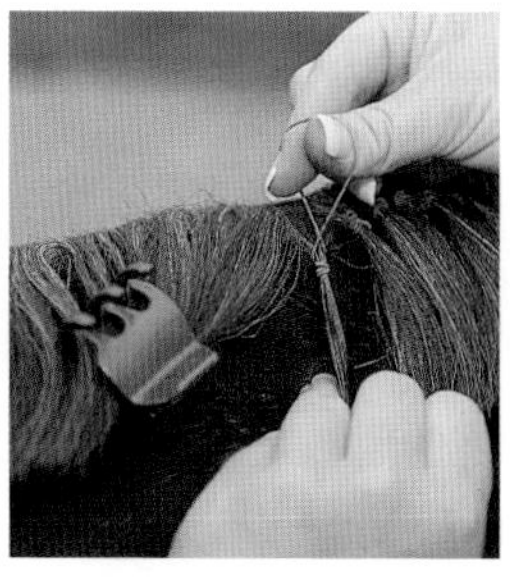

4 TIE THE BANDS
Wind the band until it is tight. Then hold the hair down and push the band up to the roots.

5 FINISH OFF
Continue down the neck until you reach the withers. It is not unusual to have 35 to 40 bands.

TRAVELLING TO A SHOW

Most horses quickly become accustomed to loading and travelling in specially designed trailers and lorries, but a bad experience will unnerve them so make your first journey with someone who is used to doing it. The vehicle must be safe and well maintained, with plenty of head-room for safety and so that the horse does not feel cramped.

PREPARING A HORSE

The most important area to protect is the horse's legs. Use either long, thick travel boots or bandages with thick padding and over-reach boots. The top of the tail also needs protection in case the horse rubs it. Take a light, wicking rug such as a cooler or fleece and use a poll-guard if necessary.

GEAR FOR TRAVELLING

Protect the horse's legs and tail, use a leather headcollar, and take a sweat sheet or fleece rug.

***A leather** headcollar should be used for travelling*

***A light** rug may be needed*

***A tail** guard or bandage stops the horse from rubbing hair from the top of his tail*

***Hind travel** boots offer protection from above the hock to below the coronet*

***Front travel** boots offer protection from above the knee to the heel*

TIPS AND TECHNIQUES

PUTTING ON A TAIL BANDAGE

A crepe bandage helps protect the top of the tail and is less expensive than a tail guard. Be careful with the tension – it must be tight enough to stay on but not cause pain. **Step 1** Start the bandage at an angle, leaving a few centimetres sticking out at the top. Hold the tail up and make the first turn at the base of the tail. **Step 2** Tuck the end under the next turn. **Step 3** Bandage to the end of the tail bone. **Step 4** Tie the tapes no tighter than the bandage itself. Bend the tail into a comfortable position.

1 **Start at the base of the tail**

2 **Tuck the end under**

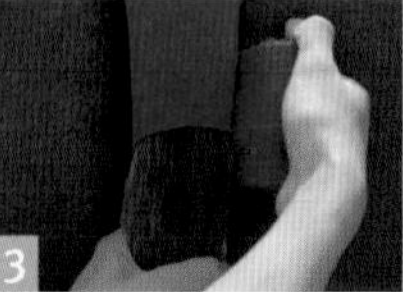

3 **Bandage down the tail bone**

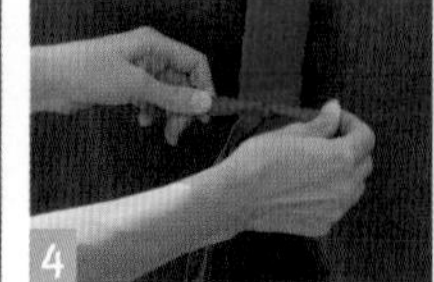

4 **Tie the tapes in a bow**

LOADING A HORSE

Learn to load a horse positively and confidently. Trying to hurry or cut corners can lead to an accident so take your time and do all the preparation carefully. Load all your equipment before loading the horse so that he does not have to stand in the vehicle any longer than necessary. If he is to travel with a haynet, tie this up securely in advance.

1 GO STRAIGHT Approach the ramp in a straight line. Parking the vehicle in a gateway or between other vehicles can be helpful.

2 UP THE RAMP Walk briskly up the centre of the ramp. Do not let the horse hesitate, either before he steps on to it or as he walks up.

3 SECURE THE HORSE Tie up the horse to breakable string attached to the metal ring, using a quick-release knot (*see* p.87). Secure the partition.

UNLOADING SAFELY

Park somewhere safe and as level as possible, where the ramp will be steady and there is plenty of space to unload the horse. Take it slowly because rushing can lead to accidents. Most vehicles have rings on the outside for tying up the horse – as ever, use breakable string between ring and lead rope – and a haynet can help take his mind off the new environment.

1 UNTIE THE HORSE Undo and secure any partitions and gates so that they will not swing or catch the horse. Untie him and turn him to face out.

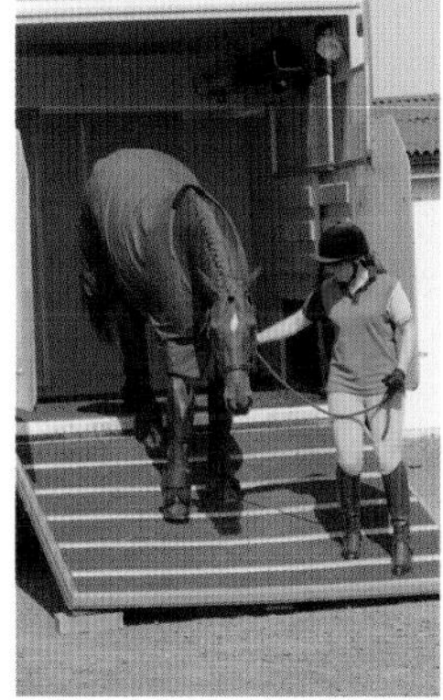

2 GO SLOWLY Lead him slowly down the ramp, letting him stretch his neck to look but not allowing him to rush forwards or jump off.

3 TAKE CARE Walk him forwards away from the ramp before turning him round to tie up at the side rings. Look out for other horses.

ENGLISH COMPETING

Because the English or Continental style of riding can be easily adapted for flatwork or jumping, slow or fast work, it can be used for a range of competitive disciplines from dressage to polo. Dressage, show jumping, and eventing are currently included in the Olympic Games and the style is also used by paraquestrian riders, who have their own, highly successful Olympics.

DRESSAGE

Essentially a demonstration of correct training, dressage tests use set movements and sequences that reflect the horse's education. Watching the experts can be truly inspiring – identifying the moves in an advanced test is puzzling at first, but you will soon begin to understand.

EXTRA INFORMATION

FULL-SIZE DRESSAGE ARENA

The instruction sheet for each dressage test specifies the size of arena that is used. If it is the full-size 60 x 20 m arena (shown below) and you only have a small area in which to practise, make sure you know where the extra markers are placed.

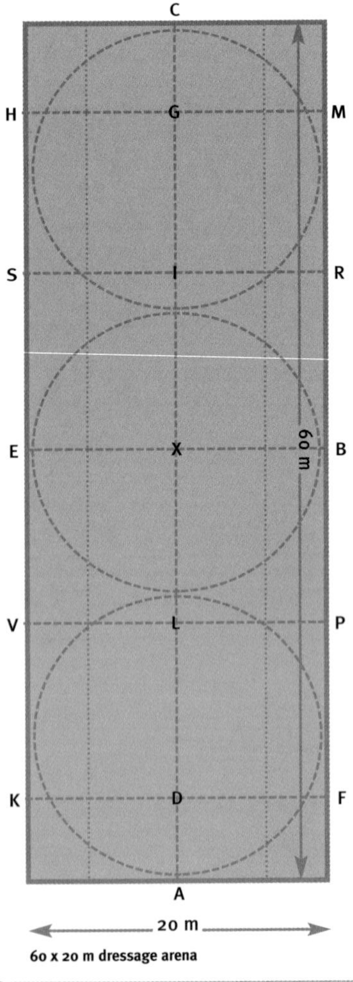

60 x 20 m dressage arena

A DRESSAGE TEST

As a novice rider, or an experienced rider on a young horse, you will start with basic tests. These are designed to show that the horse can perform tasks such as circles and transitions between halt, walk, trot, and canter, at specific points of the arena, in an obedient, forward-going yet submissive manner. At this stage, showing impulsion and a willingness to accept the bridle is more important than being truly on the bit. The judge is looking for a willing, supple, balanced, and submissive horse – collection (*see* pp.158–159) is not required at this stage and will follow naturally when all the pieces fall into place.

HOW TO PREPARE FOR A TEST

Find out whether you are allowed to have someone read out the test as you ride it. It is still sensible to learn it though – you might find you cannot hear your reader

TACK AND TURNOUT

Check the rules regarding tack – they are very specific. In general, anything not permitted in the arena is not allowed in the warm-up area either – with the exception of boots and bandages.

PRACTISING AT HOME
Working progressively through the official tests is a good way to pace your training at home and gives you a goal to aim for.

above other noise. Drawing the test on a diagram of an arena with all the markers is a good way to learn it.

Check that you and the horse can do, or at least make a reasonable attempt at, everything that is required in the test. Stick to tests that contain tasks within your current limitations – your training will dictate when it is time for you to try a more demanding one.

Start from the lowest level and work your way up, because the tests are specially written to complement the horse's training and natural physical development.

Make sure you understand each instruction. For example, for "free walk on a long rein" you must be seen clearly to offer the horse enough rein to stretch through his back and his neck without hurrying the pace. A relaxed horse working through from his quarters will do this naturally, but a tense horse is likely to jog.

Practise riding a test in sections – do not ride the whole thing more than once or twice, otherwise the horse will learn it too and will start to anticipate. Some tests are symmetrical and therefore easier to learn, but be warned – some are not!

WHAT TO EXPECT

HOW A TEST IS MARKED
A test is broken down into sections which should flow seamlessly together when you ride them but are marked separately. Each is worth 10 marks but note the breakdown. Example from FEI CCI* (*see* p.287) Test (A): "V: turn right. L: transition to walk for three to five steps, proceed in working trot. P: turn left" is one set of movements worth 10 marks together, whereas "A: working canter left" is worth10 marks on its own. Judges can only award marks for movements you have done – if you miss a transition or jog through the entire free walk section, they have to give you zero. Collective marks are awarded at the end for paces, impulsion, submission, and riding. Then the total is converted into a percentage.

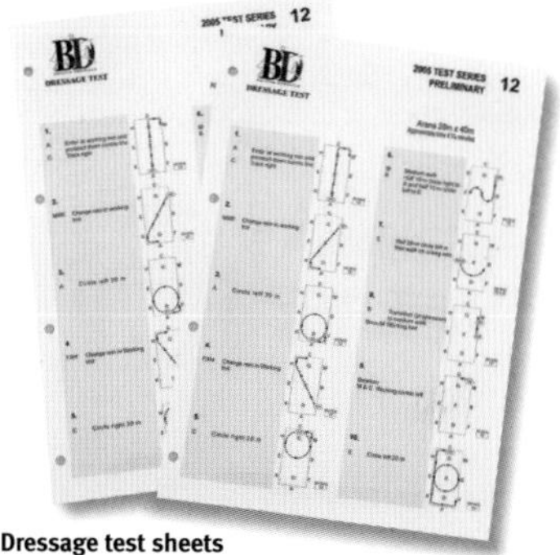

Dressage test sheets

WARMING UP

On arrival, find out whether your class is running to time so that you can organize your warm-up accordingly. The amount of warm-up you need depends on the individual horse and whether you hacked or drove to the show. He needs enough warm-up to loosen and supple his muscles, relax his mind, and become attentive and obedient to your aids without getting bored or tired.

Do not run through the test itself. Concentrate on getting the horse going forwards then use transitions to make sure he is listening. You will not have space to perform lateral movements in a busy warm-up area.

Be considerate towards other riders who are using the warm-up area. Do not ride too close to other horses, always pass left-to-left, and do not stop suddenly or change the rein in a way that interferes with another horse.

Keep an eye on the time, let the collecting ring stewards know you are there, and be ready to go into the arena when they call you. If the horse was wearing boots for the warm-up, remove them before you go in. Make sure your number is clearly visible.

A GOOD IMPRESSION
Use a plain white, black, or brown saddle cloth or thin numnah. Plaiting is not mandatory at the lower levels, but it is a courtesy to the judge.

WHAT TO EXPECT

THE JUDGES
For most tests, there is one judge at C, but at high levels there are usually three, positioned so that every aspect of your test is seen by at least one of them. Judges are skilled riders and trainers themselves, and to officiate at affiliated competitions their judging skills are assessed so that standards are consistent.

Riding in front of the judge

RIDING A TEST

When you enter the arena, it is polite to call out your number to the judge, and you should be given 60 seconds before the starting bell sounds. (If the judge is sitting in a car rather than an official "box", the bell will probably be the car horn.) You are not allowed into the marked part of the arena before the bell, so use this minute as an extension of the warm-up. Keep the horse moving around the edge and take the opportunity to trot past any unfamiliar distractions such as pot plants or spectators.

When the bell sounds, you must start your test straight away. The test officially begins from the moment you enter the arena at A and finishes after you have saluted the judge. If someone is reading it aloud for you, which is often permitted at lower levels and smaller shows, they can say only what is on the test sheet; extra comments would be counted as outside assistance and you could be eliminated.

At preliminary level, concentrate on getting the horse going forwards well rather than worrying about whether he is on the bit. This level is designed to reflect early stages of the horse's training, so the judge should be looking for a good way of going that shows the horse is obedient and understands what he is being asked to do.

At the end of your test, make a nice, clear salute and remember to take the reins in one hand as you do it. The usual way is to drop your right arm by your side and bow your head.

GAINING MARKS

If you do not reach the right marker or ride the correct size of circle, you are not performing the movement correctly, so you will lose marks.

RIDERS' TIPS

- **The judge** wants to see that the horse goes correctly and that you can do what the test asks – no more and no less.
- **Ride as** accurately as you can – for example, "canter at C" means strike off when the horse's shoulders are level with the C marker. You can lose marks through inaccurate riding.
- **Use all** the space and time at your disposal. There is no need to hurry.
- **Set up** each movement and transition well, using half-halts to rebalance where necessary.
- **If you** have trouble riding a straight line, subtle use of shoulder-fore can help correct the problem.
- **Volunteering to** write for judges is a useful way to find out what they are looking for.

SHOW JUMPING

Show jumping takes place in an arena using fences made of coloured or rustic poles that often have fillers and decorations, such as coloured blocks and pot plants. A good schooling and dressage foundation is important for this discipline because you need to be able to ride the horse in balance, with plenty of impulsion, in order to safely negotiate a course of jumps.

SHOW JUMPING COURSES

Courses are carefully designed and measured. The simplest keep the striding as well as the fences straightforward, and involve nothing more complicated than a basic combination, or double. Plenty of space will be allowed for turns and the approach to each fence, and the maximum fence size will be stated in the show schedule, so you can choose the most appropriate class. Clear-round classes are a good place to start as they give you experience of jumping in a show situation without any pressure. You get a rosette for a clear round, but are not competing against anyone else.

In a competition, a "jump-off" may be needed to determine the winner and other placings. This can be run separately, when everyone jumps their first round and those who qualify come back for a second round, or concurrently, when those who go clear the first time proceed straight to the jump-off course without a break.

TERMINOLOGY

- **Bounce** – two elements of a combination sited so that the horse lands from the first one and immediately takes off for the next without a stride in between.
- **Combination** – obstacle with two or three elements. A double (two elements) is usually separated by one or two strides; a treble (three elements) might have one or two strides between the first and second fences and two or three strides between the second and third.
- **Elimination** – disqualification when you break a rule in or out of the arena, incur three refusals, fall off, or the horse falls.
- **Faults** – penalties incurred for knocking down or failing to jump a fence.
- **Jump-off** – when several competitors have an equal score after the first round and jump again over a shorter, higher course, often against the clock.
- **Practice fence** – the jump provided in the warm-up area.
- **Refusal** – when the horse is presented at a fence but hesitates too long, steps back, crosses his tracks, or does not jump.
- **Related distance** – when fences are sufficiently close together that you need to jump the first one in a way that sets you up for the next.
- **Retirement** – when you decide voluntarily to stop your round.
- **Run-out** – when the horse ducks past a fence without jumping it.
- **Stride** – the average length of a horse's canter stride.

FOLLOWING THE COURSE
You can choose your route between fences but you must jump them in the right order.

A TYPICAL NOVICE COURSE

Designed to be encouraging for newcomers, a novice course will have a straightforward route with easy turns and it will probably include one or two combinations.

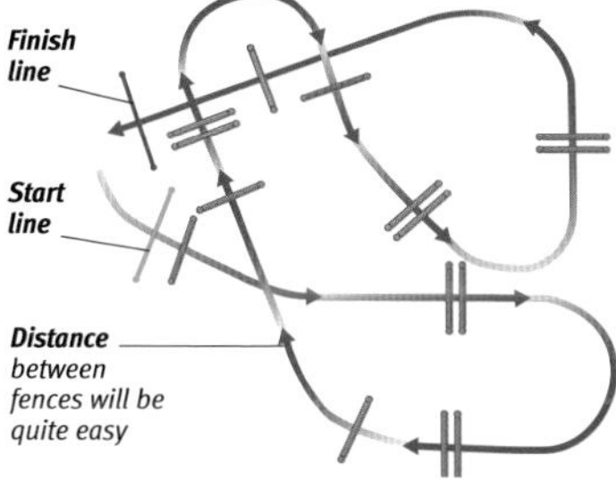

A TYPICAL ELEMENTARY COURSE

Needing more skill and experience from both horse and rider, an elementary course has a more complex route, the turns may be tighter, and you should expect several related distances.

WHAT TO EXPECT

UPRIGHT

You need lots of impulsion but relatively little speed to jump this. It is hard to judge as there is no sloping outline or ground line.

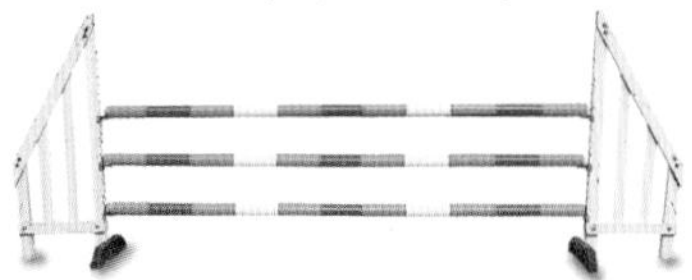

PARALLEL BAR

A fence requiring plenty of forward-going impulsion because the horse needs to jump high and wide.

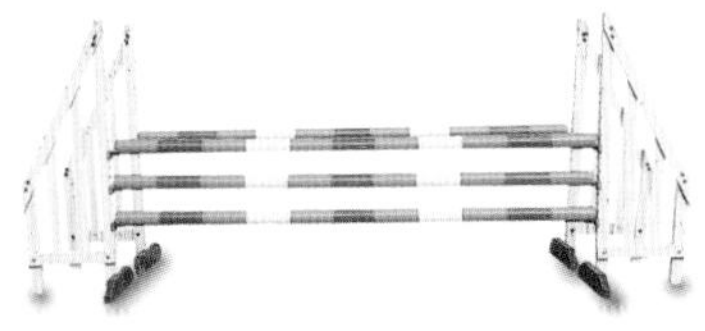

WALL

Made of plastic blocks, not real bricks. Jump as for an upright fence. Its solid appearance makes it easier to judge than upright poles. Often used in puissance competitions.

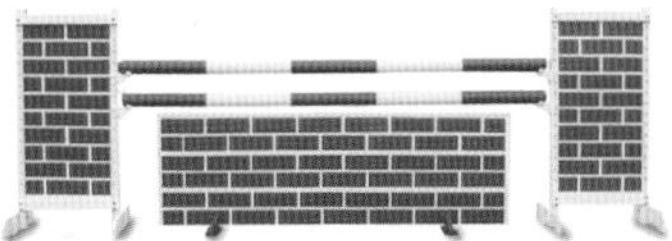

SPREAD

Requires more speed and a longer outline than an upright so the horse can stretch over its width. An inviting slope from the nearest, lowest pole to the highest one makes it easier for the horse to judge.

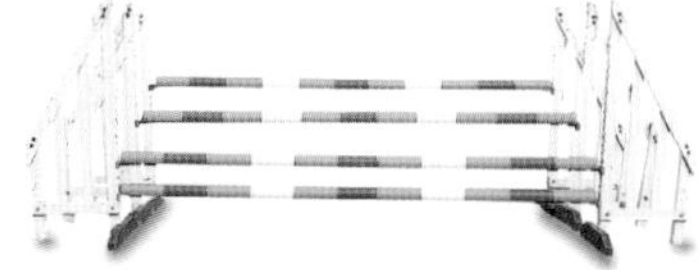

ASCENDING OXER

An inviting fence for the horse, because its outline reflects the shape his back makes as he jumps, but he can easily knock the back pole if he is not concentrating.

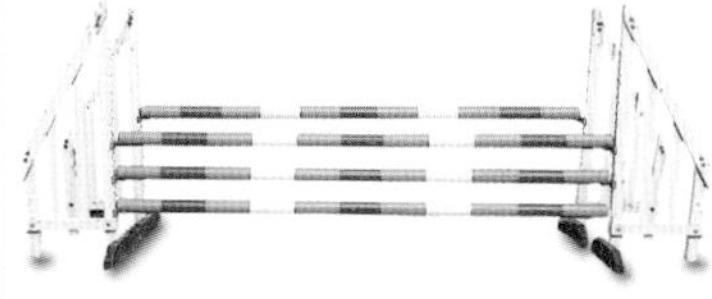

WALKING THE COURSE

Find out if there is a designated time to walk the course before the class starts and whether there will be a separate opportunity to walk the jump-off course. Learn the route and decide how to ride each fence – for example, a spread requires some speed but if it is followed by an upright, you have to quickly balance the horse back on to his hocks after landing. Count the number of strides in combinations and related distances. Practise at home and get to know how much space your horse needs and how many of your strides relate to one of his.

MEASURING STRIDES
Two of your strides from the base of the fence will be roughly where you land, then four of your strides equal one canter stride.

WARMING UP

The purpose of warming up is to get the horse listening and ready to do his best. Let the collecting ring steward know you are there and find out whether your class is running to time so that you do not end up rushing or going off the boil. The steward will call you before your turn but it is up to you to keep an eye on the time.

Start with some flatwork such as trot and canter circles and transitions to help you and the horse concentrate, then introduce some lengthening and shortening of the canter. There are usually only one or two practice fences and it is helpful to have a friend there to put them up for you. They will be flagged to show which direction you are allowed to jump them in (red on your right, white on your left) and you must always be considerate towards other riders.

Experience will dictate how much warm-up your horse needs: in general, start with a small cross-pole to get him focused and picking up his front legs, then make the fence into an upright and pop over that a few times. As you move up the levels, you will need to build other fences, but accuracy and control are more useful than height. Finally, build it up to the maximum height for your class and finish with one good jump over that.

JUMPING A ROUND

You have a few moments to ride round the arena before the starting bell. Keep the horse moving briskly in trot or canter so he does not have a chance to lose concentration. If he spooks at anything, try to ride past it again but do not make an issue of it as this is not the place to start an argument. You are not allowed to give him a close look at any fence, but watch the professionals and

RIDERS' TIPS

- **Look out** for distractions such as the judges' box or the entrance to the collecting ring being sited near a fence. Most distractions will be more in your mind than the horse's, but horses do sometimes gravitate towards the collecting ring so ride positively past this part of the arena.
- **Ground conditions** are another consideration and there are special studs you can put in the horse's shoes for extra grip (*see* p.196). The ideal ground is firm yet springy and kind on the horse's legs while giving him some grip; however it could easily be wet and muddy or dry and slippery.
- **At outdoor** shows the ground might not be level, so look out for inclines where you need to hold or push on more.

you might see them canter quite closely round an obstacle – as long as you keep moving and only go round once, you should not be in breach of any rules.

The show jumping phase of eventing (*see* p.287) differs from pure show jumping in that four penalties are given for a first refusal and elimination for a second. If you knock a fence down, do not worry – even if it puts the horse off his stride, rebalance as quickly as you can and focus on the next fence. Nor should you worry about the spectators; you might feel as if all eyes are on you, but once you learn to ignore distractions, the horse will do the same. Ride according to the conditions: for example, if the ground is slippery, keep the balance and impulsion and allow plenty of time for turns.

FAULTS AND PENALTIES

SCORE	PENALTIES
Knocking down a pole	4 faults
1st refusal at fence	3 faults
2nd refusal at fence	3 faults
3rd refusal at fence	Elimination
Run-out	3 faults
Fall of horse or rider	Elimination
Starting before bell	Elimination
Crossing the start line more than once	Elimination
Jumping the wrong fence	Elimination
Exceeding the time	Progressive time faults

SAVE THE BEST
Use the warm-up to get the horse concentrating – save his best jumping for the arena.

CROSS-COUNTRY

It might be every eventer's dream to ride at Badminton, but for those with more modest aspirations there are plenty of other competitions, from local hunter trials to affiliated one-day and three-day events. Cross-country can be thrilling both to ride and to watch, but it can also be dangerous so must be tackled with skill and sense.

RIDING ACROSS COUNTRY

Cross-country is not for beginners and the potential dangers of jumping mixed fences should not be underestimated, but the fun of watching it gives many riders the motivation to improve enough to have a go. With fences based around natural features of the countryside, such as hedges, ditches, water, and timber, courses are often beautifully designed to blend in with their farmland or parkland settings as well as to challenge competitors, making an enjoyable day out for riders and spectators alike.

Before you compete, you must gain experience of this type of riding as it presents a completely different set of problems to anything arena-based. Get used to fast hacking over all kinds of terrain, practise jumping in a field rather than a manège and take cross-country schooling lessons. Many permanent courses hire out their facilities and making use of them will also show you how fit both you and the horse need to be.

BETWEEN THE FLAGS

Make sure the red flag is on your right and the white on your left. You will be eliminated for jumping a fence in the wrong direction.

***The red** flag indicates the right-hand side of the fence and you must jump inside it*

STARTING SMALL

When you are ready, try a small novice class at a hunter trial. Unlike eventing, which also includes dressage and show jumping, hunter trials involve only cross-country, but the course may include a gate that has to be opened and shut.

Stick to novice or height-restricted classes to begin with. These courses will be quite straightforward, but fences can have width as well as height, they can be sited on slopes, and their solidity makes them look quite daunting. Do not put yourself under pressure. You must maintain enough impulsion to jump safely, but if it is your first competition and you feel happier trotting the downhill stretches, do so.

In open classes or eventing, the length and complexity of the tracks require a high level of skill and a solid foundation in schooling and jumping techniques. Do these only if you and the horse are both sufficiently experienced and confident.

WHAT TO EXPECT

PHEASANT FEEDER

An inviting shape that needs plenty of impulsion to clear the spread. Can be taken at a good pace but keep the horse together, especially if the fence is sited on a slope.

ZIG-ZAG

If the fence is flagged at either end, you can choose whether to jump directly through the V or over a straight section, which might take a few seconds longer.

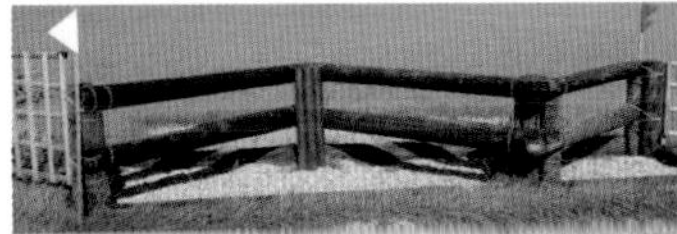

WALL

Solid and unforgiving, but usually a straightforward jump though it may be followed by a sunken road. Unlike the show jumping version, in cross-country it will probably be a real stone wall.

TRAKEHNER

A log suspended over a ditch or hollow. Try to ignore the gap underneath; come in with plenty of impulsion but not too fast, so the horse has time to assess the fence but stays focused on jumping.

HEDGE

The horse needs to clear the top of this so ride it with that intention in mind. Do not confuse it with a bullfinch, which allows the horse's legs to brush through the top.

WALKING THE COURSE

The same basic rules apply at every level. Allow plenty of time and try to walk the course more than once. Assess the ground conditions and the obstacles, and plan your approach to each jump.

Some conditions will change according to the weather and time – for example, patches of shade or sunlight will move, and in wet weather the horses that go before you will churn up the take-offs and landings. Learn the whole route and take note of hills, turns, and open or enclosed spaces. Most courses involve a water jump and the ground around the exit can become slippery as the day goes on.

As the courses become more difficult, there will be a mixture of inviting and more difficult fences; walk them with someone who knows the traps to look out for. A big spread might look daunting but in fact be an inviting, straightforward leap designed to help horses get into a forward rhythm, whereas a smaller fence might be sited awkwardly and need more thought. If a fence has an alternative, learn both routes in case you have to change plan. It can also be helpful to look back from each fence to the previous one you might spot a better line than the one you walked.

Keep the course map with you as you walk round to make sure you have not made the surprisingly common mistake of missing out a fence. Learn the route in your head, with a preferred plan and a contingency plan for each fence. Before you start your round, run through the course in your mind and go in with a positive mental image.

PLANNING YOUR APPROACH
Work out your approach carefully. Fences are often sited on or near a turn or a tree that you have to decide on your own route round.

PREPARING THE HORSE
Cross-country horses need to be warmed up to get their muscles and windpipe working well. If they are very fit it takes the edge off so they are not too fizzy when you start jumping.

WARMING UP

At a one-day event you will have show jumped before you go across country, so all you need to do is give the horse a canter to open his windpipe (known as a "pipe-opener") and jump a couple of small fences to sharpen his mind. At a hunter trial, warm up as for show jumping but include a decent canter if possible. Use transitions and variations within the canter, as despite the scope to go fast between fences you still need steering and collection.

A thorough warm-up before cross-country is important, not just for the horse's muscles and ligaments but also because very fit horses can be prone to a condition known as "tying-up". This occurs when glycogen accumulated in the muscles is used up too quickly, creating a surge of lactic acid which causes the muscle fibres to swell and degenerate. The horse becomes stiff, often almost rigid in its back and quarters, and needs immediate veterinary treatment.

CHECK LIST

RIDER CLOTHING

Body protectors are mandatory and must meet any standard specified in the schedule or rules, usually the highest available. The same applies to hats and the fitting of both must be correct. Wear long boots and non-slip gloves.

HORSE CLOTHING

Use strong, non-slip reins such as leather with rubber grips or webbing with leather bands, and an overgirth if you have one. Leg protection is essential: use brushing or tendon boots with over-reach boots, or specialized boots with added shock absorption. Whichever you use, make sure they fit when the horse is moving and will not twist, slip, or rub.

EQUIPMENT FOR THE DAY

Essentials include water for drinking and for sponging down the hot horse; sponges and sweat scraper; cooler rug; studs for the horse's shoes; hoofpick; first-aid kit; filled haynets; refreshment for yourself, as you can make mistakes if a tired or dehydrated.

BEFORE YOU SET OFF

Warm up the horse and check him carefully for physical problems. Check all your tack before you mount and again just before you go to the start. Make sure your hat and body protector are correctly adjusted and fastened. Take plaits out of the horse's mane in case clothing catches on them.

Checking the girth

YOUR ROUND

All your preparation has been done: now it is all about focus and fitness. You do not have to stand in the start box or at the line – it is often better to walk around until the starter counts you down from about ten seconds to go.

Set off at a positive but unhurried pace and, with your original plan in mind, be prepared to think quickly and change it if necessary. Reasons to do this could include diverting to an alternative route if the round is not going as you expected, or being able to ride by instinct if striding does not work out the way you walked it. Either way, you will realize why it is so important to have walked the course thoroughly.

A consistent rhythm is safer and more efficient than bursts of speed and if you feel the horse having trouble with a take-off, curb the instinct to lean forwards: instead sit up and keep your weight off

IN THE START BOX
Arrive at the start in plenty of time but try to keep the horse walking close by until you are being counted down.

STAY FOCUSED
Quick thinking and a calm head will help you in situations where your original plan has to be changed on course.

his shoulders with your legs wrapped round to maintain impulsion. A clever, well-ridden horse will often manage to get himself out of trouble, but interference at the wrong moment can be disastrous.

Adapt your riding to the ground conditions. For example, on slippery or wet ground you need to really hold the horse together, while dry or sticky ground can be especially hard on his legs. If the mud gets deep, the horse has to work especially hard and will tire more easily.

Keep riding all the way. It is easy to relax too much and lose concentration when the last fence is in sight, only to find the horse does the same and something goes wrong. Once you are through the finish, pulling up suddenly can strain the horse's tendons so slow down gradually and avoid sudden turns. You will probably want to give him a big pat but do not drop the contact, as he is tired and could easily fall on to his forehand. Dismount, loosen the girths, walk him around – and give him all the praise he deserves.

EXTRA INFORMATION

EVENTING

Horse trials is the original name for eventing, a sport that originated in Europe as an all-round test for cavalry horses over three days. It includes dressage, cross-country, and show jumping, the idea being that the extremely fit horse shows its obedience in the dressage, its bravery and stamina across country, then its toughness to come out supple enough to show jump on the final day.

Not everyone can attempt a three-day event – one-day events are more accessible. Many riding clubs and equestrian centres organize these, but most events are run by each country's governing body. These provide a points structure for moving up through the levels – for safety reasons you are not allowed to enter a class for which you have not qualified – and guarantee that the courses meet specific standards.

International competitions are called CICs (one-day events) or CCIs (three-day) with star ratings of one to four. There are only five four-star events in the world: Badminton and Burghley in the UK; Lexington in the USA; Adelaide in Australia; and Luhmühlen in Germany.

Andrew Nicholson at the Badminton Lake

OTHER COMPETITIONS

Show jumping, eventing, and dressage tend to grab the headlines but there are plenty of other equestrian competitions you can try. From in-hand showing to fast, frenetic polo and the challenge of endurance riding, there is something to suit almost every rider, from those who just want a fun day out to the ambitious who want to reach the top.

SHOWING CLASSES

Whether you have a cob, a pure-bred native pony, or even a child who wants to compete on the lead-rein with you on foot, there is a range of opportunities. There are classes for anything from veteran horses and coloured horses to hunters and hacks, and the deciding factor is how the animal looks, moves, and behaves. Skilful riding is an advantage, presentation is important, and patience is an asset for both horse and rider. Some classes are judged purely on turnout and these are a nice way for nervous first-timers to find out what competing feels like.

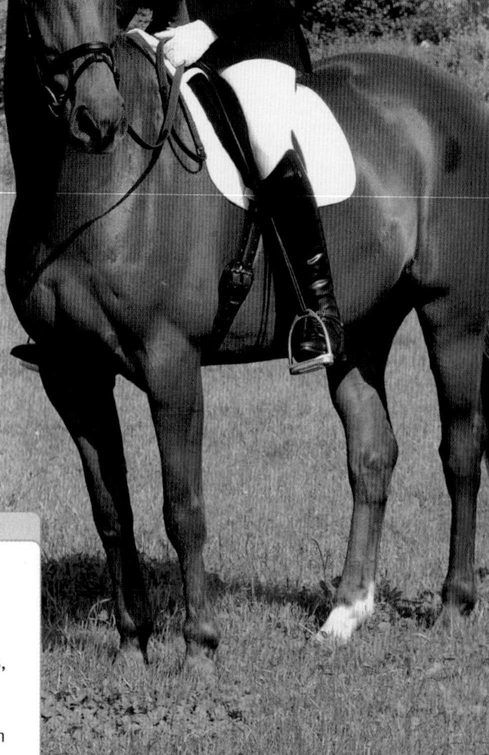

GOOD TURNOUT
Presentation of both horse and rider is a key element of showing classes.

SHOWING LINE-UP
Competitors are called to the centre for the judge to take a closer look and decide on the final placings.

EXTRA INFORMATION

OTHER COMPETITIONS

- **Some "showing"** shows provide the venue for mounted games which, while often treated as a bit of fun and great experience for kids, can lead to some quite serious competitions in their own right.
- **Vaulting is** an official competition discipline which is especially popular in Germany.

LE TREC

Originally devised as a contest between professional trekking guides in France in the late 1970s, Le Trec has really taken off in recent years. The full competition is divided into three sections: orienteering, in which you are tested on your map-reading skills and judgement of speed; control of paces, in which you might have to canter up and walk back along a set track; and an obstacle course that could include slopes, ditches, and gates that you would be likely to meet out hacking. You can miss out any obstacle you do not fancy trying – you will lose marks but you will not get eliminated.

ENDURANCE RIDING

There are a variety of endurance riding classes, from 32 km (20 miles) pleasure rides to set-speed, graded and race rides over distances up to 160 km (100 miles). If you enjoy spending a long time in the saddle and are prepared to follow maps and route markers at speed, while taking great care of your horse, this is for you.

Only in race rides do you compete against other riders; in other classes it is about completing the ride in an optimum time with your horse in optimum condition. Vet checks take place at the start and finish, as well as during the ride on longer distances. Seasoned endurance riders become familiar with every nuance of their horses' stamina and fitness – in itself a fascinating aspect of the sport.

POLO

Although polo lessons are not especially cheap and usually take place at specialist clubs and polo schools, almost anyone can try it. You do not have to be an experienced rider, but you probably do need a certain amount of bravery, fitness, and balance. Polo is the fast, furious, and glamorous end of equestrian sport.

PLAYING POLO
High-goal, or top-level, polo is frenetic and glamorous, but there is plenty of scope for beginners to have a go too.

A TEST OF STAMINA
The lower levels of endurance riding do not require great speed but there is a time limit for each class, so this is much more than a stroll in the countryside.

WESTERN COMPETING

Whether in a rodeo arena or in a show pen, going around the edge of an arena, or performing a pattern, Western competitors ave a wide variety of events in which to show ff their skills. Some classes are judged solely on he horse's way of going; others emphasize the ider's equitation. A few events are against the clock, and some add the variable of cattle.

WESTERN PLEASURE

A Western pleasure class is a "rail" class, in which all competitors go round the edge of the arena together to show off their horses to a judge. The judge is looking for the horse that is the best mover, and the winning horse will be one that is obedient, keeps a slow, easy pace, and is therefore a pleasure to ride.

HAVING AN IDEAL HORSE

To win a Western pleasure class, your horse will need the aptitude for it, with the correct physique to move well, and a good disposition – a horse that is naturally blessed with a level topline, the flat-strided gaits that are required in a Western horse, and a quiet personality will be easier to train and compete.

A good pleasure horse will be able to move at a consistent, slow speed without breaking gait – a horse that is constantly having to pass other competitors will not be placed. With his energy coming from his hindquarters and over his back, the horse should still move forwards and

AN ENJOYABLE RIDE
A horse in a Western pleasure class should have balanced gaits, with legs swinging freely from the shoulders and hips, and a loose, flat stride.

SHOW CLOTHES
Riders dress to make a show for a Western pleasure class, wearing customized chaps, Western hats, colourful Western shirts, and silver buckles.

make smooth transitions without any signs of resistance, such as head-tossing and tail swishing.

Of great importance is the horse's "headset", or head and neck position. This is scrutinized because it shows whether or not the horse is travelling in balance. If the head is too low, it is a direct reflection of the horse being too heavy on the forehand. If the head is held well above the withers, the horse's back will be hollow and his stride will be short and choppy.

PRESENTING YOUR HORSE

Horses are meticulously groomed to accentuate their level topline and excess hair is trimmed away. The mane is pulled short and banded (*see* pp.268–269) so that the neck appears thinner. The tail is left long and full, and cut blunt at the end to emphasize the horse's frame. Any white areas of hair, called "chrome", are made whiter with French chalk or corn starch. Hooves are painted with varnish.

RIDERS' TIPS

- **Present a** calm picture to the judge.
- **Although it** is the horse, not the rider that is judged in this class, you can help to create a good impression if you sit tall, keep your head up, put your shoulders back, and look forwards.

WHAT TO EXPECT

GAITS IN A PLEASURE CLASS

In Western pleasure, the horse must walk, jog, and lope willingly and responsively on a loose rein. A horse will be penalized if he "cheats" in the jog by walking at the front and jogging at the back, or shows a four-beat lope.

Walking

Jogging

Loping

TRAIL CLASS

Using obstacles based on elements that might be found on a real trail ride, the trail class is a challenging event for both horse and rider. During the trail class, a competitor may be required to lope over logs, walk over a bridge, ride between shrubs, back along narrow pathways, open and shut a gate, and even put on a raincoat.

OBSTACLE COURSE

During a trail class, the horse will be asked to negotiate a series of obstacles. Work is performed at the walk, jog, and lope. The obstacles must be completed in order, known altogether as a "pattern", or the rider is eliminated. Every obstacle represents a unique test, and the horse is judged on how well he finishes going over or through it. There is no time limit for a competitor, so the rider can take time over each element on the course.

Each competitor performs the pattern individually, and horse and rider are judged on precision, ability, and pattern completion. The horse should be calm, obedient to the rider's aids, and be willing to perform each task.

A horse will be given a higher score if he works obstacles at a regular speed – not rushing to get through them, but not dawdling through them either. He should have the ability to work his way through the entire course and be responsive to all the rider's aids, regardless of the difficulty of the obstacles he tackles. The judge will deduct points if the horse is disobedient, fails to complete an obstacle, knocks down an obstacle, or shows nervousness.

CHOOSING AN IDEAL HORSE

Any breed of horse can compete in a trail class, but the ideal horse is patient and willing and should take his time going through the trail course pattern. A horse that balks, spooks, jigs, or carries his head above the bridle will not be considered to be in control and will be judged poorly. The horse should, however, show an interest in each obstacle that he encounters.

WHAT TO EXPECT

ELEMENTS IN A TRAIL CLASS

A horse may be asked to pivot in a box on the ground to show, by placing his feet carefully, that he is aware of his surroundings. He may be asked to side-pass over a pole or lope over a series of poles set up in a straight line, or in a curved, zigzagged, or raised configuration. The horse must negotiate all these obstacles without touching the poles.

Pivoting in a box

Side-passing over a pole

Loping over poles

THROUGH A GATE

The rider must open the gate, pass through, then close it. She may place the reins in the other hand to open and close the gate, if the change is made prior to opening the gate and after closing it.

RIDING A TRAIL CLASS

It is important to memorize the course thoroughly so as not to get lost in the middle of the pattern. When approaching difficult obstacles, allow the horse to pause slightly to look at it before proceeding. This allows him to assess the situation, just as a horse should assess something unusual in his path when out on the trail.

OVER A BRIDGE

A raised bridge challenges the horse to put his feet on an unusual surface.

REINING

In a reining class, the horse is judged both on technical merit as well as stylistic elements. It is a performance class in which riders compete one at a time through a series of specified manoeuvres, including loped circles, sliding stops, and spins.

REINING PATTERNS

Competitors in a reining class are required to perform one of ten approved patterns. They will have to perform small slow circles, large fast circles, flying lead changes, roll-backs, spins, and sliding stops, which should all be done on a loose rein. Judges look for accuracy, willingness, obedience, and controlled speed. Circles should be round and should be executed without the horse swinging his haunches out or shoulders in. There should be a quick, easy run on the large circles then a definite slow-down to a relaxed lope on the small circles, with little change in rein contact. Flying lead changes should be executed smoothly, and at the proper point in the circle, with no apparent change in gait or rhythm.

SCORING

The scoring for a reining pattern is quite complicated. A horse will win points for finesse and speed control, and lose points for resistance, executing a movement too early, or performing a sloppy pattern. Any deviation from the pattern results in heavy penalties, or even a no-score. The more sedate movements, such as lope circles, have just as much importance as the spectacular moves like the slides.

The horse and rider start out with 70 points and, during the pattern, judges will award or remove points. Individual manoeuvres are scored in 1-point increments, from a low of −1.5 if they were executed poorly, to a high of +1.5 if they were executed excellently. The total of the manoeuvre scores is combined with the starting score of 70 to give a gross manoeuvre score. Any extra penalties are then deducted to calculate the pair's final score. There are about eight judged manoeuvres within a reining pattern, so a competitor can obtain a score as high as 82 or as low as 58.

WHAT TO EXPECT

ELEMENTS IN A REINING PATTERN

Much emphasis is placed on the geometry of a reining pattern, but the run work (controlled gallop) is also vital. This is where speed control becomes evident, and also where the rider can cash in on the swiftness and brilliance of his horse's pace.

At certain parts of a reining pattern, the horse is also required to "hesitate", where he stands motionless and relaxed.

Run down

Hesitate

LEG PROTECTION FOR REINING
Because a horse's legs are taxed in reining, he is allowed to compete in protective leg gear, in the form of neoprene support boots and skid boots for the hind fetlocks.

WESTERN PATTERN EVENTS

Some people want more than to merely ride along the rail in competitions. They want to enjoy the challenge of testing their own skills, rather than being judged on their horse's way of going. There are options where they compete in various Western competition classes, known as "pattern events".

WESTERN RIDING

For riders who enjoy the challenge of performing manoeuvres like the flying lead change, Western riding is the ideal class. The judges award and deduct points according to the riding qualities of each gait, the flying lead changes, the horse's response to the rider, manners, disposition, and intelligence.

Each rider competes individually, riding a pattern selected by the judge. Judges can select one of four patterns. Depending upon the one chosen, the horse may have to zig-zag across the arena and change leads in the middle, or lope down a line of cones performing a serpentine in and out of them with flying changes.

The pattern is outlined in the arena by small plastic cones. The horse lopes across to the cones, where he must lope the pattern and perform either seven or eight flying lead changes, as designated by the pattern. As in a reining class, each rider begins with a score of 70 and can be awarded or deducted points on various judged elements.

It is important that the horse is a good mover, but the headset is not as crucial as it is in pleasure classes. Horses are judged mainly on how well they can negotiate the course and change leads at the appropriate time. The Western riding horse must also move at a more forward lope and perform the set tasks precisely and calmly. He should be highly responsive to his rider and able to make this extremely demanding discipline appear effortless.

Dress, tack, and grooming for Western riding is similar to that for pleasure, and many riders will not change for this class.

WESTERN RIDING CLASS
To perform his Western riding pattern, the horse first jogs over a ground pole then lopes towards cones in the arena.

WESTERN HORSEMANSHIP

In Western horsemanship, the rider is judged for his or her ability to control and guide the horse through a set of manoeuvres chosen by the judge. This class does not emphasize conformation, breeding, or movement but rather the skilfulness and accuracy in which the rider makes the horse complete the pattern. The rider should exhibit poise, confidence, and good equitation.

The pattern is selected prior to the class by the judge. Every pattern could include a walk, trot, lope, halt, and back-up. Depending upon the difficulty of the class, circles, lead changes, turnarounds, and speed transitions can also be included. Competitors complete the pattern individually and then the entire class competes together on the rail in the form of a Western pleasure class.

HORSEMANSHIP ATTIRE
Horsemanship outfits are classic and understated. Apparel that is bulky, dirty, or otherwise detracting from the rider's silhouette reduces the rider's chance of winning.

Competitors in a horsemanship class start with a basic score of 20 but, unlike in reining and Western riding, points are deducted for errors and not awarded for good movements. The rider and horse should perform in balance, so the rider's position in the saddle is crucial. As in dressage, the horsemanship rider must think ahead to the next part of the pattern to ride accurately and effectively. An excellent Western equitation position is needed to influence the horse, and the rider should ride with light, not loose, contact.

WHAT TO EXPECT

POINT DEDUCTIONS
Besides having an effective, classic riding position, it is essential that riders follow the selected pattern accurately. In Western riding, points are deducted for bad lead changes – such as when a horse changes before or after the marker or kicks out at a lead during the pattern. In horsemanship, riders will have points deducted for careless transitions, knocking over or stepping on cones, severe aids, and disobedience.

"THERE NEVER WAS A HORSE THAT COULDN'T BE RODE. THERE NEVER WAS A COWBOY THAT COULDN'T BE THROWED."

Cowboy saying

BARREL RACING AND POLE BENDING

Performed at rodeos and county shows, barrel racing and pole bending are both exciting speed events. Horse and rider have to race round barrels or snake in and out of a line of poles, so a successful ride requires precision, agility, and speed.

BARREL RACING

A barrel racer competes only against the clock: the fastest time wins. The horse must gallop around three barrels placed in a triangle formation, called a cloverleaf pattern. He races into the arena from an area outside called the alley, or from behind a start line, turning to go round the outside of one of the barrels on the side of the triangle. He then crosses to the top side of the opposite barrel, making a figure-of-eight in the middle of the arena. Having turned around the outside of the second barrel, the horse heads to the barrel at the top of the triangle, racing around it and then back towards the start of the pattern. If the horse or rider touches a barrel, there is no penalty, but if the barrel is knocked over, five seconds are added to the time.

BARREL-RACING TECHNIQUE

Riders race in an exaggerated forward position in the saddle when galloping around the barrels. They should keep their eyes up, and after turning around a barrel should already be looking for the next one. The final seconds of galloping home are crucial – riders will spur their horses on with every stride and do not stop riding until they have crossed the finishing line.

ROUNDING A BARREL The rider must maintain balance through the turn so the horse does not drop his shoulder into the barrel and possibly knock it over.

***The horse** must turn as tight as possible round the barrel*

POLE BENDING

Horse and rider have to bend in and out of a line of six poles. As with other speed events, the fastest time wins. If the horse knocks down a pole, five seconds are added to his time. He will be disqualified if he goes off-course, breaks the pattern, or the rider falls off.

The pole bending run starts with the horse outside the arena, in the alley. He races forwards, down the side of the line of poles to the end, then turns and begins winding in an out of the poles back towards the alley. As he bends through the poles, he performs a flying lead change with every change of bend.

At the sixth pole, he performs a sharp pivot turn and then weaves back through the poles. Once he has finished the poles in this direction, he makes another sharp pivot turn and races for home.

HINDQUARTERS ON LINE
It is important that the pole-bending horse is able to keep his hindquarters on the same path as his front end.

POLE-BENDING TECHNIQUE

Above all, the rider has to be aware of where he is in relation to the poles because they are easy to knock down if the timing is off. The horse must be flexible through the spine and supple through his entire body so that he can change his bend and manoeuvre quickly through the poles. He must use his hindquarters to follow the proper track, so he does not drift out, and he must respect the poles, just as a show jumper must want not to hit a fence.

TURNOUT

Barrel racers and pole benders wear casual dress – jeans, a Western shirt, roper boots, and a Western hat. Many riders now wear safety helmets to prevent head injuries. Horses have protective legwear and often wear a breast collar to stabilize the saddle. The riders use saddles that are cut with small, round skirts and high cantles to lock them in position.

TURNING TIGHTLY
Every moment of time counts, and winning times are often under 20 seconds. The horse can lose precious tenths of seconds by running too wide between the poles.

COW HORSE EVENTS

Some of the most exciting Western events are based on traditional uses for the Western horse. These activities place a great deal of emphasis on the horse's innate "cow sense". Cow horse events include reined cow horse, team penning, and team sorting.

REINED COW HORSE

If reining is "cowboy dressage", the reined cow horse division is "cowboy eventing". The sport developed to perpetuate the Spanish traditions of the working reined stock horse. This competition has three different phases: rein work, fence work, and herd work.

The rein work, also known as dry work, is a reining pattern that includes the same circles, flying lead changes, roll-backs, and sliding stops as ordinary reining classes, and the horse will also perform work with live cattle.

In fence work, the horse demonstrates its ability to bring a cow at a gallop through the arena under control, then direct it alongside the fence, circling it once in each direction. This is arguably the event's most exciting phase. Speed and control are imperative, but a good position in the saddle is also essential as many riders risk falling off. In herd work, the horse cuts an individual cow from the herd and holds it away from the others.

A lot of training is needed to obtain a winning ride. Successful horses not only need good cow sense, but must also adapt

WHAT TO EXPECT

COW SENSE

To succeed in cow horse events, a horse must control a cow without upsetting it. A very proficient cow horse will "crouch" slightly, watching the cow and matching it step for step without any obvious cues from the rider. Judges look out for good balance and smooth changes of direction.

TEAM PENNING

A down-to-earth event, team penning is ideal for riders who prefer its utilitarian style to the glitz and glitter required in much of the show world.

well to the training. They need to be obedient in all phases, fearless among cattle, athletic, and responsive.

Horses for reined cow horse classes are groomed to reflect their working roots. Their manes are kept long – the longer the better – and, while beautifully groomed, they are not pampered like show horses, but are tough and fit. Their tack is also more utilitarian than that of horses in other classes. Dress for riders is more functional than fashionable too, but competitors can still express individuality with a patterned shirt or custom toolwork on their chaps.

HERD WORK
The horse and rider pair separates a cow from the herd, working it from side to side and preventing it from re-joining the other cows.

TEAM PENNING AND TEAM SORTING

These are some of the newest Western sports. In team penning, three riders make up a team that has only 90 seconds to complete its task. Ten sets of ten cows are numbered with collars from zero to nine. The riders are given a number and have to cut the cows with that number from the sets and put them into a pen.

Team sorting is an offshoot of penning. Teams of two or three riders move ten numbered cattle from one pen to another, beginning with a randomly called number between zero and nine. If a cow crosses the line out of sequence, the run is over. The teams are awarded points for time and the number of cattle successively penned.

Riders and horses in both team penning and team sorting compete in functional, but smart, clothes and tack, as in reined cow horse events.

RIDING WITH FRIENDS

HACKING AND HOLIDAYS

There are a variety of ways in which you can enjoy camaraderie with fellow horse lovers, from leisurely hacks and trail rides, or riding holidays in far-flung regions, to camps and courses that teach better horsemanship, and events organized through riding clubs. Friendships take on a wonderful perspective from the back of a horse.

CHOOSE WHAT SUITS YOU

Riding is an individual activity, but it need not be solitary. There are plenty of riding activities that you can take part in with other people.

If you are keen to learn more about horses, you can participate in riding courses, where you will spend a day, week, or longer at a riding centre learning everything from basic horse care and riding skills, to mastering a particular discipline.

If you want to have training and compete, you should join a riding club. Riding clubs provide a host of benefits to their members, including unique educational opportunities and reduced entry fees to their competitions, as well as social events. Local tack shops may also give discounts to riding club members.

RANCH HOLIDAYS
During a stay at a ranch in the USA, you will be able to follow the cowboy way of life.

A riding holiday is one of the best ways to experience horse riding. Different packages are available all over the world to cover virtually every type of riding, from dressage to cattle drives, and for all levels of rider.

TRAIL RIDING IN NEW ZEALAND
Well-known for its quality horses and spectacular scenery, New Zealand is one of the best places to go for a riding holiday.

CHECK LIST

WHAT TO TAKE ON A RIDING HOLIDAY

- **Pack your** normal riding boots and chaps, and a safety helmet.
- **Your riding** clothes should include long-sleeved shirts; breeches, jodhpurs, or jeans; a pullover sweater; a jacket; and riding gloves. Make sure you have a change of riding clothes in case your clothes get soaked. Include a warmer jacket with a rain hood if you are taking your holiday in the winter. Shirts and breeches made of moisture-wicking fabrics will help keep you cool and dry in a warm climate.
- **If you** are taking your own horse with you, take his passport and vaccination certificate as well as his tack, rugs, and food. Label his bridle and/or headcollar with a contact telephone number in case you fall off and he gets lost – the area will be strange to him and he will not be able to find his way home. When someone catches him they will be able to ring you.

CHECK THE WEATHER

If you are planning a trip away from home, make sure that you are aware of any seasonal differences – do not choose the time of year based on your own climate experience. For example, in Australia, remember that January is the middle of the summer and the hottest month of the year. Similarly, a desert ride in southern Arizona, USA, should not be taken between the months of June and October, when temperatures soar above 37°C (100°F). A horse camp in Florida should be avoided in late summer, particularly September and October, because this is the hurricane season.

BE PREPARED

When a large part of your holiday will be spent on a horse, you need to be prepared for long hours in the saddle. You will enjoy the holiday so much more if you are not stiff and sore after the first day. Having a good level of overall fitness helps, so put yourself in a quality exercise programme so that you have good strength in your legs and your lower back. But nothing prepares your physique for days astride a horse like more time in the saddle, so work in a couple of extra riding sessions before you depart. Concentrate on riding up and down slopes at various paces, and even testing the gallop on the flat.

RIDING CLUBS

If you want to take up competitive horse riding, as opposed to enjoying mainly leisurely riding activities, you should think about joining a riding club, where competing is often the main goal. You can join training sessions and hone your skills among other riders of the same level, so you can compete at various horse shows.

THE BENEFITS OF MEMBERSHIP

When you join a riding club you will have to pay an annual membership fee. This will cover club administration, but you will probably have to pay to attend organized training sessions or lectures, albeit at a much lower cost than normal. You can save money by joining a riding club, because you can often get discounts on everything from horse insurance to riding holidays.

There are a host of other advantages to being a member of a riding club, which may include access to organized clinics and workshops; information on horse management and health; a video rental library; free guided walks around cross-country courses with professional riders, veterinary updates on diseases, and other issues of horse and rider welfare. Many riding clubs provide an awards programme where members' hard work is recognized. Riders who are placed at club shows are awarded points, and those with the most points at the end of the year receive trophies and rosettes at the annual meeting or dinner.

HAVING LESSONS
Expert instruction in most riding disciplines can be found within riding clubs, for individuals and for teams.

A riding club will keep members in touch with one another, often providing a rulebook and newsletter with club competition results. Members will also receive updated information about local shows. Running a club is hard work and you may want to consider joining the committee to help organize shows, training, and social events.

At riding club shows, most organizers adhere to strict safety guidelines that are in accordance with the national equestrian federation rules. In some countries, many clubs are affiliated to a national organization and club teams compete against other affiliated clubs in various disciplines at regional and national level.

SPONSORED RIDES

If you enjoy participating in activities that promote good causes, sponsored rides, also called fun rides, will appeal to you. These are riding events held to raise money for a particular aid organization or charity. They are open to riders of all ages and often have large numbers of entrants.

SIGNING UP

A variety of charities use sponsored rides to raise money. The entry fees for a benefit short-course endurance ride often go to local charities too. Some of the charities are horse related, such as Riding for the Disabled and equine rescue organizations, while others are not horse related, such as research for spinal injuries or cancer. Some sponosred rides will be organized over a cross-country course, while others will be an extended trail ride.

You raise money for the charity by asking friends and colleagues to sponsor you for taking part in the event. The organizers will provide the forms and information you will need, and all you have to do is find a horse to ride and get pledges from sponsors. Often, the rider who raises the most money on the ride will win a valuable prize, such as a saddle or tickets to a major horse show. If you do not want to ask friends for money you can still participate in the ride – you can just pay a minimum entry fee that covers a donation to the charity.

Sponsored rides are fun and low pressure, so many riders like to gather several friends together to participate with them for the cause. You can take part in a ride without the stress that comes with competing, but your horse will probably find it very exciting and could be more difficult to control than usual.

You and your horse need to be fit to complete the ride. It is not fair to ask a horse to go out on a long trail ride if he is out of shape. And if you are not used to jumping anything other than cross poles in a sand-school, do not try to jump higher fences for the first time on a sponsored ride – it would be dangerous.

NUMBERED RIDERS
You will usually be asked to wear a number when you ride so that the organizers know when you have returned safely.

RIDING COURSES

When you go on a riding course, it is like going back to school, and you will have concentrated instruction in horse care and riding. Some courses take place at equestrian establishments, but many courses are run in places that offer other activities too – everything from swimming and hiking to wine tasting.

INSTRUCTION

Some riding courses teach rudimentary horse care and riding, while others allow you to perfect your skills in a certain riding discipline, such as basic dressage, show jumping, and cross-country jumping. Many cover several disciplines, and you may even be given instruction from an international-level rider or coach. A bonus provided on courses that focus on a particular discipline is that you may be able to ride a schoolmaster horse – an older but talented horse that has perhaps retired from top-level competition. Schoolmaster horses can often teach a rider more in a week than a typical school horse can in several months.

ALL THE TASKS
Students will learn to do a variety of things, including tack cleaning and care.

OPPORTUNITIES FOR ALL
The facilities that are provided for most riding courses means that serious equestrians, as well as novices, can improve their skills.

You will be able to find courses that offer English or Western riding, or perhaps both. If you are particularly interested in Western riding, you could consider a trip to the south-western USA where most courses specialize in this discipline.

A WEEK-LONG COURSE

Staying at an equestrian facility for a week is a great way to experience horse ownership before you commit yourself to the responsibility. On a typical morning, you will bring "your" horse in from the field and give him his breakfast, watch a horse-care demonstration, and have a riding lesson. In the afternoon you might go for a hack, see to your horse again, and attend another discussion on horsemanship. While the work can be intensive, it is also great fun to be surrounded by others who are there for the same reason as you.

BED AND BREAKFAST

A bed-and-breakfast getaway is a charming way to spend time in an out-of-the way place and experience the country way of life. A bed-and-breakfast establishment that will also cater for your horse can be a home away from home for a few days, or a relaxing and comfortable place to stop for one night during a multi-day ride around the area.

TYPES OF ACCOMMODATION

Although it is possible to find traditional style bed-and-breakfast establishments that also have accommodation for your horse, most are located on a large ranch or farm, or even a breeding facility. Some may charge an all-inclusive price per day, while others may have separate charges for board, feed, and bedding, allowing you to select what you need from their "menu." One great benefit of the bed-and-breakfast experience is that if you are holidaying with friends who do not ride, most establishments are located in areas where there are other activities to enjoy.

At many equine bed-and-breakfasts you will have a room or a cottage to yourself, and you will be able to enjoy a hearty breakfast as well as the company of your fellow guests. Some hosts may even pack a picnic lunch for you to take on your rides. Some properties, for example in the western USA, can be more rustic, with cabins and horse corrals instead of cottages and stables. But they will almost always be operated by people who are horse owners themselves, so you can be sure that they will provide everything that your horse needs.

ON HOLIDAY
Many facilities provide opportunities, such as large paddocks or pastures, that some "city horses" never get to experience.

RIDING FROM YOUR DOOR

Trails on and adjacent to most properties allow you to ride straight out of the stable yard and into the heart of the countryside. Your hosts will often be able to show you little-known bridlepaths, picnic areas, and short-cuts, which will help you get to know the area.

If you prefer, you can ride to a new establishment each day, instead of returning to the same place. There are companies that will arrange everything for you – booking the accommodation, arranging for your luggage to be taken on to the next stop, and providing detailed routes and maps to follow. If you arrange your own accommodation, book it in advance – it is more difficult to find somewhere to stay at short notice if you have a horse to cater for too.

CHECK LIST

WHAT TO TAKE

- **If you** are bringing your own horse to ride, you will need to pack his tack and grooming equipment, as well as your own riding gear.
- **You may** need to take your horse's passport and certificate that shows he has been vaccinated.
- **If your** horse requires any unusual feed or supplements, make sure you remember to take them with you.

GUEST RANCHES

If you do not have your own horse but want to do a large amount of riding for a week or more, take a holiday on a guest ranch, often known as a dude ranch. Guest ranches offer riders and horse lovers a great opportunity to get away from the demands of modern living by providing a holiday based on traditional ranching activities.

ORIGIN OF THE GUEST RANCH

At the turn of the 20th century, with most Americans east of the Mississippi river living in towns or bustling cities, many people longed to escape to a picturesque wilderness, even for just a holiday. Enterprising cattle ranchers, as an offshoot from their business, decided to open their doors to a select few – mainly extended family and friends – and the dude ranch, or guest ranch, was born. Each ranch developed its own unique identity, reflecting its owner's character.

TYPES OF ACCOMMODATION

Today, some ranches reflect their rustic origins, and you can expect plenty of home-cooked meals. Others have the attributes of a luxury resort and spa. Guest houses range from log cabins to spacious suites away from the main lodge. Many ranches have swimming pools, bars, lounges, and pool tables to help visitors wind down after hours in the saddle. Entertainment such as country music and dancing is also sometimes provided.

Guest ranches appeal to riders and non-riders alike. As well as horse-riding, many ranches also offer other activities such as fishing, canoeing or kayaking, hiking, and even whitewater rafting.

THE RIDING

Many ranches offer all-day excursions as well as shorter rides. Horses are matched to the riders' ability and riders at the same skill level are often grouped together. Most ranches will not let you ride out alone – even if you are an accomplished rider, you will be unfamiliar with the trails and the terrain, so an experienced ranch-hand, or "wrangler", will always accompany you on a ride.

WHAT TO TAKE

For riding you should take lightweight, cotton, long-sleeved shirts; jeans, jodhpurs, or breeches; pullovers; a rain jacket; and gloves. Take the riding boots and chaps you normally ride in, and it is a good idea to take a helmet, because you may not be allowed to ride without one.

LEARNING THE ROPES
At some guest ranches you can try your hand at cowboy skills such as how to handle a rope.

WORKING RANCHES

Like the dude ranches of yesteryear, today a large group of working cattle ranches invite guests to their property to offer a glimpse of what it is like to be a real cowboy. Most cattle ranches can only accommodate a small group of guests at a time, but it is an experience most equestrians treasure for years after.

EARNING YOUR KEEP

A working ranch is different from a guest ranch, mainly because guests work side by side with their hosts, assisting in any ranch chores that need to be done. Besides riding and moving the herd, you will help with branding, vaccinating, and castrating cattle. Because you will be there to experience working on a ranch, you must be a proficient rider and be able to control the horse at a walk, trot, and lope. Many ranches do not allow guests under 16 years old to participate in the ranch work. During your stay, you will live in a cabin on the ranch and eat your meals "family-style" with other guests, but when working cattle, lunch will be "on the trail".

GOING ON A CATTLE DRIVE

Spring and autumn are the times when you can take part in a cattle drive. This is when the cattle are moved to better grazing or gathered to be transported off the ranch. While you might get the chance to chase after an errant heifer, most of your riding will be done at a walk, which is the pace at which the cattle are driven. You can expect to spend most daylight hours in the saddle, and as you will be moving the cattle from one place to the next each day, you will probably camp out at night in a tent.

THE COWBOY LIFE

Cattle drives have been much the same for over 100 years. By taking part in one you will really be living the life of a cowboy.

TAKING A PACK TRIP

A pack trip is like a cattle drive, but without the cattle. You will be able to explore the countryside over several days and camp under the stars at night. You can select a pack trip that operates from a base camp that you will return to each evening, or a progressive camp that moves to a new location each day.

If your pack trip involves a progressive camp, you will have to pack up your camping equipment each time you move, but your ride and your surroundings will be different each day. Since many pack trips take place in mountain areas, rides are usually kept at a walk. On most pack trips, you can expect to sleep in a tent, but camp amenities vary.

WHAT TO TAKE

For working ranch holidays, take your normal riding clothes, but you should include a heavy jacket to protect you from the cold. You may also need a helmet. If you are concerned about the long hours in the saddle, take a fleece saddle cover to give you extra comfort.

TRAIL RIDING

Arena work is ideal for mastering skills or training the horse, but sometimes you may want to "hit the trail". An appealing aspect of trail riding is that it gives you the opportunity to see the world and experience different cultures and traditions. You will still need the skills you learnt in the school, and you will acquire a few new ones too.

THE TRAIL HORSE

A good trail horse is worth his weight in gold to a trail rider. He needs to be surefooted and light on the forehand. And he has to be fairly fit for activities such as climbing hills, picking a path through rocky terrain, and jumping the occasional fallen log.

THE TRAIL RIDER

The rider must possess a good seat at all gaits and be confident in the saddle in all weather conditions and in all types of countryside, from steep mountain paths to wide open spaces. You should also be able to help the horse find his way safely through varied terrain. As a rider, you should ensure that you are trail ready by getting fit. Gradually build up the time you spend in the saddle everyday so you are ready for long rides.

TRAIL SHARING

You may meet other people, such as cyclists and walkers, on the trail. It is important to be an ambassador for all equestrians so be courteous to other trail users. Thank them for giving you the right of way and be patient and tolerant. Do not leave litter on the trail and keep on designated trails to reduce land erosion.

SANTA MONICA MOUNTAINS, CALIFORNIA
Trail riding is the ideal way to "get away from it all". On many trails you will have spectacular views.

When taking a break, be considerate of trees and bushes – do not let your horse eat the bark and roots.

WHAT TO TAKE

The best clothes to wear are a long-sleeved shirt to protect you from branches and the sun; comfortable jeans, jodhpurs, or breeches; boots with ankle support; and an approved helmet. Take a small first-aid kit and a mobile phone for emergencies.

TRAIL TIPS

CHALLENGE	HOW TO RIDE
Water	Select the safest way across; move purposefully but carefully forwards.
Ice	Do not go any faster than necessary; do not make any sudden weight shifts.
Rocks	Go slowly; stay attentive and help the horse select the safest route.
"Runaway"	Sit up straight; give a rhythmical heavy pull and release on one rein; turn a circle.
"Spook"	Ride assertively past whatever the horse has seen; make the horse focus on you.

NAVAJOLAND

ARIZONA/UTAH, WESTERN USA

The states of Arizona and Utah are known for their dramatic, colourful deserts that were – and still are – home to Native American peoples. For riders who are looking for the opportunity to see past cultures and are willing to give up modern civilization for a few days, riding in this area is the perfect way to see a truly wild part of America.

UNSPOILED AMERICA

The Navajoland area of Arizona and Utah, named after the Navajo Indian Americans who still live there, is famous for its soaring, red-walled mountains, and uncompromising terrain. Although this guarantees spectacular views for riders trekking through the area, it also makes for a challenging trip. The sun-baked terrain can mean that riding is uncomfortable, while riders who are confident enough to tackle the foothills of Navajo Mountain should be prepared for steep climbs. The American Quarter Horse is known for its gentle temperament, and its versatility is ideally suited to this varied landscape.

ANCIENT NAVAJO CLIFF DWELLINGS
Navajoland contains the ruined settlements of the ancient Anasazi people, which date from 900CE.

CANYON DE CHELLY
Riders who enjoy high speeds will find that the plains are well-suited to a gallop, though they may find the mountains and canyons frustratingly slow.

ESSENTIAL INFORMATION

HORSES Predominantly Quarter Horses

TACK Western

RIDING ABILITY Intermediate upwards

ACCOMMODATION Camping

TERRAIN Challenging: often steep, dry, and rough underfoot

BEST TIME OF YEAR May or September

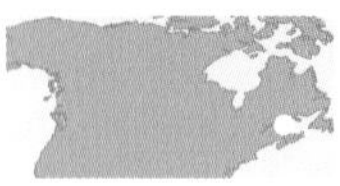

THE GASPÉ PENINSULA

QUEBEC, EASTERN CANADA

The Gaspé Peninsula is an ideal destination for intermediate riders looking for a varied ride through beautiful, untamed countryside, without having to sacrifice the luxuries of home. There are many opportunities to see the area by riding from inn-to-inn, a method that will allow you to rest comfortably after a long day in the saddle.

FORESTS AND LAKES

A variety of terrain can be ridden in the Gaspé Peninsula: hill riding gives commanding views of the region, the coastline of the peninsula is perfect for riders looking for a challenge, while the open meadows of the area cater for those wishing to gallop. Visitors can also take a trip around the Tartigou River Valley to visit the Petchedez River, where you can stop for a swim, weather permitting. Canadian horses are characteristically versatile, and are known for their strength and docility.

NATIONAL PARK
The Parc de Gaspesie contains more than 100 km (60 miles) of scenic trails with extensive views over mountains, lakes, forests, and rivers.

ESSENTIAL INFORMATION

HORSES Quarter Horses and Canadian horses

TACK Predominantly Western

RIDING ABILITY Strong intermediate upwards

ACCOMMODATION Inns and private homes

TERRAIN Moderate: forests, rough tracks, and meadows

BEST TIME OF YEAR June to October

AUTUMN COLOURS
Part of the trail follows old logging trails that pass through maple and pine forests. The maple trees are ablaze with colour in the autumn.

CENTRAL PACIFIC

WESTERN COSTA RICA

The western coast of Costa Rica is teeming with tropical sea and bird life, and is a beautiful location for warm coastal riding. Riders can explore the shores and trails in the sparsely populated province of Guanacaste from the backs of Criollo horses, and will be able to observe exotic wildlife in its natural habitat.

RIDING ALL YEAR ROUND

Costa Rica offers a pleasant climate for riding all year round, although riders wishing to stay dry should avoid the rainy season (May to November). The terrain in the central Pacific region is predominantly flat, while coastal beaches offer great opportunities for a gallop. The local Criollo horses are built to endure, which is essential for days in the saddle that often last longer than six hours. A number of rides are available that cover more than one area of Costa Rica, interspersing travel on horseback with motorized transport. A ride from La Trinidad de Orotina in the Central Pacific up to the National Park of Guanacaste in the north-west is a great way to experience the country.

RIDING ON THE BEACH
Some rides are along the beach, and there are opportunities for riders to swim in the warm waters of the Pacific Ocean with their horses.

ESSENTIAL INFORMATION

HORSES Criollo/Arab horses and Quarter Horses

TACK English, Western, and Australian

RIDING ABILITY Intermediate upwards

ACCOMMODATION Haciendas, hotels, and ranches

TERRAIN Moderate: sand, forests, and rough tracks

BEST TIME OF YEAR January to April

ARENAL VOLCANO
A climb up the Arenal volcano (one of the most active volcanoes in the world) is a unique, if demanding, riding experience.

PATAGONIA

SOUTHERN ARGENTINA

Although the cowboys of North America have been consigned to the past, the ranch hands of Argentina, known as gauchos, still play a part in the country's rural economy. With their distinctive ponchos and neck scarves, they are a constant reminder of Argentina's agricultural past and the horse's role in the nation's rural life.

GAUCHO TRADITIONS

Horse-riders who are keen to experience the age-old lifestyle of the gauchos and their traditions can ride with them through the Andes of western Argentina. Rides are available that take in the snow-covered peaks of the Andes mountains, the Tierra del Fuego region where the Atlantic and Pacific oceans meet, and vertigo-inducing canyons. The area is perfectly suited to the strong novice rider who wants an authentic experience of gaucho life in truly impressive surroundings. Those who enjoy riding at speed may be frustrated by the steep terrain and slow pace, but most days feature long hours in the saddle.

CRIOLLO HORSES
Argentines are particularly proud of their national horse, the Criollo, which has been bred to be robust, fast, and easy to handle.

ESSENTIAL INFORMATION

HORSES Criollo horses

TACK South American

RIDING ABILITY Strong novice upwards

ACCOMMODATION Hotels and camping

TERRAIN Challenging: often steep and rough

BEST TIME OF YEAR December to April

PATAGONIAN GAUCHOS
Gauchos are a symbol of Argentine history. The early gauchos, the "wanderers of the Pampas", owned nothing of value except their horse and their long knife, called a *facon*.

KJOLUR TRAIL

ICELAND

Riders on this journey get a chance to touch history – the Icelandic Horse is a purebred descendent of the horses the Vikings rode centuries ago. The Kjolur Trail takes riders "tolting" across Iceland, giving a rare opportunity to ride the unique gait that comes naturally to this small but hardy horse.

GLACIERS AND DESERTS

The Kjolur Trail follows an ancient Icelandic trading route through the central highlands of the country. You have the option of journeying from Skagafjordur in the north to Reykjavik in the south, or vice versa. The riding is exciting, with plenty of opportunities to gallop, and the chance to ford rivers on horseback. Consequently, this trail is not suited to the novice rider. Accommodation is likely to be in rustic mountain cabins and inns – they are comfortable without being luxurious. It is worth timing your visit to coincide with the Landsmot, the Icelandic National Horse show, which takes place in late June and early July.

SPECTACULAR LANDSCAPE

The trip is geographically varied, taking in everything from glaciers and volcanoes to deserts, geysers, and green fields.

ESSENTIAL INFORMATION

HORSES Icelandic Horses

TACK English and Icelandic

RIDING ABILITY Intermediate upwards

ACCOMMODATION Inns and mountain cabins

TERRAIN Varied: plains, desert, and rough tracks

BEST TIME OF YEAR June to September

ICELANDIC HORSES

The Icelandic Horse is renowned for its tolt, a gait that allows a steady pace to be maintained, with minimum disturbance for the rider.

ATLANTIC COAST

COUNTY SLIGO, WESTERN IRELAND

Ireland is renowned the world over for its affectionate relationship with horses, and the north-west region of County Sligo provides a stunning backdrop for trail riding. Thanks to its proximity to the Atlantic Ocean, riders visiting this area can experience stunning coastal scenery alongside beautiful mountains and lush forests.

UNSPOILED COUNTRYSIDE

The terrain of County Sligo is varied, and suited to riders of all abilities. Exploring the farm tracks, hills, and woodland gives a unique insight into Irish rural life, while the sweeping, quiet beaches of the coastline are ideal for riders who want to gallop. There is a wide range of accommodation in the area, so discomfort need not be part of the experience. Enthusiasts may want to coincide their trip with the Gurteen Agricultural and Horse Show, which takes place in late August, and features show jumping and other entertainments.

ESSENTIAL INFORMATION

HORSES Predominantly Irish Hunters

TACK English

RIDING ABILITY Novice upwards

ACCOMMODATION Bed and breakfast

TERRAIN Moderate: sand, meadows, and woodland

BEST TIME OF YEAR July to August

VERSATILE HORSES
Irish Hunter horses are durable and powerful. They can handle a long walk through mountains and a bracing gallop along the beach.

DARTMOOR

DEVON, SOUTH-WEST UK

Any visitor travelling through the south-west of England will probably drive through the home of the Dartmoor pony at some point. Dartmoor is the largest wilderness in England. The rough and boggy grasslands provide more than 800 square kilometres (300 square miles) of unrestricted country in which to ride.

OPEN MOORLAND
The terrain includes large swathes of predominantly soft turf, broken up by rocky outcrops and peat bogs.

RUGGED TERRAIN

Dartmoor's link with horses is indisputable, as it is home to the instantly recognizable, and always endearing, Dartmoor Pony. Riders of all abilities can ride without restriction on Dartmoor. The large swathes of soft turf and sandy tracks offer plenty of galloping opportunities. Those riders looking to practise their jumping can use the many natural obstacles presented by small brooks. English weather is frequently unpredictable, so a visit during the summer months is essential to maximize potential riding time.

ESSENTIAL INFORMATION

HORSES Irish Hunters and other types

TACK English

RIDING ABILITY Novice upwards

ACCOMMODATION Bed and breakfast

TERRAIN Moderate: open moorland, hills, and tracks

BEST TIME OF YEAR March to September

DARTMOOR PONIES
Numbers of these quietly dignified ponies are closely monitored, as the population is prone to fluctuations.

PROVENCE

SOUTHERN FRANCE

The scenic landscape of Provence, located on the sunny shores of the Mediterranean Sea in the south of France, is even more breathtaking when viewed from the back of a horse. Summers are hot, although not uncomfortably so, and the region is perfectly suited to a sedately paced riding holiday.

ROLLING HILLS

Provence is an ideal location for riders of a novice standard. The terrain is predominantly gentle, and principally comprises meadows, hills, and forests. A base at one of the many riding centres in the area lends itself to a riding experience made up of one- and two-day trips with an overnight stop. A variety of horses can be ridden in the area, from the notoriously sure-footed Camargue horses, to the naturally athletic and gregarious Selle Francais. Provence is a historically rich area, and riding can be interspersed with a visit to one of the region's many castles, such as the perfectly restored castle in the village of Entrecasteaux, which dates from the 11th century.

LUBERON VALLEY
You may well ride through the Luberon area of Provence, which is a valley nestling in rugged hills. Much of the area is a national park.

FIELDS OF LAVENDER
The large amount of sunshine in the area means there are huge areas of lavender, vineyards, and olive trees.

ESSENTIAL INFORMATION

HORSES Selle Francais horses and other breeds

TACK English

RIDING ABILITY Novice upwards

ACCOMMODATION Farmhouses and guesthouses

TERRAIN Moderate: meadows, hills, and forests

BEST TIME OF YEAR April to October

ANDALUCIA

SOUTHERN SPAIN

Andalucia is an area of southern Spain with a strong horse-riding tradition. For many years, Andalucian horses have been trained in the *vaquera* (cowboy) style to help Spanish farmers control their cattle. Taking a trek is an excellent way of experiencing the working, rural life of southern Spain.

GREAT VARIETY

Andalucia offers a feast of different terrain and types of riding holiday. From the rocky mountains of the Sierra Nevada and Alpajurras to the sandy trails of the Atlantic and Mediterranean coastlines, the area offers something for everyone. The horses of Andalucia have a reputation for being responsive, accommodating, and comfortable to ride. Horse enthusiasts who wish to experience the energy of a Spanish fiesta, as well as seeing equestrianism at its very best, can time their trip to coincide with the Jerez Horse Fair, which takes place in the first week of May.

JEREZ HORSE FAIR
The Jerez horse fair features some of the world's finest horses and riders competing in endurance trials, coach driving, and dressage competitions.

VILLAGE OF ALORA
You will have the chance to visit countless towns and villages of historical interest, such as the village of Alora with its 17th-century church and ruined Moorish castle.

ESSENTIAL INFORMATION

HORSES Andalucian horses

TACK English and Spanish

RIDING ABILITY Novice upwards

ACCOMMODATION Hotels

TERRAIN Moderate: bridle paths and mountains

BEST TIME OF YEAR April to October

TUSCANY

CENTRAL ITALY

Tuscany is equally celebrated for its splendid rural scenery and rich horse life. Stunning countryside of undulating hillsides, meadows, forests, and rivers, combined with wonderful food, excellent wine, and camaraderie with other horse lovers will make for a memorable week's holiday.

ROLLING HILLS

Although a horse-riding holiday in Tuscany is unlikely to appeal to intrepid enthusiasts, hilly terrain, historic villages, and bustling cities make the region ideal for those who wish to combine riding with other interests. Most holidays are based at one of the many riding centres in the area, which offer day treks in the surrounding countryside. The locally bred Maremma horses are sturdy and reliable, and were traditionally used to herd cattle.

PARADING FOR THE PALIO
The Palio horse race, held in Siena on 2 July and 16 August every year, is a must-see for anybody who enjoys a unique spectacle.

ESSENTIAL INFORMATION

HORSES Maremma horses

TACK English

RIDING ABILITY Novice upwards

ACCOMMODATION Hotels and guesthouses

TERRAIN Moderate: meadows and forests

BEST TIME OF YEAR April to September

SITES TO SEE
There are opportunities to visit medieval churches, castles, and abbeys, as well as to sample the region's famous Chianti wine.

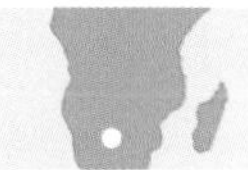

OKAVANGO DELTA

NORTHERN BOTSWANA

The Okavango Delta is the world's largest inland delta, a network of lakes and swamps interspersed with floodplains that occupy over 17,000 square kilometres (6,560 square miles) on the edge of the Kalahari Desert. The area is rich in wildlife, and provides a home to many animals, including predators, game, and exotic birds.

NATURE WATCHING

A guided trek through the delta is a fantastic experience for the horse-riding enthusiast who wants to get closer to nature. This is not, however, an area for the novice. Although the floodplains are perfect for galloping at speed, riders must exercise caution as dangerous wildlife may be encountered – an irritable elephant, for example, or a herd of buffalo. However, the rewards of a ride in the Okavango Delta are obvious. There are very few other places in the world where riders can see zebras, wildebeest, and giraffes in the wild, from horseback. Temperatures are at their hottest in October, November, and December, while May to September is the rainy season. This time of year is not recommended for riders who do not feel confident enough to wade through deep water on horseback.

WATCHING WILDLIFE

The horses are used to the presence of wild animals, and if there is no danger, will be happy to stop while you watch the wildlife.

ESSENTIAL INFORMATION

HORSES Boerpede horses and Saddlebred horses

TACK English

RIDING ABILITY Strong intermediate upwards

ACCOMMODATION Camping

TERRAIN Challenging: floodplains

BEST TIME OF YEAR March and April

LIMPOPO PROVINCE

NORTH-EAST SOUTH AFRICA

Coming face to face with a white rhino, a majestic giraffe, or a zebra herd is a once-in-a-lifetime experience. A horse-riding holiday in South Africa is an opportunity to combine exciting riding with the thrill of spotting indigenous creatures.

HOST OF WILDLIFE

The landscape in Limpopo Province is diverse, ranging from unbroken bushveld savannah, grasslands, and wetlands, to the impressive Waterberg mountain range. The grasslands are perfectly suited to fast riding, but the mountains must be explored at a gentler pace. From October to March the weather is hot, and thunderstorms are frequent, but South Africa's climate is conducive to riding all year round. The indigenous Boerperd Horses are renowned for being calm, full of stamina, and surefooted.

RED HARTEBEEST
An impressive variety of wildlife can be seen in Kruger and Marakele National Parks, such as red hartebeest, warthogs, and antelope.

ESSENTIAL INFORMATION

HORSES Arab horses and Boerperd horses

TACK English and Australian

RIDING ABILITY Strong novice upwards

ACCOMMODATION Lodges, huts, and camping

TERRAIN Moderate: plains and gentle hills

BEST TIME OF YEAR June to August

ON THE TRAIL
Most riders base themselves at one of the many riding-centres and lodges in the Limpopo Province, and explore the area through a series of one-day or overnight treks.

RAJASTHAN

NORTH-WESTERN INDIA

Located in the north of India, Rajasthan is immersed in the lore and history of horse-riding. The city of Jodhpur, in western Rajasthan, lends its name to the traditional trousers worn by jockeys today. The terrain in Rajasthan is varied – the north is sandy and includes the Great Indian Desert, while the southeast is fertile and forgiving.

DESERT AND MOUNTAINS

In high summer (April to June), temperatures can reach 48°C (118°F), which makes conditions unsuitable for riding. This is a good reason for visitors to plan their trip for November, which is also the time of the Pushkar Fair – the world's largest camel fair. You will be riding the local Marwari horses, whose ears point inward, occasionally causing the tips to form an arc above their heads. They are friendly but spirited horses, with a reputation for being easy to ride. Although the terrain is mostly desert, it is varied, from the spectacular mountain ranges near Ghatwa, to the Salt Lake at Nawa. The riding is enjoyable, although it is not for those who enjoy the thrill of speed – the soft, sandy ground may prove frustrating.

MARWARI HORSE

The horse is important to the people of Rajasthan, and in wedding rituals, the groom will often ride to the bride's house on a horse.

KUMBHALGARH FORTRESS

The remote hilltop fortress of Kumbhalgarh is well worth a visit. It contains 360 temples, and the view stretches far into the Aravalli hills.

ESSENTIAL INFORMATION

HORSES Marwari horses

TACK Indian "sawar"

RIDING ABILITY Strong intermediate upwards

ACCOMMODATION Hotels and camping

TERRAIN Varied: desert and some mountains

BEST TIME OF YEAR March and November

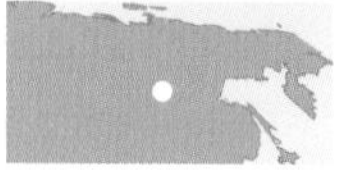

MONGOLIA

MONGOLIA

Few countries have such a strong historical link with the horse as Mongolia – the first domesticated horses are thought to have emerged on the Eurasian steppes between 4,500 and 2,000BCE. The horse is still the main form of transport in Mongolia, especially for nomadic families, whose horses are methods of transport and status symbols.

NOMADIC WAY OF LIFE

Mongolia offers great opportunities to those wishing to experience the nomadic way of life. A variety of rides are possible, from crossing mountain passes to pack-trips across the vast steppes that make up much of the country. You will also have the chance to ride one of the oldest breeds of horse, the indigenous Mongolian Pony, which is built for fortitude and endurance. Traditional Mongolian tack includes wooden saddles decorated with large silver studs, but most visitors will use more conventional English or Russian tack. It is worth timing your trip to take in the Naadam Festival. These are Mongolia's national games, and are held in July each year. The most spectacular event of the festival involves horses racing along open grassland for as much as 30 km (19 miles), ridden by children between the ages of five and thirteen. Winning horses are feted in song and poetry, and earn a place in the country's cultural heritage.

ESSENTIAL INFORMATION

HORSES Mongolian Ponies

TACK English or Russian

RIDING ABILITY Strong novice upwards

ACCOMMODATION Hotels and camping

TERRAIN Varied: mountains, steppes, and grassland

BEST TIME OF YEAR August and September

EAGLE HUNTERS OF MONGOLIA
The centuries-old tradition of hunting with eagles is still practised among the Khazak horsemen of Mongolia. In early October the Eagle Hunting festival in Bayan Ulgii attracts the best hunters and birds.

TAUPO

NORTH ISLAND, NEW ZEALAND

A safari trail in Taupo, in New Zealand's North Island, allows riders an authentic glimpse of rural life in one of the country's most popular destinations. Rides take in the backcountry of the region, home to a variety of native birds, deer, and game and there are even two active volcanoes close by – Mount Ngauruhoe and Mount Ruapehu.

VOLCANIC CRATERS

The wide expanses of open land and hills in the Taupo region make for great gallops, while riders curious about the workings of a traditional New Zealand sheep farm can even try their hand at sheep mustering or sheep shearing. The most commonly used horses in the area are reliable Quarter Horses, and the varied landscape means that riders of all standards will find something to suit them. New Zealand's National Equestrian Centre is based at Taupo, and frequently runs high-standard competitions during the summer months (October to March), including the New Zealand National Breeding Show Jumping Championship in early December.

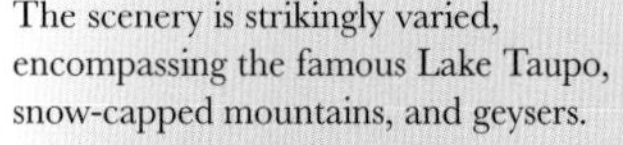

LAKE TAUPO
The scenery is strikingly varied, encompassing the famous Lake Taupo, snow-capped mountains, and geysers.

MAORI GATE CARVING
There are many historical Maori sites in the Taupo region. You can also visit a living Maori village and meet carvers, weavers, and musicians.

ESSENTIAL INFORMATION

HORSES Quarter Horses and Thoroughbreds

TACK English and Western

RIDING ABILITY Novice upwards

ACCOMMODATION Ranches and cabins

TERRAIN Varied: meadows, tracks, and mountains

BEST TIME OF YEAR October to April

GLOSSARY

There is a huge number of terms used specifically in connection with horses and horse riding, and until you are familiar with them they can be confusing. Here are some common terms with their definitions, which you may find helpful as you learn about horses.

Aids The way the rider communicates with the horse; divided into *natural aids* and *artificial aids*.

Artificial aids Devices designed to help reinforce *natural aids*. These include spurs, whips, and *martingales*. Artificial aids should never replace the natural aids or be used to punish a horse.

Bars Part of the Western saddle *tree* that determines the size and shape of the saddle. **also** the narrow gap between the horse's incisor and molar teeth on which the *bit* sits.

Bit Device used in the horse's mouth to aid control.

Body brush Soft brush for removing dust and grease from the horse's coat.

Body protector Reinforced garment that helps absorb the impact of a fall and protect the rider's internal organs.

Bolting When a horse goes fast and refuses to stop.

Bosal Stiff *noseband* attached to a Western *headstall*. It is teardrop shaped and ends in a knot, called a heel knot, to which the *mecate* is tied.

Breeches Riding trousers that finish above the ankle, designed to be worn with long boots or *half-chaps*.

Bridle horse Term used to denote a Western horse that is fully trained to respond to the curb *bit*.

Browband Part of the bridle that lies across the horse's forehead to stop the bridle from slipping back.

Brushing boots Boots put on the horse's lower legs to protect them from blows inflicted by the opposite leg.

Canter Smooth, three-time pace.

Cantle C-shaped back of the saddle that rises up to cradle the rider's *seat*. An important part of the saddle, the cantle along with the *pommel* keeps the rider secure in the seat of the saddle.

Cheek pieces Straps on either side of the bridle that connect the *bit* with the *headpiece*.

Cinch Western saddle's *girth* that keeps the saddle secured to the horse's back.

Clicker training Type of training using a clicker device to mark the horse's correct behaviour.

Clipping Process in which the horse's coat is shorn to allow him to work without sweating too much. It is usually the winter coat that is removed, and a clipped horse must wear a rug to replace this.

Cold bloods Horses that have European origins and are known for their large size, compliant nature, and strength.

Collection Slow but very powerful version of a *pace* that demonstrates great control, willingness, and obedience.

Contact A friendly connection that a rider feels from the hands through the *reins* to the horse's mouth, signifying good communication.

Cooler Lightweight rug used to keep wet horses warm while they dry; made of fabric that lets moisture pass through into the air and dries quickly.

Counter canter *Canter* in which the rider asks the horse to take the wrong *lead*; used to develop and demonstrate the horse's balance.

Crib biting A *vice* where the horse latches on to and chews any protruding object. He may *windsuck* at the same time.

Cross-country Jumping outdoors over fixed fences, best known as the most exciting phase of *eventing*.

Cross-surcingles Straps used to fasten rugs under the horse's belly.

Curry comb Metal device used to clean the *body brush*. A rubber curry comb can be used to loosen mud from the coat.

Dandy brush Coarse-bristled brush used for removing dried mud and sweat from a horse's coat.

Dismounting Getting off a horse.

Double bridle Bridle that has both a snaffle and a curb *bit*. Used with two sets of *reins*, it gives a fine degree of control and is most often used in *dressage* and *showing*.

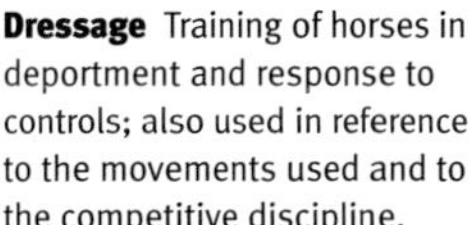

Dressage Training of horses in deportment and response to controls; also used in reference to the movements used and to the competitive discipline.

Drop fence Jump where the landing side is lower than the take-off side.

Dude or guest ranch Holiday ranch found in western parts of North America where guests can ride horses among their other activities.

Eventing Sport in which horses and riders compete in *dressage*, *show jumping*, and *cross-country*; divided into one-day and three-day events.

Extension Version of a *pace* in which the horse's stride is lengthened while maintaining the same tempo.

Farrier Qualified practitioner who trims and shoes horses' feet.

Flank billet Strap on the back of some Western saddles for attaching an extra *cinch* to.

Flehmen response Horse's facial expression that is a reaction to an unusual smell or taste, or is performed by a stallion trying to locate a mare in heat.

Flexion When the horse is asked to bend his neck slightly in one direction.

Forward position Used by riders for fast work and jumping, the upper body is inclined forwards without compromising the centre of balance. Usually requires shortened *stirrups*.

Frog Sensitive, V-shaped part of the underside of the hoof that feels spongy and acts as a shock-absorber.

Gait Another word for any of the horse's *paces*.

Gaited Term that describes horses that exhibit *paces* different from the normal *walk*, *trot*, and *canter*. Gaited horses demonstrate tendencies to perform these unique paces naturally, but training brings them out to the fullest.

Gallop Fast, four-time *pace*, which can reach speeds of up to 70 km/h (45 mph).

Girth Long, wide strap that holds the saddle on the horse; usually made of leather or synthetic material with two buckles at each end.

Grid Series of ground-poles or jumps used to improve athleticism and jumping technique in horse and rider.

Grooming Process in which brushes are used to clean the horse's coat, boost his circulation, and promote good health.

Hackamore Bitless bridle with a hard *noseband* over the horse's nose and a curb chain below the chin groove.

Hacking Riding out in the countryside for pleasure.

Half-chaps Informal style of gaiter worn with *jodhpur boots* or *paddock boots*.

Half-halt Brief halt *aid* followed immediately by a release so that the horse pauses almost imperceptibly; used to rebalance, especially before a turn, *transition*, or school movement.

Half-pass Advanced *lateral* movement in which the horse moves sideways and forwards at the same time.

Hand The standard measurement used for horses in non-metric countries; equivalent to 4 inches (10 cm) and derived from the average width of a person's hand.

Haute école ("Airs above the ground") Highest form of *dressage*, where the horse executes manoeuvres in the air, originally to protect the mounted soldier.

Haynet Rope or nylon net used for feeding hay to horses; stops horses from eating too fast as they have to pull the hay out through the mesh.

Headcollar Item of tack used for leading or tying up horses.

Headpiece Top part of the bridle that sits behind the horse's ears.

Headset Term used for the head and neck position of a Western horse.

Headstall Leather portion of a Western bridle that fits around the horse's head.

Hoofpick Blunt, hooked device used to pick debris out of the horse's feet.

Horn Short "handle" on the *pommel* of a Western saddle, developed from a cowboy's need to use a rope and have leverage against a steer at the other end.

Horse trials Original name for *eventing*.

Hot bloods Horses that have desert origins and are known for their athleticism, extreme sensitivity, and intelligence.

Hunter trials *Cross-country* competitions originally used to test the skill of hunters.

Imprinting Training method that exposes a foal to various stimuli during the first few hours after birth to teach it to accept training and handling later in life.

Impulsion When a *pace* has power from the hindquarters without excessive speed.

In hand When the horse is led rather than ridden, especially as in *showing* classes.

Jodhpurs Full-length riding trousers that can be worn with short boots.

Jodhpur boots Short, slip-on boots for riding.

Jog Western version of the *trot.* It is highly *collected* so that it is easier for the rider to sit.

Lateral work School movements in which the horse is asked to move sideways or forwards and sideways; used to develop balance, suppleness, and obedience.

Latigo Long leather strap that attaches the *cinch* to the Western saddle.

Lead Leading foreleg in *canter*.

Leg straps Two straps on a rug that fasten around the horse's hind legs.

Leg yield *Lateral* movement in which the horse is asked to move both forwards and sideways across the arena.

Le Trec Sport based on trekking. Includes riding over varied terrain, opening gates, jumping, and demonstrating the horse's obedience.

Lope Slow, relaxed version of the *canter* which is easier to sit for a great length of time.

Lungeing Way to exercise or control a horse from a distance by asking him to work in a circle around you via a long, soft lunge-rein.

Manège French word for "the art of horsemanship", but the term is colloquially applied to an enclosed area for riding.

Markers Letters used to identify specific points in an arena or *manège*.

Martingale *Artificial aid* sometimes needed for greater control. The most common types are the running and standing martingales.

Mecate Heavy rope that is tied to the heel knot of a *bosal* to form *reins* and a lead rope.

Medium paces *Paces* with impulsion and slightly lengthened strides.

Moment of suspension Part of the footfall sequence when all the horse's feet are off the ground.

Mounting Getting on a horse.

Mounting block Step or block on the ground that makes it easier for a rider to get on a horse. It also relieves stress on the horse's back from the rider pulling up from the ground.

Natural aids Parts of a rider that are used to communicate with the horse. These are the legs, hands, *seat*, and voice.

Natural horsemanship Non-forceful training method in which trainers study the horse's nature and body language and use equine psychology.

Near side Horse's left side.

Noseband Part of the bridle that goes round the horse's nose. Some forms, such as the drop noseband, give extra control, while the plain cavesson is worn loose.

Numnah Pad that can be used under the saddle.

Off side Horse's right side

Over-reach boots Small boots in a "ring" design that fasten around the horse's coronet to protect the front heels against blows from the hind feet.

Oxer Jump with a round-topped outline.

Pace Way in which a horse steps. The common paces are *walk*, *trot*, *canter*, and *gallop*. **also** *Lateral* two-beat *gait* in which the horse moves its legs in unison on each side. A horse has to be taught to pace.

Pacer Horse that has been taught to *pace*. Both legs on one side reach forwards at the same time with the help of guides called hobbles around the top of the legs.

Pacing *Vice* where a horse incessantly walks a fence line back and forth.

Paddock boots Short, informal boots designed for riding or stable work, usually fastened with laces or a zip.

Polo Game played on horseback using long-handled mallets and a wooden ball.

Pommel Front of the saddle. Along with the *cantle*, it keeps the rider secure in the seat of the saddle.

Pony Equine that measures 14.2 *hands* or less.

Reining Type of Western riding that includes performing spins and sliding stops.

Reins Two straps connecting the rider's hands to the horse's mouth or nose.

Related distance When jumps are close enough together that the way you jump the first directly affects your approach to the next one.

Riding club Organization that promotes rider training and organizes competitions; possibly affiliated to a national organization, as in the UK.

Riding helmet Safety hat that fastens with a secure harness around the ears and under the chin, that protects the rider's skull in the event of a fall.

Riding school Establishment dedicated to the training of riders.

Rope halter *Headcollar* used by some Western horsemen that gives the handler a little more control.

Roper boots Sturdy boots with heels worn by Western riders.

Sand-school Enclosed area used for riding, also called a *manège*. The surface can be made of a variety of materials, including sand and rubber.

Schooling Exercising the horse for suppleness and obedience rather than *hacking* for pleasure.

Seat Refers to the rider's bottom as it sits in the saddle and plays a part in controlling the horse. A rider with "a good seat" is someone who sits well and rides effectively.

Shoeing Process of having a horse's feet trimmed and shoes nailed on.

Shoulder-fore *Lateral* exercise to straighten and supple the horse, in which his shoulders are brought slightly off the *track* as he moves forwards.

Shoulder-in Similar to *shoulder-fore* but the horse is bent in the direction of travel.

Showing A competitive discipline with a huge variety of options, from breed or height-specific classes to hack and hunter classes, in which the horse's presentation and manners are crucial. Classes can be ridden or *in-hand*.

Show jumping Competitions in which courses of coloured fences are jumped.

Shying Action of a horse when he sees a frightening object and has an extremely quick reaction to step sideways.

Side-pass Step in Western riding, when the horse crosses his feet while moving sideways.

Side-pull Bitless bridle that uses direct pressure against the horse's nose to guide.

Side-saddle Type of riding that evolved in medieval times so a lady could ride a horse without having to sit astride.

Split reins Two Western *reins* that do not fasten together at their ends.

Spooky Horse that is easily startled and reacts by *bolting*, *shying*, or whirling around.

Spread Wide jump that the horse needs to stretch out over.

Stall walking *Vice* where a horse walks round and round its small living quarters.

Stirrups Supports for the rider's feet.

Stock Long strip of material wrapped around the neck and tied in a knot. Traditionally used for hunting, it keeps the rider's neck warm and can be used as a bandage. Ready-tied stocks are often used in *showing* but do not have the original, practical use.

Sweat scraper Plastic or rubber strip used to wipe sweat or water off the horse's coat.

Test Set series of movements performed by *dressage* riders.

Throatlash Part of the bridle that fastens loosely under the horse's throat to help stop the bridle slipping forwards.

Tie down Western standing *martingale* that dictates how high the horse can lift his head.

Tolt *Gait* performed by the Icelandic horse. It is a lateral four-beat gait and is similar to a running *walk*.

Track Path you follow in the *manège* **also** "turn" as a command, e.g. "at C track left".

Transition When a horse changes from one *pace* to another, e.g. from *trot* to *canter*, or from one variation of a pace to another, e.g. from *collected* trot to *medium* trot.

Tree Internal structure of the saddle.

Trot Two-beat *pace* in which the horse moves its legs in diagonal pairs.

Trotting poles Poles placed on the ground that the horse trots over; used to practise jumping position with novice riders and to encourage horses to pick up their feet.

Turnout Leisure time that a horse spends in a field or arena. **also** how a horse and rider pair are dressed, particularly for a competition.

Upright Jump built without any spread.

Vice Bad habit that a horse can develop – often through boredom or by copying other horses e.g. *crib-biting*, *pacing*, or kicking in his stable.

Walk Slowest *pace*, with a four-time beat.

Walking the course Process of learning a jumping course thoroughly on foot before you ride it.

Weaving *Vice* where a horse will stand in front of his stable door and rock from side to side.

Windsucking *Vice* where a horse latches on to a stable door, fence, or other horizontal object with its teeth and gulps in air rhythmically. This releases endorphins in the horse's brain and gives him a comforting feeling.

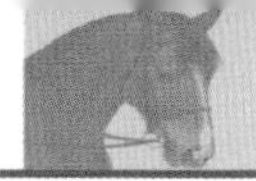

USEFUL ADDRESSES AND WEBSITES

Whether you are planning a riding holiday, want to learn English or Western riding, or want to know about local events and competitions, these pages will provide you with a selection of useful addresses and websites to help you find all the information you need.

UK AND IRELAND

BRITISH EQUESTRIAN FEDERATION

National Agricultural Centre
Stoneleigh Park
Kenilworth
Warwickshire CV8 2RH
The recognized governing body for horse sports in the UK, representing thirteen member bodies and co-ordinating their common policy issues.
Website: www.bef.co.uk
Telephone: 02476 698871
Email: info@bef.co.uk

The following organizations are affiliated to the British Equestrian Federation:

ASSOCIATION OF BRITISH RIDING SCHOOLS

Queen's Chambers
38/40 Queen Street
Penzance
Cornwall TR18 4BH
The representative body for professional riding school proprietors in the UK.
Website: www.abrs.org
Telephone: 01736 369440
Email: office@abrs.org

BRITISH DRESSAGE

Website: www.britishdressage.co.uk
Telephone: 02476 698832
Email: office@britishdressage.co.uk

BRITISH EVENTING

Website: www.britisheventing.com
Telephone: 02476 698856
Email: info@britisheventing.com

BRITISH HORSE DRIVING TRIALS ASSOCIATION

Website: www.horsedrivingtrials.co.uk
Telephone: 02476 303339
Email: bhdta@horsedrivingtrials.co.uk

BRITISH HORSE SOCIETY

Website: www.bhs.org.uk
Telephone: 08701 202244
Email: enquiry@bhs.org.uk

BRITISH REINING

Website: www.britishreining.com
Email: council@britishreining.com

BRITISH RIDING CLUBS

With more than 400 affiliated clubs and over 35,000 members, the BRS is affiliated to and contactable via the British Horse Society.
Website: www.bhs.org.uk
Telephone: 08701 202244
Email: enquiry@bhs.org.uk

BRITISH SHOW JUMPING ASSOCIATION

Website: www.bsja.co.uk
Telephone: 02476 698800
Email: bsja@bsja.co.uk

ENDURANCE GB

Website: www.endurancegb.co.uk
Telephone: 02476 698863
Email: enquiries@endurancegb.co.uk

NATIONAL FEDERATION OF BRIDLEWAY ASSOCIATIONS

An organization providing a contact network to inform, support, and encourage people working to improve bridleway access in England and Wales.
Website: www.rightsofway.org.uk
Email: nfba@rightsofway.org.uk

RIDING FOR THE DISABLED

Lavinia Norfolk House
Avenue R
Stoneleigh Park
Warwickshire CV8 2LY
A registered charity that works to enable disabled adults and children to enjoy the experience of riding or carriage driving.
Website: www.riding-for-disabled.org.uk
Telephone: 0845 658 1082
Email: info@rda.org.uk

WESTERN EQUESTRIAN SOCIETY

A body dedicated to promoting and improving the standard of Western equitation in the UK. It has a register of approved instructors.
Website: www.wes-uk.com

EQUESTRIAN FEDERATION OF IRELAND
Kildare Paddocks
Kill County Kildare
Ireland
The EFI is the National Governing Body for all equestrian sport in Ireland, with the exception of horse racing.
Website: www.horsesport.ie
Telephone: +353 45 886678
Email: efi@horsesport.ie

The following organizations are affiliated to the Equestrian Federation of Ireland:

ASSOCIATION OF IRISH RIDING CLUBS
Website: www.airc.ie
Telephone: +353 818 270227
Email: info@airc.ie

DRESSAGE IRELAND
Website: www.dressageireland.ie
Telephone: +353 59 9771728
Email: info@dressageireland.ie

EVENTING IRELAND
Website: www.eventingireland.com
Telephone: +353 45 886674
Email: headoffice@eventingireland.com

IRISH PONY CLUB
Website: www.irishponyclub.ie
Telephone: +353 56 8832966
Email: ponyclub@iol.ie

RIDING FOR THE DISABLED ASSOCIATION
Website: www.rdai.org
Email: rdaisecretary@eircom.net

SHOW JUMPING ASSOCIATION OF IRELAND
Website: www.sjai.ie
Telephone: +353 45 842300
Email: info@sjai.ie

INTERNATIONAL

EQUESTRIAN FEDERATION OF AUSTRALIA
Postal address:
PO Box 673
Sydney Markets, NSW, 2129
Australia
The governing body of equestrian sport in Australia, covering disciplines including dressage, eventing, jumping, show horse, paraequestrian, endurance, and reining.
Website: www.efanational.com
Telephone: +61 2 8762 7777

RIDING FOR THE DISABLED ASSOCIATION OF AUSTRALIA INC
Postal address:
PO Box 2410
Werribee, Victoria, 3030
Australia
A voluntary, not for profit, organisation that provides riding instruction and other activities associated with riding for people with disabilities.
Website: www.rda.org.au

NEW ZEALAND EQUESTRIAN FEDERATION
Level 4, 3–9 Church Street
PO Box 6146
Wellington
New Zealand
The governing body of equestrian sport in New Zealand, covering eventing, show jumping, and dressage.
Website: www.nzequestrian.org.nz
Telephone: +61 2 8762 7777

NEW ZEALAND RIDING FOR THE DISABLED ASSOCIATION
Postal address:
PO Box 58–110
Whitby, Porirua
New Zealand
NZRDA provides the training, health and safety policy, advocacy information and advisory services for 52 member groups. The general fields covered are: Therapy and Rehabilitation; Education, Behaviour Modification and Social Contact; Horse Riding for Sport and Recreation for people with disabilities.
Website: www.rda.org.nz

FÉDÉRATION ÉQUESTRE INTERNATIONALE
Av. Mon-Repos 24
PO Box 157, 1000 Lausanne 5
Switzerland
The International Federation of Equestrian Sports is the governing body that regulates horse-riding competitions all over the world.
Website: www.horsesport.org
Telephone: +41 21 310 47 47

INTERNATIONAL LEAGUE FOR THE PROTECTION OF HORSES
Anne Colvin House
Snetterton, Norfolk NR16 2LR
United Kingdom
A registered charity established for the protection, rehabilitation, and rehoming of horses and ponies worldwide. It operates a horse loan scheme.
Website: www.ilph.org
Telephone: 08708 701927
Email: hq@ilph.org

INDEX

M

N O

P Q

R

S

Publisher's acknowledgments

Dorling Kindersley would like to thank the following for their help in the preparation of this book:

Katie, Lucy, and Jane Driver; Matthew Wilkes; Mr and Mrs John Burbidge and team at Parkwood Stables, Somerset; Stockland Lovell Manor Equestrian Centre, Somerset; Coach House Saddlery, Stockland Lovell; all staff and students at Hartpury College Equestrian Centre, Gloucestershire; Jane and Chris Reece; Hannah Payne; Mr and Mrs Philip Ellicott, Trapnells House Stables; Martyn England, Priors Cottage Stables; The Quantock Riding Club; Quantock Saddlery; Deborah Cook; Bob and Chrissie Mayhew at Dumpford Manor Farm, Hampshire; Carley Yeates; Micheal Langford; Tim and Lou Petty at Petty Quarter Horses, Florida, USA; Rachel Gregg; all at Classic Farms, Kentucky, USA; Mark Rafacz; Cindy Garden; Wendy Sasser; Carol Derry; Bennie Sargent; Jason Stefanic; Amy Elizabeth Kash; and Dale Rudin.

They would also like to thank Christine Bernstein for the index, and Nicky Munro, Lettie Luff, and Jackey Lennard for editorial assistance.

The publishers would also like to thank the following for their kind permission to reproduce their photographs:

ABBREVIATIONS KEY:
b=bottom; c=centre; l=left; r=right; t=top.

1, 2-3, 5, 6-7, 8-9, 10-11, 12tl, 12-13b: Kit Houghton; 14-15: © Araldo de Luca/CORBIS; 16cr: Harry Taylor © Dorling Kindersley, Courtesy of the Natural History Museum, London; 17tr: Alan Hills and Barbara Winter © The British Museum; 17br: Alan Hills © The British Museum; 18tl: Colin Keates © Dorling Kindersley, Courtesy of the Natural History Museum, London; 18-19b: Jerry Young; 19cr: Geoff Dann © Dorling Kindersley, Courtesy of the Wallace Collection, London; 20cl: The Art Archive/ Eileen Tweedy; 20bl, 20bc, 20br: Kit Houghton; 21: Heritage Image Partnership © The British Library; 22b: Charge of the Light Brigade, Balaclava, 25 October in 1854, Woodville, Richard Caton II (1856–1927) (after)/ Private Collection/Bridgeman Art Library; 22t: © Jerry Cooke/ CORBIS; 23, 24-25, 26, 28c, 28b, 29tr, 30b, 31t, 32b: Kit Houghton; 33tr: Coco; 35c, 37, 42-43, 84tr, 95c, 95cr, 95br, 104bl, 105, 107tr, 108, 109r: Kit Houghton; 110: Bob Langrish; 113tr: Kit Houghton; 120, 121b: © Michael St. Maur Sheil/ CORBIS; 158br, 174b, 181tl, 184: Kit Houghton; 192-193: © Mike Finn-Kelcey/Reuters/Corbis; 203tr, 206-207, 209bl, 211tr: Kit Houghton; 214-215: © David Stoecklein/CORBIS; 245tr: Bob Langrish; 258-259, 266tr, 267tr, 273t, 278-279b: Kit Houghton; 287br: Bob Langrish; 289cr, 289b: Kit Houghton; 290-291, 291cr, 291br: Bob Langrish; 296c, 296b, 297: Sharon P. Fibelkorn; 298cr: Bob Langrish; 299: Sharon P. Fibelkorn; 302, 303c, 303br: Bob Langrish; 304-305b: © CLiX/ Shawn Hamilton; 306-307: © Bill Ross/ CORBIS; 308t, 308-309b: Kit Houghton; 310, 311, 312b: Bob Langrish; 313: Kit Houghton; 314: © Macduff Everton/ CORBIS; 315: Kit Houghton; 316: © Phil Schermeister/CORBIS; 317b: © Stocknet/ CORBIS; 317cr: © David Muench/CORBIS; 318b, 318c: © Wolfgang Kaehler/CORBIS; 319b: © Kevin Schafer/CORBIS; 319tr: © Danny Lehman/ CORBIS; 320t, 320b: Kit Houghton; 321b: © Jay Dickman/CORBIS; 321c: © Layne Kennedy/ CORBIS; 322: © Dave Bartruff/CORBIS; 323t: © Andrew Brown; Ecoscene/CORBIS; 323b: Kit Houghton; 324b: © Gavriel Jecan/CORBIS; 324c: © Nik Wheeler/CORBIS; 325r: © Carl & Ann Purcell/CORBIS ; 325b: ©/CORBIS; 326tr: © Owen Franken/ CORBIS; 326b: © Sergio Pitamitz/CORBIS; 327: © Anthony Bannister;Gallo Images/ CORBIS; 328l: © Peter Johnson/CORBIS; 328r: Franco Barbagallo; 329bl, 329r: Kit Houghton; 330: © Hamid Sardar/ Corbis; 331c, 331bl: © Robert Holmes/CORBIS; 338: Kit Houghton.